Praise for

SIX PIXELS OF SEPARATION

"Inspirational...practical advice...an eminently readable guide to harnessing the various tools available across the virtual landscape." —*Publishers Weekly*

"Deeply satisfying...extremely useful...a great guide to the changing world." —HuffingtonPost.com

"A first-rate debut by Mitch Joel, SIX PIXELS OF SEPARATION shows us how our world of commerce has changed, using real-world business examples and written with the entrepreneur and business person in mind."

—Chris Anderson, editor in chief of *Wired* magazine and author of *The Long Tail*

"Engaging, witty, and wise, with book smarts and pop-culture savvy...If you're enticed by all you've heard and read about the benefits of deploying online tools like LinkedIn, Facebook, Twitter, podcasts, blogs, search engines, and the rest for your business or personal enterprises but were not sure what to actually do and where to begin, this terrific tome will help hook you up."

—*Miami Herald*

"Social media in all forms are becoming the dominant form of interaction on the Net, whether blogging, Twittering, Facebook, LinkedIn, etc. SIX PIXELS OF SEPARATION clearly describes this new family of media, offering realistic ways to get involved and productive in a hurry."

—Craig Newmark, founder of Craigslist

"This book is really about how to market in a new age . . . Joel gives you the tough medicine you need to hear . . . I love the against-the-grain statements that throw the new conventional wisdom on its head."   —*Fast Company*

"Whether you are a *Fortune* 500 CEO, an entrepreneur, or a college kid dreaming about starting your own business, SIX PIXELS OF SEPARATION is an essential road map to our intricate and complex social connections. Mitch Joel helps us understand this emerging world, and turn its force into our ally."

—Dan Ariely, author of *Predictably Irrational*

"In today's world of constant Twittering, pinging, poking, and Facebooking, connecting your business to your customers is essential. Trouble is, the old rules won't help you much. Today, as Mitch Joel explains in this terrific book, survival depends on creating real value, speaking authentically, and building trust. For anyone looking to understand the new media landscape, SIX PIXELS OF SEPARATION is the ultimate guidebook."

—Daniel H. Pink, author of *A Whole New Mind*

"First, there was a gulf, then a chasm, then a gap. Now, of course, there's nothing in the way of making the connection. Mitch takes you on a detailed, fun tour of what it means to connect online—with your customers, your colleagues, and even your competitors. If you've been waiting to catch up on what's been going on, here's your chance. Better hurry."   —Seth Godin, author of *Tribes*

SIX PIXELS OF
SEPARATION

**Everyone Is Connected.
Connect Your Business to Everyone.**

MITCH JOEL

**BUSINESS
PLUS**

NEW YORK BOSTON

Business Plus
Hachette Book Group
237 Park Avenue
New York, NY 10017
www.HachetteBookGroup.com

Business Plus is an imprint of Grand Central Publishing.
The Business Plus name and logo are trademarks of
Hachette Book Group, Inc.

Printed in the United States of America

Originally published in hardcover by Business Plus.

First Trade Edition: October 2010

10 9 8 7 6 5 4 3 2 1

The Library of Congress has cataloged the hardcover edition as follows:
Joel, Mitch.
    Six pixels of separation : everyone is connected : connect your business to everyone / Mitch Joel.—1st ed.
        p. cm.
    Includes index.
    ISBN 978-0-446-54823-6
    1. Business enterprises—Computer networks. 2. Electronic commerce.
    3. Internet marketing. 4. Entrepreneurship. I. Title.
    HD30.37.J64 2009
    658.8'72—dc22

                                                    2009002999

ISBN 978-0-446-54822-9 (pbk.)

Book design by Charles Sutherland

Cells before Pixels . . .

Ali and Julien—I love you with all of my heart, soul, cells, and pixels. You are my inspiration.

Contents

INTRODUCTION   ix

CHAPTER 1
I Google You . . . Just Like You Google Me   1

CHAPTER 2
The Trust Economy   22

CHAPTER 3
Entrepreneurship 2.0   45

CHAPTER 4
*Faith-Based Initiatives, Viral Expansion Loops,
and the Long Road*   64

CHAPTER 5
Know Control   87

CHAPTER 6
The Real World   108

CHAPTER 7
You Are Media   124

CHAPTER 8
From Mass Media to Mass Content   143

CHAPTER 9
Digital Darwinism   161

CHAPTER 10
From Mass Media to "Me" Media   178

CHAPTER 11
Burn the Ships   197

CHAPTER 12
Tribal Knowledge   215

CHAPTER 13
Digital Nomad   234

CHAPTER 14
Participation 2.0   252

ACKNOWLEDGMENTS   275

INDEX   277

ABOUT THE AUTHOR   287

Introduction

Since 2003, I have been putting my thoughts, ideas, inspirations, and frustrations into a blog called "Six Pixels of Separation—The Twist Image Blog."

Admittedly, this was never my intention or plan. From the mid-1980s on, my career was in journalism. Sure, I would write the occasional piece for free to build credibility, prove that I could write for a well-respected editor, or get into a publication I admired, but the cardinal rule was: Never write for free. After all, what kind of business could I possibly generate if I was giving away the final product?

When I joined my fellow business partners at Twist Image in 2003 to build our vision of a modern-day digital marketing and communications agency, I took one look around our closet-sized office space and asked, "How are we going to build this business and get our name out there?" At the time, we had one employee and a client list you could count on one hand of a bad high-school woodshop teacher. The prospect of building Twist Image was daunting. Then it struck me: I have a lot of thoughts about the marketing, communications, and advertising business as it currently is. I have a passion for helping others to achieve their business goals, and I was still more than slightly interested in writing.

FROM PAID TO FREE?

But I ran into an immediate hurdle. No marketing industry magazines would let me write for them. I was unproven. I was a part of a start-up. They could not give me valuable pages in their magazines to wax poetic about the power of new media. Around this time I heard about a new online service called Blogger. Blogging was still very nascent and it was much more about being an online journal than a commercial and viable way to grow your business.

My first posts were pretty embarrassing, but slowly I began to find my voice. I began to realize that the process I had used to publish my own magazines (several years before joining Twist Image) was now extinct. In the old days (about two years before 2003), you would write an article, it would go to the editor, he or she would send it off to the production team, they would mock it up onto a page, sell some advertising, produce final films, print it, and distribute it, and by the time it hit the streets I had forgotten what I had written. But now I could type my thoughts on a word processor, copy and paste them into Blogger, hit the publish button, and— *voilà*—my words were available to the world (and those who were interested in finding them). Slowly, the blog started getting the attention of mainstream media. Between offers for speaking gigs and being asked to be a source in print publications and in mainstream media, I had a realization that writing for free was an amazing way to build community and get clients in the door.

YOU'LL NEVER KNOW UNLESS YOU TRY

People are constantly saying things like "Okay, Mitch, we get it, but can you show me someone who has really grown their business by doing all of this stuff?" Most people see my company as it is today: multiple offices, over seventy employees, and world-class clients. They wonder where I find the time for all of this social media stuff. Here's the truth: *All of my past and current personal successes in life, from the growth of Twist Image to the mass media attention to the publishing deal that put this book in your hands, has been because of these online channels.* Nothing more. Nothing less. It's sometimes hard for me to say this because I don't like using myself as an example. The reality is that my business partners and I have built a multi-million-dollar business by doing everything you're about to read on the following pages.

IT'S SERIOUS

The advantage is that most businesspeople still see the digital channel as a joke. They don't take it seriously. They think it's nothing more than a time suck. The good news is that the more people think like that, the wider the opportunity is for you to do your thing, make your own noise, and grow your online community and business while they look around wondering what's happening to their market share.

Most businesspeople still don't read blogs. They don't listen to podcasts, and they're not even thinking about smartphones and Netbooks. This book is meant to "break the fishbowl." It is meant to give the entrepreneur, the business manager, the vice president, the CEO, and anyone else in the business world who is not engaged in these channels a better understanding not only of what they are and why they are important, but also of how to use them. Not in technical speak and not in online jargon, but in business talk. *Six Pixels of Separation* is filled with stories of individuals and personal anecdotes of people who have used these channels and what they did to make their mark.

Whether the economy is still in a slump or clawing its way back to life by the time this book hits the shelves, one thing will still be for certain: all of us are going to be doing a lot more with a lot less. The digital channels were meant to do just that. Your business has been forced to change over the past couple of years. As a result, there has never been a more important time to understand the myriad digital channels and free publishing tools that are right here in front of you—at your fingertips—and are relatively cheap, or free, and easy to use. By using these tools, you are going to learn how to do more with less.

By understanding how this information flows online, by being engaged and connected, and by creating your own content, you will begin to unravel how much more efficient you can be as a business. I wrote this book to explain how I did it, so that you can do it too.

FROM DEGREES TO PIXELS

We all know the story of Six Degrees of Separation, the idea that we are all connected through fewer than six degrees— meaning that I know someone, who knows someone, who knows someone, who knows someone, who knows someone, who knows someone—who knows you. The theory has been around for ages. It has been tested, refined, and tinkered with over the years, but it is no longer relevant. *In the digital world there are no degrees of separation between you and your customers*. You are connected. You're even connected to those who are potential customers.

The Internet, the many online social networks, and new media tools have taken the degrees away—and we're down to pixels. This changes everything we know about business and how you can connect your brands, products, and services to your community.

Everyone is connected. It's time to connect your business to everyone.

SIX PIXELS OF
SEPARATION

CHAPTER 1

I Google You . . .
Just Like You Google Me

MAYBE ALL YOU NEED IS A HUG?

On June 20, 2004, Juan Mann was feeling low. So he did something about it. He made a simple sign that said FREE HUGS and walked through the open Pitt Street Mall in Sydney, Australia, holding it over his head. For about fifteen minutes people walked by, stared, snickered, and muttered words behind his back.

Then someone—a total stranger—came forward and took him up on his offer. Suddenly, all sorts of people started to follow suit. Folks throughout the mall started to hug spouses, kids, whomever.

In the months leading up to that first free hug, Juan Mann (a pseudonym for "One Man") was going through his own personal turmoil until he received a hug from a total stranger. In a post–9/11 world, that simple act of kindness sparked Mann to heal not only himself, but to heal the world. It wasn't just Mann. After he walked around the open market with the FREE HUGS sign, other strangers began making their own signs and handing out free hugs alongside him. The movement continued to grow until the authorities stepped in and forced the antics to stop because these people had not acquired the proper permit and licensing. But after accumulating 10,000 names on a petition, the free hugs movement was allowed to continue.

During this time, Mann met Shimon Moore. Moore was fascinated with what was happening and spent close to two months video recording the free hugs (and the petition process). Along with hours of footage that he was editing down to just a few minutes, Moore layered over the video a song that his own band, Sick Puppies, had recorded entitled "All the Same." During this time, Moore (and his band) decided to move from Sydney to Los Angeles. In 2006, word reached Moore that Mann's grandmother had passed away. As a gift, Moore sent Mann the video of him giving out free hugs, along with the accompanying music. Ultimately, that video was uploaded to YouTube.

To date, the video has had more than 40 million views and has sparked free hug movements in places like Taipei; Tel Aviv; Boulder, Colorado; Korea; Jordan; and just about anywhere and everywhere in between.

Chances are you have probably seen the free hugs video and are now wondering, *What do Juan Mann, a successful video on YouTube, and the beginning of a hippy-esque movement like "free hugs" have to do with my business and increasing my sales?*

Everything.

Like Juan Mann, you and your business have a mission. Juan's core brand values were about directly connecting to real people in a day and age where people were separating themselves from one another. He decided to use the Pitt Street Mall as a focus group to test-drive his idea and started offering his free hugs to anyone who would take one. Once you know that your product or service resonates with its intended audience, the next phase is to spread the message far and wide.

The traditional channels of marketing, communications, advertising, and public relations can be costly and prohibitive to some businesses. Mann and Moore did something very interesting. They leveraged the power of the many free and easy-to-use tools online to spread their message to anyone and everyone who would be willing to listen. It cost zero dollars to upload their video to the online video-sharing service YouTube. They used these online channels in lieu of buying ads on TV or sending out a press release. They knew that if their message could find their intended audience, those people, in turn, would help them spread the message as well. They used online tools and empowered the people who were connecting with their message to spread it further. They used free channels to communicate. They set up groups, responded to comments, and became active participants in their self-created community.

The greatest businesses and the most engaging brands understand how to use the more costly and traditional marketing channels (television, radio, print, and billboard advertising) to get their messages to spread. These newer channels—the ones that make Six Pixels of Separation possible—seem confusing, counterintuitive, and even scary to some corporations. They're worried about "opening up." What choice does any business have in this new world of radical transparency?

One of the biggest challenges that every business faces is figuring out who the target audience is, how to connect to them, and how to build on those relationships. But traditionally, the cost of these activities, the cost of growing that base and getting it to multiply, has always been expensive. Very expensive.

That's the beauty of what Juan Mann did with his free hugs online video. The same tools he used to connect to millions (the actual online population is closing in on over 1.5 billion worldwide) are readily available to you as well, and, for the most part, they are free (or cheap). Juan Mann's story should resonate powerfully for you and your business because Juan is not a high-paid digital marketing strategist, he is not a .NET programming sherpa, and his technological acumen is not all that Steve Jobs–ish. He's a regular person, just like you and me, with fairly limited technical and Internet skills. That is the point: *You don't have to be a computer whiz or a member of the Geek Squad to make the online channel and communities work for you.*

In the end, it's not the hugs, and it's not YouTube or the Internet celebrity it brought Juan Mann. Along with the free and easy-to-use tools, the reason Juan Mann was able to make his message connect is because through these digital channels *we are all connected*. And that is the main point of this book.

SIX PIXELS OF SEPARATION = WE ARE ALL INTRINSICALLY CONNECTED

We no longer live in a world where there are Six Degrees of Separation (where any one person is connected to anybody else through fewer than six degrees of separation). We are all intrinsically connected through technology, the Internet, and our mobile devices. These digital channels break down the notion of "it's who you know," because we all now live in a world where we can know everyone—and everyone can know us. And we're not connected by degrees anymore; we're simply connected. I don't need an introduction to you through someone else, and you no longer need one to me. We are all a click (or a pixel) away from one another. This means a big change for business. This means a change in how you sell people your products and services. This means that building relationships and turning those relationships into an online community is more powerful and more important than ever before.

These new online channels give you the full power to make this happen. It's no longer about how much budget you dump into advertising and PR in hopes that people will see and respond to your messaging. The new online channels will work for you as long as you are working for them by adding value, your voice, and the ability for your consumers to connect, engage, and take part. This new economy is driven by your time vested—and not by your money invested.

YOU AND I ARE CONNECTED AND ARE A PART OF THIS EVER-EXPANDING COMMUNITY

In the digital world, we are all intrinsically connected. Individuals, people like you and me, are able to develop not just our businesses, but our personal brands as well. Because of Six Pixels of Separation, the people who are connecting in these channels are growing personal brands that have the size, power, audience, and influence to rival the corporate branding powers of the biggest companies. It's a happy problem to have if you are the owner of your own business, but this core idea is changing business as we know it. New breeds of entrepreneurs are emerging daily, and even those working for a company are becoming entrepreneurs within.

Six Pixels of Separation is all about what you can do to grow your business. Many people see the Internet and think it's just a bunch of pimply-faced teenagers with underdeveloped social skills who sit at home all day and engage in massive multiplayer online games. Or they think they're simply too old to learn new skills, that the technology has passed them by.

It hasn't.

Six Pixels of Separation is your guide to understanding what these digital channels really are and how best to work within them to connect, communicate, share, and grow your business.

NEWS FLASH: "YOUR BRAND IS NOT WHAT YOU SAY IT IS . . . IT'S WHAT GOOGLE SAYS IT IS"

So says Chris Anderson (editor-in-chief at *Wired* magazine and best-selling author of *The Long Tail*). Now, more than ever, people's first interaction with a brand is happening at the search box. That first page of search results defines you. It defines your brand and either taints you or teases the consumer to push on and read more, comment, or get others' perspectives.

Think about the last time you bought a car or thought about buying one. Odds are you were sitting around chatting with family and friends and someone suggested a specific make and model. What was your next move? Did you run down to the nearest dealership, or did you hop online to do a quick search and see what came up? Did you go to multiple car dealers or did you do a side-by-side comparison online and read a bunch of reviews submitted by happy (or unhappy) customers?

Did you trust what the salesperson at the dealership had to say when you finally made it down to the retail level, or were you fully up to speed based on hundreds of reviews from people you didn't even know and all of the research you had done online already? We trust one another over industry veterans who have sold thousands of cars. Why is this happening?

Chris Anderson is alluding to this new phenomenon where that first page of search engine results has become a digital collage of corporate speak, press releases interspersed with real individuals' thoughts created through channels like blogs, forums, and reader reviews. They all interact on a level playing field, and this is creating a fundamental shift in business, how we communicate, and how people buy. When an individual's personal review sits on equal ground with the millions being spent on advertising, marketing, and communications from corporations, the traditional mass media model begins to crumble. It also places a strain on any business that has relied so heavily in the past on having "expert" salespeople. *We live in a new world where people go online if they are not feeling well and then tell their doctor what the diagnosis is and the appropriate medical intervention—including medication and dosage.*

Some see this as a new virus, others see this as the cure.

THIS IS WHAT HAPPENS WHEN THE COST OF PUBLISHING IS FREE (OR CLOSE TO IT)

The old poker saying is all that you need to make millions is "a chip and a chair." When it comes to these online channels, all you need to publish for free is a computer and an Internet connection. Within the next few chapters we will look at how, in a few simple clicks, anyone can have his or her own publishing platform, be it for text, images, audio, video, or all four. As easy as the setup is, the implications are massive. What we're really talking about is your newfound ability to build your own media channel, or multiple channels, and how to turn them into your own media empire (or mini empire). The reason this is so profound is that, for the most part, people are spoiled. They tend to look at some of the tools currently available to us online with a sense of entitlement. ("You mean I can't upload my entire photo set to Facebook?" Pshaww!) I'll urge you to show some respect. Being able to publish to the world for free is a big (huge) deal. When the cost of publishing any piece of content is free and offers along with it a global audience, you, as a business owner, have only one choice: to get involved, build the awareness of your company, brand, product, and service, and to use these tools to eclipse your competition.

That's what *Six Pixels of Separation* is all about.

While many still see the Internet as a virtual Wild West of ridiculous pictures of kittens and videos of hockey brawls, what we're really seeing is an entirely new marketing and communications channel emerge where brands are all treated equally (sometimes equally badly, sometimes equally well). We're seeing a place where consumers are free not only to speak their minds about brands, but also to mash them up into their own interpretations. We're seeing a new world where people are building huge networks of connections that foster community, conversation, and commerce. These individuals, in and of themselves, are becoming highly sought-after media properties (whether they realize it or not).

Even though we're just at the beginning stages of these shifts in society and business, we're already starting to see people grow personal brands that are rivaling some of the biggest corporate brands in the world. As an entrepreneur you understand the value of "getting in early," and while this is not a quick fix for your business growth, it is a free channel that is ready, willing, and welcoming. The goal of this book is to help you become your own media channel, producing content that stimulates the industry you serve and helps establish you as a recognized authority.

We're quickly reaching a place where entrepreneurial individuals are creating, curating, and nurturing personal brands that are helping to build their profiles, grow their businesses, make more money, get the jobs they want, and connect to other like-minded individuals to effect change in the world (yes, it's that big and it's that serious).

A PERSONAL ANECDOTE ABOUT WHERE A PERSONAL BRAND IN THESE DIGITAL CHANNELS CAN TAKE YOU

This story is about me and how I came to understand the concept and power of a Six Pixels of Separation world, but really this story is about you. It's going to illustrate how the little things we do as entrepreneurs to get our messages "out there" are now creating big opportunities that are connecting us—and our businesses—to opportunities that were not available to us before the advent of the Internet.

A podcast is like an online radio show. I have two. One of them is about the intersection of digital marketing and personal branding, and it is called "Six Pixels of Separation" (it's also the name of my blog). I have another podcast that is called "Foreword Thinking—The Business and Motivational Book Review Podcast." I'm certainly not as diligent with it as I am with "Six Pixels of Separation—The Twist Image Podcast" (which I do weekly), but the real spirit of "Foreword Thinking" is based on my passion for reading both business and motivational books. I love "Foreword Thinking" because all I really do is connect and have wonderful conversations with some of the best authors out there. More importantly, I get to choose whom I talk to, and I also decide how frequently (or infrequently) a show gets produced.

In 2007, I was asked if I would be interested in interviewing Dan Ariely. Dan is a well-known behavioral economist. He was also about to publish his first book, *Predictably Irrational: The Hidden Forces That Shape Our Decisions*, in about six months' time. Clearly, I had never heard of Ariely (his book was not out yet), but I liked the idea that he was going to bring some different thinking into what motivates people to do things.

We immediately hit it off. By the end of our conversation, I was recommending that he get in touch with my speakers bureau and he suggested that perhaps I would be interested in connecting with his literary agent. At the time I had met with a few literary agents but nothing had really clicked.

So Dan made the digital introduction. At that point, his literary agent, James Levine from the Levine Greenberg Literary Agency, hopped over to "Six Pixels of Separation—The Twist Image Blog," and started snooping around. He checked out my speakers bureau's Web page and dropped me an e-mail expressing an interest in meeting to see if something could be done.

We met at his Manhattan office. I showed him some of my presentations and top-line concepts for the book you hold in your hands. But here's something Jim doesn't know: I could not concentrate. Sure, there's a palpable energy in the air when you're sitting with a Manhattan-based literary agent, and the thought of having him hunt down a serious publishing deal was equally exciting. But in truth, I could not keep my mind off of his socks.

Yes, his socks.

They didn't match—not even close.

Now, let's be clear, Jim is not a young guy (but he ain't old, either) and all I could think was, *Is this guy wearing Little Miss-Matched socks?*

I first heard about Little MissMatched socks on the blog of Seth Godin (he is well regarded as one of the leading marketing presenters in the world, and one of his better-selling books is *Purple Cow*). The premise of *Purple Cow* is that brands can't afford to be ordinary. According to Seth, in this day and age you're either remarkable or invisible. To illustrate the story in live presentations, Seth talks about Arielle Eckstut. Arielle started a different type of clothing company—she sells socks to young girls. The big idea is that you can't buy a single pair of socks. You can only buy them in sets of three. Oh, and one more thing: none of them match. It's a remarkable idea that has grown Little MissMatched into a unique franchise of clothing, furniture, books, and beyond. While the philosophical spirit of the business is about empowering young girls to be different and creative, Little MissMatched works because little girls like to talk and show off their new and freaky socks.

I had to ask: "Jim, are those Little MissMatched socks you're wearing?"

He looked almost as surprised that I knew what they were as I was that he was wearing them. It turns out that Little Miss-Matched was not Arielle's first venture. Her first gig was working alongside Jim at his literary agency. On top of that, the Little MissMatched offices were only a couple of floors down in the same building.

During our lunch break we went down to meet Arielle. In a strange twist of good timing, just that week I had blogged about Little MissMatched because someone decided to make a Seth Godin action figure and the toy is decked out with mismatched socks (no, I'm not making this up). Arielle had not heard of the action figure until I brought it to her attention.

There's a point to this story.

What was nothing more than a step above a hobby for me (my "Foreword Thinking" podcast) had led me on this amazing adventure that includes a book deal with one of the biggest publishing houses in the world and personal encounters that have not only been interesting, but have led to new business opportunities and introductions. All of them were perfectly linked through my activities in online channels (blogging, podcasting, online social networking, etc.).

My point is, if I can do this, so can you. Every single pixel in that story was connected to me—either through someone I follow online or someone who follows me—and while those looser pixels had never directly connected, I was suddenly confronted with four connections that linked perfectly together.

Ultimately, your business needs to sell more stuff and sell it fast. You may be thinking that you simply don't have time for all of this online stuff or you're equally jaded because of the many "time suck" articles you have read about these channels in the traditional media. Let's look at some reasons why you should care and take the time to understand this new medium. It will change your business forever. Here's why.

YOU CAN MAKE MORE MONEY

Competition is fierce. Advertising is expensive. More and more consumers are looking for products and services that fit their specific needs. When Henry Ford was selling his Model T automobile in the 1920s he was noted as saying, "You can paint it any color, so long as it's black." In today's world of personalization, customization, and individualism we're beginning to see our modern-day Model T's offered in a prism of colors with full customization. Making real money as an entrepreneur is all about adding value.

The new digital channels give businesspeople unprecedented opportunities to share their insights, information, additional levels of customer service, and, most importantly, access to you and the brands you represent. But there's another shift in thinking that needs to take place, and very few people understand or talk about it.

Google, Yahoo! and Microsoft are making their billions from pay-per-click contextual advertising in their respective search engines. When you do a search using the Google search engine, you'll notice either colored sponsored search results at the top of the page or additional search results on the right-hand side of the page. Both of them say "sponsored links," meaning a business has bought a targeted keyword and appears when a user searches for those specific terms.

It's powerful because you're "catching" a potential consumer while he is in active search mode, and you only pay for that ad if the user clicks on it. (Granted, the system is so robust that if your ads are not converting into clicks, most engines will automatically boot you off the system.)

It's the perfect dream for advertising: Match your products and services up to consumers who are looking for them.

Think about that for a minute.

How much money does your company spend on traditional advertising? It could be TV, print, radio, billboards, or whatever. Here's the thought process: "Let's take out an ad in hopes that some of our potential consumers will see it, remember it, and then think of us if they're looking for what we're selling."

During that process, do you know how many thousands of people have searched online for information or pricing on the exact same products and services?

Are you there?

Thousands of potential customers are raising their hands every day and saying, "Hey, I'm looking for you!" and yet most businesses consider Google, Yahoo! and Microsoft's search engine marketing opportunities an afterthought. Most businesses would rather put their advertising dollars in media that are—pretty much—a hope and a prayer. *Most businesses don't even know if their traditional advertising campaigns worked until they are over.*

Most businesses are not present enough in the search engines and they're leaving big money (and clients) at the table (or for their competition).

It's not that all of the search engines have figured out a better mousetrap for sales and marketing. It's that they've managed to place your messages with potential clients when they're in the mood for them.

It's a sales funnel unlike any other. These search engines act as virtual sales representatives, making their presence known and felt by how well structured those few sentences are when someone types in a search related to your product or service. If you're wondering where the number-one source of traffic to your corporate website currently comes from, you don't have to bother to look at your Web analytics package. I can tell you right now: It is the search engines.

And while pay-per-click advertising is picking up steam, it is not the only way to rocket to the top of search engines. We'll look at how being present on many of the online communities and creating your own publishing platforms will move you all the way up to the top of every major search engine.

YOU ALREADY HAVE A COMMUNITY . . . ARE YOU A PART OF IT?

Why does your business work? (Or why is it struggling?) It's a fundamental reality that most successful businesses flourish because they are operating in a community that is flourishing. You can't have a strong business without a strong community.

Online communities have been around since the advent of the Internet. Early BBSs (bulletin board services) were the new bazaar as people connected through their telephone lines and pioneered the first virtual communities.

We've come a long way since then (just look at Facebook, FriendFeed, Twitter, and the myriad other popular online social networks). The misconception is that online social networks are just for fun and games. They aren't. Individuals are building strong community ties that are spilling over into real-life introductions and business opportunities.

In November of 2006, the U.S.–based Center for the Digital Future surveyed over 2,000 people during a six-year research project to study the attitude of individuals and the Internet. Did you know that 43 percent of Internet users surveyed in this study felt as strongly about their online communities as they do about their real-world communities? These online interactions were also discovered to be much more than online flirting, too. According to the survey, individuals meet in person an average of 1.6 of the people they had connected to online.

COMMUNICATE WHO YOU REALLY ARE

Throughout this book you will be able to underscore all of the information and tactics and weave them through one long thread of authenticity. These many online channels will empower you to take control of your brand by enabling you to communicate and connect with those who share your values.

All too often we get caught up in our industry acronyms or wander into the world of bloated marketing chatter using terms like "best of breed" or "world class." The fact remains that the Internet is all about real people looking for real interactions. They give you and your employees the ability to connect, solve problems, and enhance customer service by speaking in a human voice. They will force you to become ever more transparent—and this is a good thing.

Candor goes a long way in the new online social channels. Your ability to speak as you would if someone were sitting across from you becomes one of the most valuable online opportunities. The more you learn how to communicate who you really are and put those thoughts out there, the less you have to worry about constantly repeating your communications to each customer on an individual basis. Search engines have memories that rival elephants'. They remember everything and will link your consumers directly to the answers they need for the questions you have already answered.

The trick is this: Don't be afraid of technology. If you are, just take a deep breath and realize that everyone from four-year-olds to forty-four-year-olds to eighty-eight-year-olds is getting more and more comfortable with these online social channels. As Franklin D. Roosevelt said in his first inaugural address, "The only thing we have to fear is fear itself." Go ahead, start using a search engine to see who is talking about your business and the stuff that matters to you. Get yourself involved in the conversation.

Right now, you have an opportunity to be a part of a conversation with millions of people. By not being afraid of technology and by using it to your advantage—in a very simple way—you will not only get the business results you have been seeking, but you will build a tremendous brand with unparalleled loyalty.

I GOOGLE YOU . . . JUST LIKE YOU GOOGLE ME

Make no doubt about it, the minute someone hears something (anything) about you, the first place they go is to their favorite search engine to see, exactly, what the story is. My point is: If you had a job promotion, opened a business, issued a press release, were mentioned in a newspaper article, were involved in a charitable organization, created a profile on Facebook or LinkedIn, there should be some kind of digital footprint for yourself and your business. This first page of search results is your personal brand and the way the world sees you. Remember, "Your brand isn't what you say it is, it's what Google says it is."

Your personal brand is becoming more critical as online social networks and social media, in general, become pervasive. Not a day goes by that someone, somewhere, is not checking out who you are, what you're about, and whether or not they are willing to invest (or divest) in you. That investment could be regarding anything: personal, business, community, or all of the above.

As our digital selves and the personal brands they represent begin to overshadow everything else (in terms of mass awareness), our real-life personal brands need to keep pace. As an exercise, before you hire your next employee, do a quick online search and see if his or her résumé and in-person meetings match up to what is being shown online.

It's not all about vanity, but there is a small vanity component to this (it's nice to know people are talking about you). The main point here is to stay focused on whether your brand is being properly maintained in the online channel. It's not a question of defending against those who think differently; rather, it's a general digital-footprint audit to ensure that who you really are and what you really do are coming through—loud and clear.

WARM UP TO THE IDEA OF NETWORKING

It's not just about buying a ticket to a local chamber of commerce event and standing at the corner bar with your buddies complaining that you are not meeting anyone. Real entrepreneurs understand the fundamental power of networking—connecting to like-minded individuals and helping them connect to others. These social circles are critical to your success, and they are magnified when you layer them into the new digital channels.

Six Pixels of Separation speaks to a new way of connecting. It's a world where mass brands are overtaken by personal brands. It's a world where individuals are building their personal brands by connecting to very specific niche content and media that they are choosing and controlling. It could lead to a world where divorce rates will decrease as more people get connected because they share similar values and life goals. It's a place where an individual brand voice is as loud as the mass advertisers'.

There are millions of new ramifications for entrepreneurs to deal with. Not only are we challenged with how to reach and connect to our customers and their rising personal brands, we now have to deal with how to market to people who have unique personal brands that share a similar audience, size, and reach.

Networking online is core to success because it's not blatant sales and marketing. You network to build your circle of influence by adding value to your community and helping others get what they want. In return, you build influence and a presence, essentially becoming the "go-to person" for the community.

Use these channels to help others grow their businesses. Use your connections to provide your clients and partners with sales leads or competitive information, or just to discuss areas of mutual interest. This will position you as a key adviser and, at the same time, will change your entire business-development funnel. It's no longer about outbound calls and pressing the flesh at industry events—it's about using these online channels to communicate how you think and how you speak, and to give an overall feeling of your business by maintaining a presence in the many online channels. Use this book to help you become a valued member of the many communities that exist and are looking for you not only to join, but also to lead.

If you look at how the Web is performing as a pure networking tool, we're already seeing great results at the relationship level with successful online dating and successful online social networking sites—and this is just the beginning.

There are many more new connections to be made.

CONNECT TO THE RIGHT PEOPLE: CONNECT TO SIMILAR OTHERS

Connecting and being validated are a huge part of our lives. Abraham Maslow, the American psychologist, will forever be remembered for his theory on the hierarchy of needs. The highest point of that pyramid (self-actualization) is where the online channels focus most. Even if you have never taken a psychology class, as a business owner you must have an inkling of interest about why humans do things, and then why they are compelled to share their experiences with others. It turns out that there is a serious connection between Maslow and the current rise and success of online social networking.

From the Center for Media Research and their "Research Brief" e-newsletter (December 27, 2007) comes this: "Emotional Business Bonding on Social Networks," by Jack Loechner, who notes that according to a recent report called "Meeting Business Needs by Meeting Social Needs," by Communispace, researchers have uncovered that human beings' needs are being met through online social networking. They have connected "Six Social Needs" in order to help entrepreneurs understand how to create better affinity with their consumers.

Here are six key points from the research:

1. Online social networks provide people with the ultimate tool for defining and redefining themselves, as evidenced in profile pages on Facebook and MySpace.
2. The need for autonomy, recognition, and achievement are essential to our sense of self-worth and are fulfilled in online communities, blogs, and social networks that provide a way to develop and manage a virtual reputation.
3. People have a need to both seek [help from] and provide help to others. Mutual assistance between strangers is a phenomenon that has been uniquely enabled by the Internet.

4. Online communities are becoming the way people find, create, and connect with others "just like me"—people who share similar tastes, sensibilities, orientations, or interests.

5. A sense of belonging or affiliation alone is not equivalent to a true sense of community. Achieving a real sense of community requires long-lasting reciprocal relationships and a mutual commitment to the needs of the community as a whole . . .

[6.] People want to be reassured of their worth and value, and seek confirmation that what they say and do matters to others and has an impact on the world around them. Meeting all 5 + 1 of these social needs generally requires the level of intimacy and facilitation that are the hallmarks of smaller, invitation only online communities.

These six points do illustrate that we are moving toward a world where online reputation and personal branding are taking hold. If people connect more to one another through their personal brands online, we are going to see the connection for emotional branding in these channels. Odds are that you have looked at these many online channels and have seen them as fads (whether we're talking about blogs, online social networks, or widgets), and have not paid enough attention to what the net result could mean: more and more people finding and making brand decisions based not on the corporate line, but on what a mass of individuals have said, done, and collected.

This can't be a trend, because it will transcend all technology and media channels. The technology (or the online social networks) will just be the platforms by which these consumers connect. Much like a search box where people now find information online, these emotional branding connections will happen in the same, easy way.

The big idea in a world of Six Pixels of Separation is to embrace community as the new currency. Understand and believe that your business and how it is perceived in the marketplace are going to get increasingly complex in the coming months. How you are positioned, how people see you, and how you speak back to them are going to be the global validation for your growth. *In a world where we're all connected, one opinion quickly turns into everyone's opinion.* How you build trust in your brand, your business, and yourself is going to be an important part of how your business is going to adapt and evolve.

CHAPTER 2

The Trust Economy

In the August 2007 issue of *Scientific American Mind* there was an article by Christoph Uhlhaas entitled "Is Greed Good?" The story describes how eBay should simply not work. After all, if you send money to a complete stranger, why would he send you anything in return? According to the article, "This is a borderline miracle, because it contradicts the concept of Homo economicus (economic man) as a rational, selfish person who single-mindedly strives for maximum profit. According to this notion, sellers should pocket buyers' payments and send nothing in return. For their part, buyers should not trust sellers—and the market should collapse."

So why does the online auction eBay work? Why do most people buy from someone they do not know, based on a bunch of positive peer reviews and ratings from people they do not know? But, people will not buy from someone they do not know based on a bunch of negative peer reviews and ratings from people they do not know. At first strike, this doesn't make any sense, but—as you will see in the coming chapters—this type of behavior is commonplace online. We have an inherent trust in those who have taken the time to publish their personal feedback.

There is a "Wisdom of Crowds" at play here (to quote best-selling author James Surowiecki) and an overriding faith in groups of individuals who have never met. The online trust economy is a powerful force that favors the crowd over companies. Look no farther than Amazon.com. When reviewing book selections, the traffic and attention given to these peer reviews is so powerful that the online merchant's description of the book from the publisher and subsequent mass media reviews pale in comparison to the conversion rate to sale that they get from the consumer-generated reviews. Ultimately, you'll trust Sally from Carefree, Arizona, over the *New York Times Book Review*.

In fact, it works so well that Amazon.com also has a feature called "Customers Who Bought This Item Also Bought," which is one of the best tools to get consumers to buy more books. After all, if you like the book you're about to purchase and other people who bought this book also found value in some other titles, they might be worth checking out as well.

Those who are part of the *participatory culture* (and give abundantly) tend to build powerful and respected personal brands. They are connected through intricate networks based on information and content as the currency, and their ability to provide value translates into their status in the disjointed hierarchy online. Among all communities, individuals hope to achieve some level of status and reputation. The pecking order online is simply bigger, and it has no face.

This unique trust economy is counter to everything you ever thought about how a business grows. A great salesperson knows that the ultimate customer is one who has given you his or her trust. Trust is earned by an overall great experience with a foundation of authenticity, open communication, knowledge, and value from that customer's perspective.

IT'S UP TO YOU

That's what it said at the checkout section on the website for the alternative rock group Radiohead when they released their seventh disc, *In Rainbows*, in October of 2007. The world sat back and jaws dropped as the rock band announced that their upcoming album would sell online for as much (or as little) as the individual fan was willing to pay (the band actually said, "It's up to you").

What do you think a new album from Radiohead is worth? Five dollars? Five pounds? Fifty dollars? Two hundred pounds? Nothing?

Radiohead, a band known for pushing creative and technological boundaries, was now mastering the art of becoming a brilliant entrepreneur by embracing the trust economy online. With close to 15,000 CDs being released by the major record companies each year in an industry that is in the middle of redefining what the business model is, some might think that selling music online is not even an option anymore. After all, illegal downloading has become easier to do and harder to trace, and it is approaching a forty-to-one ratio in relation to legal purchases, according to some recent surveys.

The Radiohead initiative was pure marketing and promotion in a digital marketing world. Value is subjective, and Radiohead trusted that the wisdom of their crowd would do right by them. While this story is well known and you probably heard about it when it was playing out, there is a bigger story here as it relates to how your business can connect online.

In a world where many people were going to download and steal the music illegally regardless, Radiohead used the promotional aspects of this specific tactic (including all the press that came with it) to, at the very least, get some of their money's worth in terms of marketing. They knew they could never stop people from downloading illegally, but by demonstrating that they trust their community, they were hoping to put a bit of guilt on the consumers. They were well aware that there exists a "shade of gray" Radiohead fan who might steal the CD if given the opportunity. They figured that those same people are probably good people, and if given a reasonable option might consider some sort of payment in kind. Radiohead's strategy was to get those people who would be willing to cough up something (anything) as an overall effort to get the masses thinking differently about paying for music. As lofty as that might sound, it did focus the attention back on to the quality of the music and away from simply downloading things illegally.

The result?

According to a comScore research report, more than half of those who downloaded the album chose to pay nothing—but the remaining 40 percent paid an average of six dollars. Further to this statistic, 1.2 million people visited the Radiohead download site (it is not known how many out of that group actually went on to download and select their payment). In the U.S. the band has sold a bit fewer than 650,000 CDs as of November 2008, according to *Billboard*. The results feel slightly inconclusive, but people did react to the initiative.

Here's what Josh Tyrangiel wrote in "Radiohead Says: Pay What You Want" (*Time* magazine, October 1, 2007):

> The ramifications of Radiohead's pay-what-you-want experiment will take time to sort out, but for established artists at least, turning what was once their highest-value asset—a much-buzzed-about new album—into a loss leader may be the wave of the future. Even under the most lucrative record deals, the ones reserved for repeat, multi-platinum superstars, the artists can end up with less than 30% of overall sales revenue (which

often is then split among several band members). Meanwhile, as record sales decline, the concert business is booming. In July, Prince gave away his album *Planet Earth* for free in the U.K. through the downmarket *Mail on Sunday* newspaper. At first he was ridiculed. Then he announced 21 consecutive London concert dates—and sold out every one of them.

One of the reasons iTunes has become so powerful is that people were revolting against the twenty-dollar cost for a disc that had only a handful of tracks they loved. They wanted the power to purchase just what they wanted. Radiohead's and Prince's approaches embrace some core social media values for their respective new disc launches. While they would never enable their consumers to co-create the actual music with them, clearly the artists are willing to stand by their music by enabling us, their community, to establish the monetary value.

As an entrepreneur, you should find this pay-what-you-want model fascinating. Beyond the action of trusting your consumers to do the right thing and the subsequent publicity that comes along with it, they have stirred up many different types of conversations online that are overshadowing what should be the biggest conversation: Is the music any good? (no doubt it is—it's Radiohead, after all). The conversation is lively and continues (to this day) to keep Radiohead in the headlines.

What was Radiohead's message to their fan base? It was something like "We know you can steal this disc on the Torrents, but, if you really like us, give us whatever you feel is right. *We trust that you will do the right thing.*"

It's a prime example of the trust economy and this new marketing value system. When you engage in a conversation and treat your consumers with respect and as your peers, magical things will happen. It worked because Radiohead has already spent six albums' worth of time and touring adding value to their community and fan base. And while it definitely did not outperform the sales of some of their past hits, the concept created an overarching halo effect that reopened the conversation around paying for music.

Here's the crux of it: You are in the business of building your own trust economy as part of your core values and foundation. In order to move forward and to engage in these conversations, nothing happens until you have demonstrated and displayed the highest levels of trust for, and within, the communities.

It's deep. It's powerful. It's true. It also takes a lot of time to develop—and that's where entrepreneurs get scared off. It's not something that can happen in Q1; it's not a campaign, it's a commitment. The truth is that it can happen faster, or it can take years to build.

THE CHANNELS, THE OPPORTUNITIES

Before we deep-dive into the real guts of how these new channels came to be and why it is so critical for your business to take part, let's look at the overall digital tool kit. Here are the many new media channels that are available for you to take part in and create.

The primary objective is, and should be, to drive consumers to take action and keep them engaged. This is accomplished by either bringing them from one of the social channels to your website or to your business in the real world.

The two pillars for building your business through the digital channels will be:

1. Permission: Having consumers give you their explicit permission to connect. You have probably seen disclaimers on web-

sites that say something akin to "We promise never to sell or give your personal information to any third party." The nature of these new conversational channels suggests that you will need to take that type of disclaimer up a notch (or five). The best way to keep your community members happy is to apply the real-world advice never to talk behind someone else's back. Same rules apply here. When somebody says something in the space you are connected in, treat the conversation as if it is private—even if, in reality, there's nothing that could be more public about it.

2. Content: Your ability to create compelling text, audio, video, and images is going to build your story and get people excited about staying connected to you.

There are also many traditional advertising and communications tactics that have been adapted for the online world. These include:

1. Cross-Channel Promotion: Driving people from your general advertising and communications campaigns to your website.

2. Display Advertising: This is typically called banner advertising. The ads come in myriad shapes and sizes and usually are seen at both the top of the page and on the right-hand side.

3. E-mail Marketing: Collecting e-mail addresses from your customers and communicating to them via e-mail with either stand-alone offers or e-newsletters. Some companies also purchase third-party lists and try this as a form of direct marketing.

4. Search Engine Marketing: Buying text-based ads that are placed in search engines when the consumers do a query on a specific keyword or keyphrase. This type of advertising is

typically purchased on a CPC (cost per click) basis, meaning that the advertiser pays only when a consumer clicks on the ad. This is also how Google makes the majority of its revenue to date.

5. Affiliate Marketing: Many companies will offer a commission or bounty if you help them sell their stuff. Amazon does this brilliantly. Any website owner can sign up for Amazon's affiliate program. The website owners are given unique identifiers that notify Amazon if anyone purchases something that was referred to Amazon by the affiliate. Many online marketers consider affiliate marketing one of the most effective forms of online advertising. People are supposedly mentioning certain products and services anyway; why not have them make a commission if that inspires someone to buy?

While it is important to understand the more traditional online advertising channels mentioned above, *Six Pixels of Separation* is going to focus on the more conversational channels where your business becomes the de facto source of insight, information, and community. These channels include:

1. Blog: A text-based online journal where an individual or group can quickly publish and post thoughts. These posts are listed in chronological order. Readers can comment on and share this information as well as subscribe to the content for free. When participants subscribe, they are notified in their readers whenever a new piece of content is created. Blogs are typically chatty, informative, provocative, and written in a very human voice.

2. Micro-Blog: Twitter, Jaiku, and Identi.ca are the better-known micro-blogging platforms. These spaces allow people to com-

municate one short message (about 140 characters long). People follow you and you follow people. Through this intimate 140-character broadcast you can share micro-content, connect, and build community.

3. Podcast: These are exactly like blogs only they come in either audio or video formats. The majority of audio and video podcasts are accessible and indexed over at iTunes and are free. That being said, most people producing a podcast house them on a blogging platform, and you can grab a podcast directly from that destination. Most people listen to or watch podcasts on their computers, and you can even download the program onto your hard drive.

4. Online Social Network: From Facebook and MySpace to LinkedIn, online social networks are where most of the people online are connecting. Individuals create their own profiles and add connections (or friends). You can do everything from creating groups and sharing photos to business networking and checking out other people's profiles. All online social networks have varying levels of security and permission, so that you don't have to share everything you're up to with the world (unless you want to).

5. Sharing Sites: You can upload a video to YouTube or do the same thing with your pictures on Flickr. Online sharing sites are popular and have some features that are very similar to the more traditional online social networks. There are even sites like SlideShare, which allows people to share their PowerPoint presentations. Along with sharing your multimedia content with the world, people can also rate, comment, link to, and embed your content in their own channels.

6. User-Generated Content: One of the highest forms of flattery occurs when your consumers create their own content—it

could be text, audio, video, or images—about your brand on their own, without your permission. It could be a parody of your products, their own personal review, or simply a mash-up of your stuff and someone else's into something completely new and different.

7. Wiki: A wiki is a website that anybody can edit. Wikipedia is probably one of the best-known wiki-based initiatives. Wikis embrace the philosophy of mass collaboration and create an online space where one piece of content can be created, adapted, changed, debated, and honored by a mass number of people.

8. Widgets: A widget is a small application that can be added onto an existing website or blog, downloaded onto your desktop as a stand-alone application, or put on your mobile device. Widgets (also known as gadgets) are used for anything and everything from weather alerts and stock quotes to sales and breaking news.

IN PRAISE OF SLOW

Entrepreneurs want everything (more sales, more brand awareness, more recall, more word of mouth, more business) and they want it fast. You can attribute this directly to the initial gold rush toward online marketing back in the early 1990s. The real excitement about online marketing was caused by the misconception that it could be done fast, much faster than a traditional mass-media campaign. More importantly, if it wasn't performing up to standards, it could be removed even more quickly. This was all very attractive.

To this day, most businesses embracing the digital marketing channels do it because they think it will be cheap, cheerful, and fast. It's simple, right? You choose a handful of keywords, link to some of your Web pages, buy some pay-per-click ads on your favorite search engine, and watch the sales ring up.

Problem is, we've got it all wrong.

Digital marketing is about being slow.

Yes, you can make fast decisions, see fast results, and optimize and change things on the fly, but real, tangible results take time. You can't quickly start a blog and get results right away. It takes time to build your content, find your voice, develop a community, and earn trust and respect.

You can't just publish a podcast and expect your cash register to start ringing.

You can't join an online social network and derive any value from it unless you take the time to meet the right people, connect, share, build, and grow.

Digital marketing is not a one-night stand. We can, literally, gauge the upward spike of business after a strong traditional advertising campaign runs. The trouble is the "vicious cycle" effect of it all. The more you advertise, the more attention your business gets, but the more you continue to advertise, the quicker you start experiencing diminishing returns.

The digital channels we're looking at in today's world are about building real relationships, both with your consumers and with your potential consumers.

Over half of all traffic to *Wired* magazine's website, Wired.com, is to the archive. This creates a media paradox of the highest order. In one sense, the magazine has to include the latest and greatest in terms of editorial content and visual design to stay ahead of the curve at the magazine rack, and where you might suspect that the website would need to be even more up-to-the-minute and fresh, it's simply not the case. The website does not get nearly as much traffic to the home page as you might suspect. People are doing a bunch of online searches for random tech and geek terms, and this is driving them to articles and pieces of content that could have been created and posted online over a decade ago. The older the content, the longer it has been online and searchable through the engines, the more people who have linked to it, shared it, and tagged it, the more valuable it is. Content that ranks at the top of Google does not get there because of how new and fresh it is. Content rises to the top of Google based on how long it has been available and how valuable it has been to the online community. It's a slow and steady process that makes content rise to the top of the search engines.

This is a profound learning for businesses trying to understand the online space. One would think that being online is all about how fast you can post the latest news with the most cutting-edge insights. Not the case. The longer content has been part of the Internet, the more catalogue that is built, the more trust that is gained by people linking to the content, the more valuable it is, and the more growth the brand will have. That being said, the quicker you post your content, the faster you can start gaining the efficiencies of the slowness.

Chris Anderson and his team at *Wired* still rush to post the latest and greatest technology news and information online (they have to compete with the other websites out there), but the true value of that content is derived slowly and over time. The speed to publish information online is, in fact, a strategy to get it indexed in search engines as fast as you can. The sooner it is available through search, the sooner people will find it, and the sooner it will become more valuable.

Slow, however, does not mean resting on your laurels and not engaging in these new channels. Slow simply means that long-term and tangible results do take time. There are no shortcuts to success in these online channels, because the people who are connecting to you will know if you're just making a "money run" at them.

As an example, if you're starting a blog and you pre-load posts with made-up questions or semi-edited snippets of old press releases just to have content for the sake of having content, you're not adding value and you are not speeding up the process. In fact, you are probably slowing it down for yourself. In this case, slow is bad. It will take you even longer to correct course and build the right conversations because your audience will read through it, and it will take even longer to rebuild that trust over time. And sometimes that trust is never regained at all.

Think about how real business-building campaigns soar. Think about the time, effort, and speed by which great stuff happens—and is maintained. There's no such thing as an overnight sensation. Everything you've seen in business as an overnight sensation was, in effect, decades in the making.

Think about how the concept of "slow" may very well be one of the best-kept secrets of truly successful businesses. The digital social spaces are built on trust and trust alone. Trust is always built slowly and over time.

TRUST + COMMUNITY = ROI

What is the ROI of building community, engaging in conversations, and working in these digital channels?

A more appropriate question might be: How much are you willing to invest in building a trust economy that builds a community around your brand, products, and services?

Return on investment in the new economy is driven by how loyal and engaged your consumers are. Businesses that build trust and engage in their community (whether they have created it themselves or take part in an existing one) are seeing real results and real ROI. Let's assume that you are delivering the ultimate experience. Your brand rocks, you offer excellent products and impressive service—you've got it all. What's next? Your ability to leverage true ROI is going to come from the level of trust you have built and the community you serve. How different would your business look if there were thousands of brand evangelists online talking about you, creating positive reviews that fill the search engine results that surround your keywords, which then builds a general loyalty that is sorely missing from your biggest competitor?

How can you start?

Here are six ways to build trust in the trust economy:

1. Consistency

As a former publisher of music magazines, I learned the lesson of consistency long before I had ever published an issue. In developing the business model, I was fortunate enough to have a conversation with the editor of a very highly regarded lifestyle magazine. During a phone call, he asked me about the format of the publication I had in mind. I was young and exuberant, and said that I'd like to start with a forty-eight-page full-color glossy first issue. He recommended a twenty-four-pager on newsprint in black and white.

Why?

Because if I had gone with the forty-eight-page full-color glossy style and a couple of issues in, the advertising dropped out or never materialized, I would be forced to reduce page numbers, lower the quality of the paper, use less color, and downgrade in other ways, but if I kept it humble and stayed consistent I could grow it to the point where I could publish a four-color cover, maybe add a spot color within the magazine, or perhaps add some pages as the demand for advertising grew over time.

While my mentor's comment was frugal from a business perspective, the point is that it's very hard to take stuff away from your consumers once you've put it out there. If you decide to start a blog and, in the heat and excitement of it all, you start posting every day, what will be the public perception if you switch to once a week? It's a letdown. Worse than that, your public's trust in you begins to fade, and it fades fast.

Be consistent in everything you do.

Don't blast out five pieces of content or join three online social networks and fade away. Choose one, stick with it, and keep at it. Think about the classic fable and be more like the tortoise than the hare. Slow and steady wins the race. Advertising is the hare and this new social channel is the tortoise. If you release a weekly podcast, don't change your production schedule to every month or so. If you start with a monthly show, you can always step it up to twice weekly (or weekly) as it grows in audience and popularity. Be consistent.

Your community will appreciate it, and as you grow and add more gizmos, bells, and whistles, they'll be thankful for the increased output, even though you would have done that right from the start.

2. Choose a Global User Name

First impressions count. The name you use to represent yourself is (and will be) directly linked to the brand you are building. Take some time at the beginning to decide on some options. If you are going to use your company name, be prepared that some people will perceive it as "cold" because it will look and read like a marketing message and not like it is coming from an individual.

Do everything you can to avoid using an anonymous user name. How often do you see a very smart (or very stupid) comment that is simply signed "John68"? Yes, the Internet does afford the power of anonymity and, in certain cases, being anonymous is what makes the content that much more relevant and interesting, but if you are interested in taking part and putting yourself "out there," use your real name. In terms of being an entrepreneur, taking part in these channels to build your business will require you to open up the kimono (just a little bit). My recommendations are as follows:

Try to use your entire full name and include your company name. For example, when you see me commenting on blogs or writing an article for a newspaper, you will probably see something like "Mitch Joel—Twist Image." By doing this, I am transparent in presenting myself and the company I represent. I also list the company name on the off chance that there is another "Mitch Joel" out there (thankfully, there isn't). This adds another layer of branding where the individual is still linked to the company. This is especially important if you, as the owner, will not be the person in these channels. By allowing one of your employees to take part and using the formula above, your brand is still tied to the concepts and spirit of the conversation.

Avoid using nicknames, too. "SkiDog73" may have seemed like a great user name for your Web-based e-mail account in college, but it's not going to help you establish yourself as a recognized and credible authority.

Also, don't forget about rule number one: Be consistent. Maintain this user name in every channel you can. Some websites allow you to create your own unique URL (Web address) once you are a member. Choose one style and stick with it. If you're ever looking for me, I should be listed as "mitchjoel," not "mitch_joel" or "mitch-joel." Choose one style and stand by it.

3. Choose One Good Picture of Yourself

Every so often on the very popular online social network Facebook you'll notice a message that says, "15 of your friends have changed their personal profile picture." The temptation is huge—you just had a baby and you want the world to see her, someone snapped a shot of you as you scaled Mount Everest, or it's time to update your profile picture because it is no longer 1978 and you're kidding no one with that photo. Whatever your reason may be, think first about what the photo is and what it represents. If all you're using these online channels for is personal communications among friends and family members, then none of this information matters.

On the other hand, if you are trying to build a presence online by connecting to like-minded others to grow your business, odds are these conversations and communities will extend well beyond one online location. *Remember that each one of us is now our own media channel.*

With that in mind, choose one picture and stick with it. Always use the exact same picture in any instance you are able to. Take a quick audit of your friends or connections on any of the major online social networks you are connected to. Which ones stand out? Which ones are memorable?

The next time you walk down the street, take a moment to look consciously at all of the signs on the stores. Which ones stand out? Odds are they are the ones with the vibrant lights, happening colors, and bolder font types. Think about Times Square in New York City (signage overload). Your picture or image needs to stand out. While I would recommend that you use a close-up headshot of yourself, I have also seen many individuals get highly creative by creating images, cartoon likenesses, and more of themselves. Any and all of these will work fine as long as you keep the same picture and use it consistently across all of the platforms you're looking to take part in. Using your company logo is also an option, as well, if you think it will stand out and add value.

The two classic clichés stand strong in a digital world where millions of individuals are striving for attention: "A picture is worth a thousand words" and "You never get a second chance to make a first impression."

Finally, think about the user experience. Someone comes to one of these environments and starts looking through a profile to see whom they know. If he's seen your picture in another space and has connected with you, seeing your familiar mug again will spark a response like "Oh yeah, I know her—we're connected on LinkedIn!" making him more likely to connect.

4. Add Value to the Conversation

No one cares about what you say until you demonstrate how much you care about them and their insights. The easiest way to build your business buzz is to add your personal insights and establish yourself as a recognized authority. The first thought most entrepreneurs have at this point is *I should start a blog*. It's not the wrong way to do things (far from it), but there is another way to build your credibility and discover whether your thoughts resonate with an audience, and that's to find the more highly trafficked blogs and online spaces that serve your industry, follow the content until you get a feel for it, and start adding your comments there.

All too often comments online are more akin to "Hey dude, I, like, totally agree with everything you're saying . . . rock on." Or "You should stop blogging. It pains me to read you." Those are your basic "high-five" or "low-blow" types of comments that add little to no value to the conversation and look more like linkbait than anything else (linkbait is when someone writes a comment with the sole purpose of having readers click over to his website, or simply of having his link listed on your site).

A simple way to build trust and community is to comment intelligently and frequently (but not too frequently). While it seems simple enough, one quick glance across a handful of the most popular online channels will demonstrate that few of the comments they contain are truly valuable. And that's the opportunity for you right now.

To date, many individuals have built the initial traffic to their brands by finding others who were creating valuable content, and by adding to their conversations. As our digital lives get increasingly complex with podcasts, Twitter, Facebook profiles, and more, taking the time to be a part of someone else's online community has been usurped by expecting others to join the ones you are creating.

Not cool.

While inspiration on other blogs and the like should encourage you to create content of your own, you need to "be out there." This way, you can keep up with what's going on, and get your ideas into new channels that have new audiences and new readership for you to connect with. Having a blog and podcast is, simply, not enough. You need to encourage the conversation in your own spaces but, more importantly, you have to get out of "lurker mode" and engage in the conversation that is taking place beyond your own RSS (Really Simple Syndication) feed. (RSS is described in chapter 3.)

5. Online Etiquette: Respond Quickly and Honestly

Believe it or not, in all of this new online chaos, some good rules of thumb are already mature, present, and, to a certain degree, expected. *Following up in a quick, timely, and honest manner will be your salvation.* Your parents always told you to say "please and thank you," and this important point is the digital extension of that concept.

When you begin to venture into these channels and get started, it is critical that you never be silent if someone e-mails you, blogs or podcasts about you, or interviews you for an article. If someone mentions you, it is now your duty—at the very least—to leave a comment back on their blog (or e-mail them directly), letting them know that you are reading, paying attention, and, most importantly, appreciative of their mentioning you.

Make this your one golden rule, and make a commitment that you will never break it.

I never forget those who respond. Now, there are instances when Google Alerts fails or a Technorati-driven ego surf does not pull in every result (more on these tools later), but more often than not you will be able to see, hear, and even feel what everyone out there is saying about you. After reading the next chapter on how to monitor what people are saying about you online, you'll have the full set of tools at your disposal to be an amazing voyeur into the life and times of your growing business and brand.

More than anything, social media and Web 2.0 (both terms that are used to describe this new form of Internet interaction and creation) and channels like blogs, podcasts, and wikis provide a global platform to share. There is the Momentum Effect that entrepreneurs are increasingly paying more attention to. The Momentum Effect occurs when consumers mention your company, brand, product, or service in their profile in an online social network and then this has an effect in the marketplace and within their social circle. This metric is becoming increasingly popular as a way for companies to measure their success in these social channels.

It's your responsibility to always respond to an inquiry. If anything, there's that Raving Fan (as Kenneth Blanchard calls them) whom you are all but ignoring. This is further amplified because the feedback is being given in one of the social media channels and on a public platform. Imagine that a potential customer discovers Raving Fan's comment via a simple search and then sees that no one ever responded. What kind of brand impression does that leave?

Nothing stinks of insincerity more than a person using these new digital channels who is not listening to the other conversations.

Having the time to respond is a huge and realistic issue, but we can't afford to have the attitude that people are too busy to respond to every comment or posting. Yes, people are busy, but they still need to respond, especially when it was this channel that gave some of these individuals access to the opportunities that are keeping them busy.

As much as you can, be responsive and be thankful. Do it now. And, as the old saying goes, "People always have time for the things that are important to them."

As your popularity grows, you are going to have to manage the feedback and conversation in a different manner. Obviously, responding to everyone personally is not scalable. You're going to need more resources and perhaps some help. Think of it as the most human kind of real customer service. What would that look like in your company?

6. Speak Like a Human Being, Not a Press Release

"On behalf of everyone at Twist Image, we would like to thank you for your patronage. You are a valued customer and we pride ourselves on providing a best-in-breed business book experience with strategic insights that optimize your supply chain and improve your business outcomes. It is through our best practices and optimization systems that we are able to serve you in an efficient manner meeting the highest standards of excellence."

Blech.

Can you believe that people still use this type of business speak to communicate on websites, in press releases, in speeches, and in corporate brochures? Let's be honest: Nobody likes it, nobody understands it, and, most importantly, nobody knows why we still use this type of communication. It's old and it's tired, and in a world where anyone can have his or her own media platform in about five minutes, it's almost a little insulting to be spoken to in that type of language.

Longtime loyalty and building trust with your consumers boils down to one hard reality: *People will buy from you and want to stay connected to you only if they are getting a real interaction from a real human being.*

There's a reason you decided to become your own boss. It might be because you figured out a better mousetrap for the industry you served, it might be because you were frustrated with how the competition did things, and it could be because you came up with a whopper of an idea. Whichever one (or combination) it is, you know better than any big business the value in really connecting with your consumers through common language. In a Six Pixels of Separation world, bland corporate speak, laden with jargon and industry acronyms, is not going to win you any customer service awards. In the online channels it will make you look like a jackass or, at best, a cold and heartless corporation that is dead inside.

HAVE FAITH IN THE TRUST ECONOMY

It's a fairly simple rule: The more human, honest, and transparent you are, the quicker you will be able to build trust and leverage it to build community and your business. It has to be sincere and it can't be done in the spirit of trying to sell people something.

Remember to have faith in the trust economy, have faith in the community, and have faith in your inherent niceness as the key driver to building your success. The serendipity of these actions is impossible to quantify as you begin to make connections and become a part of communities where your best interest is served through what you give back to the community and the individuals who make it up.

CHAPTER 3

Entrepreneurship 2.0

As the saying goes, "This is not your father's Oldsmobile." Being a successful entrepreneur has never been harder. At the same time, making the choice to become an entrepreneur has never been easier. And that's the paradox and challenge you're going to have to overcome as we launch ourselves into the digital world.

QUICK AND PERSONAL STORY

A few years ago, one of my friends became interested in opening up a store. He had indirect retail experience but felt that his concept was strong and would perform well on a particular street in a trendier area of a major metropolitan city. I inquired about his online plans; he confirmed that he would have a website to let people know what was on sale, what events would be taking place, how to contact him, store hours, and news. When I pushed him further, asking about e-commerce and an online loyalty-and-reward program and about how he would manage the many social places to connect, he was hesitant and said he wanted to see how the retail location performed before making the commitment to the online channel.

In other words, he was busy test-driving his father's Oldsmobile.

Admittedly, the concept for the store was new and different, but from a pure entrepreneurship perspective it was baffling. Why try to grind it out on one specific street in one specific city of one country instead of going full-out online, which offered unlimited market opportunity, many fewer headaches in terms of infrastructure and setup, and the ability to really see how his idea would perform on a global scale?

As you know, the digital revolution has re-invented what it means to be an entrepreneur. We've gone from slugging it out on a local level for small contracts to build credibility, to a world where people can make the choice to break clean from a corporate gig, fire up their laptop, develop a website, start joining the more social spaces to demonstrate their industry knowledge, hook themselves into some key online social networks to connect with like-minded individuals, and even advertise using their specific keywords on a pay-per-click basis on one (or all) of the major search engines. Without even an office or a business card, your business (and your brand) is linked to millions of people and connected to thousands of potential business opportunities.

ONE LAPTOP...ONE CONNECTION...GLOBAL SCALE

As for my friend, his store is closed. It didn't fail completely, but it certainly didn't perform as he had hoped. Ironically, someone had a similar idea but launched it as a pure-play online initiative. At last look, that business is still going strong.

In form and function you can no longer be hesitant about connecting your business online. Here's the bigger reason: Tier-one companies are already on the Web and, as a first point of online marketing indoctrination, they try their hands at some search engine marketing. Quickly they realize that the threat is not their direct competitors anymore. In fact, it's not even the tier-two companies in their vertical. It's the small and hungry entrepreneur who saw the opening and availability, bought the keywords, engaged the community, became a part of the conversation, and is, ultimately, the market leader. The big telcos are not winning the VOIP (voice over Internet protocol) war; a small start-up called Skype is (they were acquired by eBay for $2.6 billion). Barnes & Noble and Borders do not own the selling of books online; Amazon does. And, at last look, people aren't letting their fingers do the walking through the Yellow Pages when they need to find something online—they're clearly using Google, Microsoft, or Yahoo!

All of these businesses were once very small start-ups that saw a change in a certain industry and, without caring about what the number-one or number-two player in the industry thought, they went after it and used the online channels not only to build their businesses but to communicate and connect.

As an entrepreneur, you don't need to be a pure-play online business, but you do need to be better at creating an online experience. You do need to get more engaged with the online community.

THIS IS NOT ABOUT TECHNOLOGY

You don't have to be tech savvy to be great at working the online channel to build your business. Most of the tools we'll talk about in *Six Pixels of Separation* are straightforward, easy to use, simple, and even free.

On top of that, even if there are some areas that cause you confusion or frustration, usually within a quick online search you can find the answer or join a community of others who are using similar tools and work through it together. Look at these tools as another way to grow your business and pay no attention to the technology behind the curtain.

For the record, I have never designed a website or programmed a line of code (I don't even understand the differences between most programming languages) and, probably like you, I use about 2 percent of the options and functionality of my laptop and am equally frustrated when something that was on my screen suddenly disappears. You are among friends here.

BE LIKE GOOGLE

In 2007, I had a rare opportunity to visit the head office of Google in Mountain View, California. I was asked to give the closing keynote presentation for a retail event that featured some of the biggest brands in the United States. One of the morning presenters was Google's then CIO (chief information officer). He brought forward a statistic that will astonish you. Did you know that 20 percent of all searches done on Google every single day are searches that have never been done in the engine before?

Twenty percent.

Imagine if we were discussing your business and I told you that it would change by 20 percent every quarter. That would be enough to make any business owner cry. With a 20 percent unknown every day within Google's main product line, everybody who works there has no choice but to be on their toes.

While it would be foolish for me to assume that as a business owner you have the same resources (and deep pockets) Google has, some of Google's work philosophies are 100 percent transferable. Namely: Be flexible. Understand that your strategy to grow and change your business is no longer going to line up with your quarterly projections, but perhaps moving toward a more organic and "live" strategy (like Google has) will help you embrace these new digital channels. Google also engenders a philosophy that the consumers and the community are going to do many things to your business that are unknown and potentially not in your control. You have to be open to this type of reality. The inventor rarely knows what the invention is for.

If you're a serious entrepreneur, you've invested some serious time in a strategic plan. I'd recommend dusting it off and turning it into a living and breathing actionable document.

YOUR STRATEGY SUCKS (MOSTLY BECAUSE YOU'RE NOT THINKING ABOUT IT ENOUGH)

Once you've resolved that you can't ignore this space anymore (and I know you have because you are holding this book in your hands), the next step is to define your strategy. We just looked at the many different tools we're going to be discussing going forward. These tools are useless unless you have a strategy. You've probably heard these questions at one time or another in your business over the past little while (in fact, I'm sure you even asked your employees and partners some of these questions):

"What are we doing on Facebook?"
"What's our game plan for YouTube?"
"What's our blog going to be about?"
"What can we do with Twitter?"

You can take out the channel and replace it with whichever online social network is popular these days, or change the word "blog" to "podcast"—you get the idea.

But the biggest and most important questions never get asked: Everyone is so busy getting excited about the channels (and tactics) that they completely put aside the strategy and the brand. Instead of asking "What," please ask "Why."

Here are those questions again (rephrased):

"Why should we be on Facebook?"
"Why would we make videos for YouTube?"
"Why would we blog and why would anyone care?"
"Why should we try Twitter?"

When you really understand the "why," you'll know:

- Why people love you.
- Why people buy from you.
- Why they tell other people about how great you are.
- Why people are loyal to you.
- Why the world needs more of whatever you do.
- Why customers would never leave you for a cheaper price.
- Why they've never bought from you in the first place.

Asking "What" simply means deciding which tools you'll use. It's deciding between a blog and a podcast. It's choosing YouTube and Facebook over MySpace and Twitter. It's about the things you can do because you already know where your consumers are, what they're saying about you, and how you can add value to the online environments they're currently occupying.

But without the "Why"—your strategy—and a deep respect for being the guardian of your brand, everything else is just a tactic or a distraction. And if you're into sports, war games, or any other form of competition, you'll know that tactics don't win anything—strategy does.

Six Pixels of Separation is meant to inspire you to shift your consumers into valued members of your community. It's not meant to add a bunch of whiz-bang gizmos to your life. Having a solid brand strategy will empower you to decide best which tools and tactics make the most sense for you and the growth of your enterprise.

YOUR WEBSITE SUCKS (MOSTLY BECAUSE IT WAS AN AFTERTHOUGHT AND NOW IT'S THE MAIN CALLING CARD FOR YOUR BUSINESS)

The intersection of growing your business, understanding the power of your personal brand, and how the digital channels can help make everything connect is all fine and dandy, but unless you have somewhere to bring your newfound customers and community members back to, all is lost and forgotten.

All too often people look at the results from an online marketing campaign and frown. They're not sure why it was not effective. More often than not, the reason is staring them (and everyone else) in the face: Their website is not all that good.

You need to have an amazing website. It's not a luxury. It's not a marketing afterthought. More and more people's first interaction with a brand is happening at the search box. Whatever they see after that first click needs to be in line with their expectations.

It's not just the design (although that could well be a part of it); a website has many moving parts, of which the design phase is only a small (but important) one. The entire process of building a corporate website has traditionally fallen into the hands of two types of companies:

1. **Web-Design Shops:** I have nothing against Web designers. In fact, some of my best friends are Web designers. But Web design is only a small fraction of what it takes to strategize, design, create the content, develop the technology, and market the website. Most Web-design shops turn out great websites, but they don't build engaging online environments that embody the strategic goals of the company and how it relates to successful marketing campaigns and findability in the search engines. Having the prettiest website is not the goal—having the most functional one, with great creative flair, is.

2. **Technology Companies:** As a general rule, you should never have a technology company build your website. That's like asking the mailman to design your direct marketing package. The mailman's job is to deliver the finished product, not create it. In the same sense, technology is the mailman. The reason technology companies (or IT departments) have held and controlled most websites to date is because entrepreneurs have a lot in common with your average marketer: they are both scared of technology. As we discussed earlier, don't let the technology part wig you out.

Who should build your site? I lean toward a full-service digital marketing and communications shop (also known as an interactive agency). I would not be much of an entrepreneur myself if I didn't slant in that direction. Ultimately, your budget will decide the type of resources you can patch together to make it work, but always keep in mind that a great website should be:

- Clean
- Easy to navigate

- Appealing to the type of consumers who will visit your website
- Written in the language that your consumers use to find your products and services
- Filled with engaging media beyond the text (this includes images, video, and audio)
- Positioned with several "calls to action" that move consumers to do something
- Tied to the other social channels where people can connect to you
- Search engine friendly
- Built to link (both internally and externally)
- Easy to update
- Constantly refreshed and refocused
- Tied to some kind of analytics tool
- Measurable through marketing and overall business goals

It's a remedial list, but it's a good checklist and starting point. Everything you do online must bring people back to your space. Before moving forward with the concepts we're about to discuss, please make sure that both your strategy and a solid Web presence are in place.

THE FIVE C'S OF ENTREPRENEURSHIP 2.0

1. Connecting

Do you remember the sound of getting on the Internet through a dial-up connection? As we move toward faster and faster connectivity, it's important to remember that we're also connecting to individuals like never before. A business has four true objectives:

1. Connecting to consumers
2. Building loyalty
3. Nurturing those connections to make more connections
4. Making money and growing

We are connected like never before.

Do you remember when the BlackBerry first came out? There was tons of media commentary around the notion that you would no longer have control over your own life, that this new device was really a ball and chain that attached you to your employer's desk. Where did all of those editorials and fear-mongering news items go?

There's been a shift in society. Being connected is a part of it. We're not talking about answering e-mails while you're on vacation (that's more about discipline and allowing the technology to control you versus you controlling the technology). We are talking about a world where someone who doesn't use e-mail or have a mobile phone is no longer wearing a badge of honor but, rather, a scarlet letter in the world of business success and opportunity. How quickly would you be willing to hire a person who said he would only work for you on the condition that he have no form of e-mail or mobile access? It sounds about as crazy as it is.

Brass tacks: We are all connected, and being connected is a big part of how you are going to grow your business. Assume that connecting is now a core business value. If you're not connected to your business, your employees, your consumers, and your business leads, the competition is.

2. Creating

It's no longer about idly sitting by and letting the media wash over you. People are using this newfound channel to create content—text, images, audio, video—to grow their businesses. One of the biggest shifts is the individual's ability to create content. When was the last time you watched an episode of *Entourage* and thought to yourself, *This is good. I should really produce my own television show*. It sounds crazy, because it is crazy. Television was (and is) expensive to produce. One of the amazing things about consuming media in the past was how undoable it was from the consumer's standpoint. Up until very recently, creating any form of content was simply not possible.

But this ideology is completely flipped when it comes to the online world. Online is all about the consumer not just consuming but creating. So much so that there continues to be online debate as to the merits of even using the word "consumer" when it comes to your business online. Is that all your customers are doing? Consuming? We've heard nomenclature like "prosumer" and other terms used to explain the strange and intertwined relationships customers have with brands. Even calling someone a "user" has become somewhat foreign.

No one is "using" anything anymore. They are creating. You are creating. It's all about creating. Think about Facebook: How fun would Facebook be if all you could do was look at other people's pictures? (Okay, that was a bad example—we all love creeping on each other's profiles.) That being said, the real power behind Facebook is that you create the experience. You add your pictures, create events, build pages, update your status, send someone a virtual beer, poke them, and more.

Your business takes on a whole new level of complication when you're not just buying content in these spaces, but, literally, building it.

3. Conversations

It is, without a doubt, the most used word in the entire social media, Web 2.0, and online world. Everybody is talking about how the best (and newest) way to grow your business is to start a conversation, join a conversation, and/or be a conversation. From comments and blogs to online forums, podcasts, Twitter, and beyond, the individuals and the conversations they are creating are the new media. Looking at any form of business-building activity in these online channels requires you to embrace the idea of a conversation. Many people think of a real-life conversation, a one-to-one conversation; but it's more like going to a rock concert where you know everybody—some people are really close, some you've just met, and some you haven't met yet but have been looking forward to the occasion to connect.

How do you manage it all?

Should you even bother to manage it at all?

The Five C's of Entrepreneurship 2.0 were established to help you identify and define the new rules of making money and how your organization is going to have to shift toward one-to-one dialogues without getting too bogged down. Depending on the industry you're in and the types of conversations happening online, getting too engaged can take the focus away from your main course of business action.

As in the real world (although I'd argue that the online world is getting more and more real with each passing day), you have to be responsive and realistic, and there need to be tangible results (a little bit of focus doesn't hurt, either).

A conversation has to lead to a connection, and that connection is community.

4. Community

Community is the new audience. Community is the new currency. Community is the new mass media. Throughout this book, you're going to read stories of people just like you. People who had a great business idea, but who went online, got connected, started creating content (both for themselves and by adding value for others), joined and led conversations, and wound up building powerful and engaging communities (and growing their businesses like crazy). Human nature is about community. There's a reason we live in populated cities, work in the companies we do, connect with certain types of people, and serve the communities in which we do business.

Think of these online channels the same way. Would you take advantage of your community? Lie to it? Do evil?

There are basic tenets to follow and adhere to when living a community lifestyle online (like acting civil, being respectful of others, and contributing). The common misstep is to think about communities like a 1960s commune. Be practical and pragmatic about this by really focusing on the real-world community in which your business finds itself. Imagine being able to magnify that. Imagine being able to replicate how you contribute to the growth of your business and community by connecting to the entire online population. Many entrepreneurs wonder how, exactly, they can make their businesses scale beyond their four physical walls. Many of the answers to those questions can be found and discovered by being an active member of the online community. That being said, what about making money?

5. Commerce

There is nothing wrong with making money, and you should not be shy about it. You should also not try to trick people into thinking you're interested in a conversation and building community if all you really want is a quick sale. There's no trick to using the digital media channels to make money. Don't push a sale on people. Much like the tools in the following chapter will suggest, building community is way more about "pull" than "push." By adding value to the community and building trust, you will grow your sales because people will come to you instead of you pushing yourself (and your wares) on them.

Many people point to the success of Gary Vaynerchuk of Wine Library when looking at how community turns into commerce. Gary turned his parents' New Jersey liquor store from a $4 million business to a $45 million business within a five-year period. He did this primarily by listening and responding to the community at large. He not only got connected on the many existing channels like Facebook and Twitter, but he used a basic video camera setup to create his own video podcast that gets over 80,000 viewers per day. He'll randomly offer up to his community free shipping or advice on which wines to try during special times of the year. By making himself available online in much the same way he would answer your questions if you walked into his store, Gary has become an Internet celebrity. His highly personable style has even turned him into a much-sought-after speaker and an expert wine connoisseur, which has led to appearances on *Late Night with Conan O'Brien* and the *Ellen DeGeneres Show*.

SIX FREE ONLINE TOOLS YOU SHOULD BE USING RIGHT NOW

In this age of new business, understanding the myriad conversations that are taking place online is not only core to having successful marketing and communications campaigns, but it's key to understanding how people actually feel about your brand, products, and services. And, most importantly, if they're buying from you, why they're buying, and what they're saying about you to their community.

The common mistake most traditional businesses make is thinking that what is being said online has no real bearing in the "real world." Nothing could be further from the truth.

Don't believe me?

Think about the last time someone told you about a brand. Odds are you did not rush down to the nearest store to check it out. You probably did a quick search online to see what's being said, and read what others are saying. We're not just doing it for big-ticket items; we're researching everything and anything— from hotels to HDMI cables to paper clips for the office (and we're also comparing prices).

Here's the multi-million-dollar question: What are people saying about you and your product or company?

Most businesses haven't the foggiest idea. Maybe someone in the communications department does an occasional search on Google to see what's ranking on the first page, but that's about it. In today's world of interconnectedness, you may be losing real-world dollars simply because you're not monitoring your reputation online. While there are countless robust (and expensive) solutions that help companies do this, there is a handful-plus of really good (and free!) ones that will take you there as well. Below are six tools every business should know about and use.

1. Reader

In order to stay on top of everything and be able to see the information in one simple and easy-to-access environment, the first step is to get yourself a reader (also known as an RSS reader or a news reader).

My personal preference is Google Reader, but you can use iGoogle, My Yahoo! Netvibes, or any other Web-based tool that enables you to subscribe to websites and blogs. Some Internet browsers even have readers built into them.

There are two very important reasons why this is the critical first step:

1. RSS is a free subscription technology that notifies you when any website or blog you are interested in has been updated. No more morning runs through the bookmarks in your Web browser only to discover there is nothing new there. The moment something is updated, you're notified. Instead of your going out to surf the Web, a news reader brings the Web to you.

2. You don't have to worry about going to a fistful of different websites every day. With a reader, you can centralize all of your content from all of the websites and blogs you like. You're going to save time and be much more efficient. Having a reader set up with the channels you are interested in is one of the great lifehacks.

Once you have one of these fancy and free readers (you'll see how easy it is to set it up and get started), you're going to need to fill it with some great content. Whatever your personal interests may be (Scottish death metal? Economics in Southeast Asia? Knitting for kittens?), there is some kind of website, blog, or podcast that covers your area of passion. Start looking for what interests you and start populating your reader.

2. News Alerts

Curious how to find out anything and everything that is being said about you—as it happens, live and in real time? You need to set up some alerts. Google Alerts is one of the best places to start. All you have to do is input your search term (I'd suggest adding individual alerts for your company name, senior management team, products, brands, services, clients, and competitors) and you can choose what to be updated on (news, blogs, video, the Web, newsgroups, etc.) and how frequently (as it happens, once a day, once a week).

Now whenever the terms you input are mentioned online, you can be notified immediately. You can create as many alerts as you want and can be notified of updates by e-mail or set them up as a subscription to run through your reader. You will also be able to manipulate, change, and delete your alerts as needed.

3. Watchlists

Much in the same way Google monitors the Web, Technorati is a search engine that monitors the blogs. At last check, Technorati was monitoring well over 130 million blogs. That's a lot of people saying a lot of things online. Technorati offers a free service called "Watchlists" where, much like Google Alerts, you can be notified as you or your company are being mentioned in these millions of spaces.

The question is, "If I have set up Google Alerts, why would I bother with a Technorati Watchlist as well?"

Google does have an excellent blog search engine (see below), but they each capture different types of content. Most of your Google Alerts will be based on when a website or news item mentions you, but Technorati focuses exclusively on blogs, giving you additional insight into what people really think. Technorati also has a ranking tool called "Authority" that allocates and ranks blogs based on how many other websites and blogs link to it.

4. Google Blog Search

Google has its own blog search engine that sometimes returns very different results than the ones you'll find on Technorati. One trick is to organize your search results by date (this way you can see the most recent conversations). You'll see the link "sort by date" in the top right-hand side. IceRocket is another search engine for blogs.

5. Search Engines

Even if Google accounts for a huge percentage of all searches done on the Internet, it's also important to know what comes up when Yahoo! and Microsoft serve search results about you. There are two things you should immediately be looking at. One is how many results appear for your given search terms (determining if the trend increases or decreases is a great way of seeing how much buzz you're building) and the second is a little-known tool. If you enter your website address like this: "link:www.twistimage.com /blog" (obviously replacing my website with yours) in the Google search box, what returns is a list of all of the websites that are currently linking to you.

Reciprocating a link back to an existing website that is valuable is a great way to build reputation. You can use Google Search, Yahoo! Search, or Microsoft Bing (don't forget to search on the .com versions of the country you live in as well). Just being clued in to why certain sites are linking to you is a powerful market research tool that you should not dismiss.

6. Google Trends and Facebook Lexicon

Not only can you find out what people are saying about you, but tools like Google Trends and Facebook Lexicon enable you to compare your brands with others. Not only do they feed back the volume of mentions, but these tools also provide some fascinating market research by region, language, and related topics of interest.

It's important to note that the fact that you're seeing a high volume of traffic doesn't necessarily mean that everything is cool. You could actually be getting a lot of traffic for negative reasons. Most of these tools are just measuring the sheer volume of traffic; you will have to dig deeper to really uncover what the voice of your customers is really saying.

The Web provides the ultimate focus group (and it's free). It's authentic because you're not locking people in a room and feeding them pizza to get their opinion. They're expressing themselves (good, bad, and neutral) without being solicited, and they're talking online with passion. Can you really put a price on that? Can you really afford not to be listening?

CHAPTER 4

Faith-Based Initiatives, Viral Expansion Loops, and the Long Road

"Marty . . . we're going back . . . to the future!" And with those words, Doc Brown from the always likable flick *Back to the Future* drove the plutonium-powered DeLorean "time machine" until it clocked eighty-eight miles per hour and took Michael J. Fox (aka Marty McFly) on the joyride of his life.

In this chapter, we're going to go back to the future to explain how you can harness the power of online communities to build your business. Many people will tell you it's too late to get involved in online communities, that if you're not involved now, you've missed the boat. But online communities are not going away. In fact, they're just getting started. There's plenty of time to get on the boat, and you can even be the captain. As old as the Internet might seem, it's still in its very early days.

Take a quick trip with me back to the world of fifteen years ago. Computers were just starting to connect to each other through the telephone jack in every household. Microsoft's founder Bill

Gates's dream of a computer in every home (running his operating system, Windows) was taking hold (against all naysayers). The Internet was slowly being discovered by the mass population; it was already well beyond its initial intent to serve as a way for government and educational facilities to share information and knowledge. Companies like AOL and Prodigy began selling subscription-based services to consumers for dial-up Internet access, and—if you were lucky—with a few keystrokes (okay, those initial URLs were way more than a few keystrokes), you would be "surfing the Web."

Back then, I was a music journalist. My first gig was interviewing Tommy Lee from the rock band Mötley Crüe in 1989 for a national teen magazine. I kid you not: it was all downhill from there. The band was just about to launch what would become the multi-platinum best-selling album (remember when we called them "albums"?) *Dr. Feelgood*, and—I don't know how or why—a short while after, I heard about two music websites that were actually using graphics and not just text (remember, it was the early days).

One website was the official online home of the heavy metal rock group Megadeth. I seem to recall it being called Megadeth, Arizona. Whoever built that website clearly understood where the Web was going, but also had no clue where it actually was. Bandwidth speeds were primal back then. I would type in the URL and, literally, go away from the computer for a few hours and come back in hopes that some server had pinged an image or two back my way and (hopefully) some fresh text as well. This worked somewhat well, but was more often than not disrupted by someone in my household who had picked up the phone to make a call and booted me off of my ISP (Internet service provider). Good times.

The other website was a music news and information site called

Allstar. More than once a day Allstar would update their home page with the latest news in the music world. While this may not seem like a big deal as you read this, try to focus on the time when this was happening. First off, there were few people online at all. Second, computer prices were high (stupid high), and purchasing a modem to connect to the Web was not cheap either. Even the notion of an Internet service provider was still nascent and everything, overall, was pretty clunky. You needed to be part MacGyver, part IBM engineer, and all geek. Sure, "geek" has become a term of endearment today (everyone wants to date and marry a geek—just watch reality television), but back then it was all black glasses with masking tape, snorting laughs, pocket protectors, and lots of Dungeons & Dragons. From a media perspective, the life cycle to get information was a monthly walk over to the corner newsstand in hopes that the magazines (or industry trade publications) you followed were in stock (and had something of relevance for you). These days, we take for granted this new world where the media are always on, updated, refreshed, and available.

Back then, the idea of getting my hands on the latest copies of *Circus*, *Faces*, *Hit Parader*, and *Metal Edge* magazine was the highlight of the month. The severe withdrawal I would get from a lack of content as I finished the last story in each and every issue was heartbreaking. I used to read some of the issues cover-to-cover twice just to get my fix. I was desperate. Allstar ushered in a new way to consume content. It enabled me (and you) to have this unbelievable access.

From there, everything changed. It seems as though I can place my finger on the exact moment when I realized content would never be the same again. And it hasn't. Being an entrepreneur was about to change forever, too.

So what if we could go back in time? What if, with a snap

of my fingers, I could take you back there with me? Your entre-preneurial drive is intact and this crazy world (that you now see coming) is right there for the taking. Would you start the first online auction? Would you start to figure out a way for others to find and sort all of this information like that small company called Google? Would you dive headfirst deep into figuring out a way to do gambling or to sell adult content online?

Regardless of the path you would have chosen or the industry and applications you would now digitize and make your billions on, one thing remains constant: you would have focused a lot more of your time and energy on the online space if you had known then what you know now. The reality is that none of us have crystal balls. None of us could look into the future and see what was about to take shape, but as we've come to a point where we're all intrinsically connected, the digital channels are ubiq-uitous, and we're edging ever closer to a world that is truly flat. If you don't believe me, grab yourself a copy of Thomas Fried-man's best-selling book, *The World Is Flat*. Through all of these virtual (and physical) signposts, there are some clear indications as to where this is all going and how you and your business can leverage these changes. This is your chance to, literally, go back to the future, and here is the message:

Now is your opportunity to harness the power that lies in online communities. The idea here is not to dive headfirst into starting your own blog or podcast. Instead, it is to create an on-line strategy by understanding what, exactly, you hope to accom-plish by connecting to the many thousands of people who are already fascinated by the industry you serve. And if you don't start thinking about defining a strategy for getting involved in these online communities, well, then you really are stuck in the past, and you're hanging out with Biff at the high school prom drinking peach schnapps.

But, you may wonder, what's the real ROI of learning how to work with online communities? Will it be worth the effort? Statistics from a variety of sources suggest that becoming a member of an online community—and, most importantly, adding value to it—will bring not only more customers to your business but more loyal customers:

- "Community users spend 54% more money than non-community users."—eBay, 2006.
- "Community users remain customers 50% longer than non-community users."—AT&T, 2002.
- "Community users visit nine times more often than non-community users."—McKinsey, 2000.
- "56% of online community members log in once a day or more."—USC–Annenberg School Center for the Digital Future, 2007.
- "43% of Internet users who are members of online communities say that they 'feel as strongly' about their virtual community as they do about their real-world communities."—USC–Annenberg School Center for the Digital Future, 2006.

Moreover, building community online is a sustainable model. The more you put in, the more equity you create, and the more loyalty and goodwill you build.

Let's look at six ways to build a strong community.

FAITH-BASED INITIATIVES

I first heard the term "faith-based initiative" from Avinash Kaushik, who borrowed the term from former President of the United States George W. Bush and then tweaked it. Kaushik wears many hats: author of *Web Analytics: An Hour a Day*, blogger at "Occam's Razor," and analytics evangelist at Google. He helps Google define what metrics are important to measure in all of their product offerings, and he helps promote Google Analytics, a free tool for measuring traffic to your website.

Why would Google give away, for free, a tool like Google Analytics? There are companies that are selling very robust and expensive Web analytics tools like WebTrends, Coremetrics, Omniture, and others, and yet if you ask professionals in the analytics space, they'll tell you that Google Analytics gives you about 80 percent of what those big-name application developers deliver, but Google does it for free.

Google understands the power of a strong faith-based initiative. By giving you, the general public, a free and easy-to-use tool that will help you better understand who is coming to your website, what they are doing, what search engine keywords drive traffic, and who is linking to your website, Google realizes that the more likely it is that you will improve how your website converts traffic into consumers. Once you start optimizing your website, odds are that your next logical step will be to advertise with Google. Google has faith that the smarter they make you and the more tools they give you to help you improve your own situation, the more loyal you will be and the more likely you will be to spend money with them.

I can hear you now: "But I'm not Google! I don't have billions of dollars or tens of thousands of employees! How do I make this work?"

You make it work by remembering the old sayings "Givers gain" or "Give and ye shall receive." The secret in creating compelling online faith-based initiatives is to forget about how you're going to make money initially and focus instead on what tool or application you can create and give away to add value to the lives of others.

One example is Due Maternity. This maternity retailer is a husband-and-wife operation that, in 2003, was launched as the destination for moms-to-be. The couple quickly realized the opportunity to sell their merchandise online. They were not, by any stretch of the imagination, the first online merchant in the maternity space. So they created several faith-based initiatives but one really stands out: a countdown clock widget. A widget is a downloadable application that resides on your computer desktop—it's always there. For the mother-to-be, the cute little countdown clock is a very useful tool, a reminder of just how close her special day is. It also happens to be branded Due Maternity. So, as the expecting parents begin working on their birthing plan and what they need to be prepared, who do you think is top of mind? Due Maternity.

How much does the development of a widget cost? It varies, but there are several online applications that let you slap together a fully customized widget for free. There's nothing wrong with starting there, seeing how your customers take to the idea, and then upgrading as customization, demand, and involvement become more necessary. What about creating an application for the iPhone or BlackBerry?

The challenge is to create a faith-based initiative that truly adds value and gets people's attention. Here are some questions to get you thinking about what faith-based initiatives you can create:

- What tools do people commonly use that have not been made available for the online world?
- What expertise and knowledge do we have, and how can we best share this with our consumers? Is it text, images, audio, video?

- Are there any Web-based tools that will let me get started with this idea for free?
- What is my competition doing? Can I do it better? What are they not doing?
- How can I use this initiative to stay connected to my consumers?
- Is there something I can create that will empower my consumers to connect to one another better?
- Once I have the idea, which existing online communities should I be connected with to let people know about it?

VIRAL EXPANSION LOOPS

Which of these two options would you prefer in building word-of-mouth for your business?

1. People pass word of your amazing brand on to others because they are enthusiastic about it.
2. The only way for people to get true value from your brand is to engage and encourage their entire personal and professional community to use it.

Option 1, known as viral marketing, is very powerful. It's the force that takes hold when people pass around something that is very cool and will earn them status, accolades, or goodwill. And it's what put Hotmail on the map as well (at the bottom of every e-mail they had a simple call to action for people to get their own free Web-based e-mail address). Movies like *The Blair Witch Project*, *Snakes on a Plane*, and *Cloverfield* have done it as well.

Option 2, which is extremely powerful and is known as a viral expansion loop, is what rapidly makes one consumer become fifteen or two become sixty-four or four become twenty-eight, eight become two hundred. A viral expansion loop is enormous in growth because it expands through networks. It's what Facebook, MySpace, and other hugely successful digital businesses—think eBay, Skype, Twitter, and Google—are premised on. It's a dynamic model for growing revenue and market valuation, and for generating more brand evangelists who, in turn, keep growing revenue.

The idea behind viral expansion loops is very social media and Web 2.0. It follows the core rules of new marketing by embracing the power of individuals and their social graphs and the power of online communities to create a collaborative experience. The very nature of these types of environments creates an atmosphere where full engagement happens as more and more interested parties enter the fold and then expand the network even further by bringing in others to connect.

You don't have to be Google or eBay or any of the other well-known giants to take advantage of viral expansion loops. Ning, created by Marc Andreessen and Gina Bianchini, allows anybody (for free) to create his or her own independent online social network. Unlike Facebook, where you create your own personal profile that becomes a part of the entire Facebook system, Ning gives you the power to create, design, and execute a centralized online community without being thrust into a larger social network structure. If Facebook is a planet, Ning is a system that empowers anybody to create his or her own separate planet. In and of itself, Ning is a meta–viral expansion loop that enables entrepreneurs to build their own, niche, viral expansion loops. Or, as co-founder Gina Bianchini commented on my blog, it's "your own social network for anything."

Spend a few minutes identifying how to bring your community together and engage them to bring in their contacts and associates. In essence, look at what Ning is doing for the average person, and think about ways you can leverage this type of online tool to build your community. A viral expansion loop makes you the hub (not the spoke). And, best of all, it works. Ning is the machine behind the new 50 Cent and Radiohead online social networks as well. While building an online social network is not a new idea, there's constant talk in the online channels of how the massive online social networks would be much more powerful if they focused on the specific niches of interest over the sheer massiveness of it all. The opening is there for you.

Take, for example, the ASPCA Online Community, which describes itself as "a great place to meet fellow animal lovers and to discuss everything from pet care to animal cruelty." The space was created by the ASPCA, the American Society for the Prevention of Cruelty to Animals, and now boasts over 20,000 community members. They are taking part in forum discussions on topics as diverse as pet memorials and the life of an emergency room veterinarian.

So why is the power of the viral expansion loop infinitely more engaging than a typical viral marketing campaign? It's real human beings creating real interactions and connections. Remember, great marketing is about real interactions between real people. For me to pass along a video because I find it engaging and I know it will make me look good in someone else's eyes is one thing. For me to be a part of something I am deeply interested in, knowing that I'm inviting other like-minded individuals to take part, is infinitely more powerful.

How powerful?

Think about your network of connections and the relationships among the people within it. As these digital channels add more and more people with more and more connections, they continue to grow. In fact, they become more useful at a faster rate. We have begun to spread and share our most important information this way. The net effect is that the connections eventually reach a point of exponential growth. Don't you find it becoming increasingly harder to abandon any online community you've become involved with because of how much time you've spent connecting?

As an entrepreneur, your best bet is to focus on creating your own niche marketing initiatives that embrace the spirit and result of the viral expansion loop. You need to create something that adds multiple layers of value for the person who takes part when he encourages his friends to take part as well. It's a big idea. Here's the bad news: There is no obvious step-by-step guide to make this happen. Prior to viral expansion loops, most marketing initiatives looked at how to get as many people as possible to see an ad and take an action. But a communications strategy that embraces the ethos of the viral expansion loop puts you, as the brand, right smack dab in the middle of a bustling community where the members are, literally, inviting everyone they know with similar interests to take part, get involved, and, in turn, tell the people they know.

Viral expansion loops are exciting because they also establish the creator as a recognized authority and enable the instigator of the program to capture information about who is connecting to whom and how strong the links are. In sum, viral expansion loops are all about making one plus one equal ten. They create a platform where you, as the entrepreneur, take on a key role in how your industry unfolds.

Marketers love drowning themselves in a sea of data. As online advertising took hold, the general consensus was that the data we were capturing, from advertising with banners to search and e-mail marketing, was overwhelming. Most businesses don't use this data to its full potential because of the complexity and density of it all. Imagine adding in the layer of a viral expansion loop.

Imagine knowing not just what an individual clicked on, but who else in his or her network might be open to your messages.

The possibilities become endless, and we can begin to appreciate how viral expansion loops will weigh heavily on the types of creative programs we can initiate within online environments and social networks. The real business leaders who will lead this charge are the ones who are spending time now investing in either developing or partnering with technology that is attempting to break down the data into bits of insight that will connect all of us more effectively to our consumers.

Prior to online social networking, ideas like viral expansion loops were, traditionally, something cared about only by those interested in genealogy or technology. But because of what's happening now online, we're all starting to realize that these online channels are not just a place to advertise, but are vast and powerful communities with many nodes and connections. The challenge is that building a viral expansion loop is not easy and does not hold the same marketing values we're accustomed to.

TripIt is a great example of a viral expansion loop. If you have played around on any of the online social networks, you soon realize that geography is not as important as finding others who have similar interests. Still, when you travel, wouldn't it be nice to meet up with some of the people you have connected to only online? Enter TripIt. Once you have your itinerary you can e-mail it to TripIt. Not only does TripIt centralize and organize all of your travel information in a useful and visually appealing way, it is also an online social network. TripIt will look at all of the friends you are connected to and let you know when someone is in your hometown, or when you will be in theirs (it can even tell you if that person is expected to be home during the same time frame). Instead of a traditional online social network for people interested in travel, TripIt amps it up into a viral expansion loop.

Yes, their tools for organizing and planning your personal trip are superior to many similar products on the Internet, but what gets the word out about TripIt is not the strong word of mouth, it's the advantage in sharing the information with everyone you know— family, friends, and co-workers—and getting them to use it too. The power to meet new and interesting people also multiplies as those people inject their social graphs into the system. Dopplr is a similar viral expansion loop for people interested in travel (and there are others). It's the network effect in effect. Neither of these networks is of any value to one person unless that person implicates his or her entire social network. The more people who are connected to the one individual, the more value the entire community derives from the service.

THINK RIPPLES, NOT SPLASHES

Traditional advertising campaigns have a striking resemblance to a big splash in a pool of water. In fact, it's not uncommon for the marketing department to get a call from the C-level suite asking to "make a splash" for the upcoming product launch.

Splashes do work (when done right), but only for a very limited time. Think about it. You drop a rock in the water, and the splash comes up high and fast, but fades just as quickly. The only way to keep your momentum is to keep making splashes, which, as you know, gets messy and confusing super quickly (after a while, people also get a little sick of getting wet all the time). Splashes are also expensive to start, execute, and then repeat.

Ripples work in an entirely different way. With less energy, you can toss a small pebble (your ideas) into a big lake and let the ripple effect take hold. True, it's not as dramatic as a splash, but it sustains itself for a longer period, covering a much wider area.

In the digital world it's actually easier and less expensive to create a ripple than a splash. Ripples are the powerful conversations that are generated when you share your content (text, audio, video, images) online with a blog, YouTube, or a social networking site. People grab the content and place it on their sites and pages, they comment on it, they Digg it, they pass it on, and they encourage others to take part. (Digg is an online space where everyday people submit and vote on what the most relevant news of the moment is.)

For over twenty-five years, Stonyfield Farm, the organic dairy producer known primarily for its yogurt, worked hard to build its brand and increase sales. "From 1983, when we were still milking cows," says CEO Gary Hirshberg, "we would write 'Let us hear back from you' on the back of the yogurt container." Then in 2005 the company embraced the new world of marketing and started blogging. Nothing fancy, just a simple blog to start speaking to consumers in a human voice.

The overall results have been impressive if you keep in mind the kind of audience that would be attracted to the Stonyfield Farm blogs. Christine Halvorson, the company blogger for Stonyfield Farm, discussed the kind of traffic they were seeing during an interview posted to the "Business Blog Consulting" blog in December 2004:

> Since we began the five blogs on April 1, 2004, we've had a total of 160,000 visitors. (That number combines all five blogs. We actually didn't begin measuring until June 6.) We have discontinued one of the blogs, so now there are four. Of those remaining four, the most recent per month visits are:
>
> Strong Women Daily News: 15,603
> The Daily Scoop: 4,049
> Creating Healthy Kids: 9,659
> The Bovine Bugle: 28,237

These have been growing steadily each month.

I like also to measure our [email] subscribers. Even though "subscribing" is not really "blog culture," I like to offer our readers that option. Subscriber numbers to date are:

Strong Women Daily News: 1,701
The Daily Scoop: 129
Creating Healthy Kids: 318
The Bovine Bugle: 276

These, too, have been growing slowly and steadily, with the exception of Strong Women, which has grown dramatically and quickly!

"I was really intrigued by the kind of immediate intimate connection created by blogging," says Hirshberg. "But what I know in my gut from 22 years of running this company is that we have an emotional connection with customers. That helps explain why we're growing at four times the category rate in some markets and three times the category rate nationally. . . . If it's done properly, I can't imagine any company that wouldn't benefit."

Whatever your business, you can use a blog to share what you're thinking, share what's going on in your industry and, most importantly, share your expertise. Ripples grow wider and bigger until they become waves. Waves never stop. They keep pounding the land, one after the other.

THE LONG ROAD

The crux of the best-selling book *The Long Tail* by *Wired* editor-in-chief Chris Anderson is that, in the Internet economy, every obscure product has at least one customer. There is a "Long Tail" of products and services in deep and rich niches that are not the "hits" of the world, and there is a business in getting the right products into the hands of the right customers. The Long Tail also works because online you can have unlimited inventory.

The Long Tail is perfect for those who have been online and adding value for years. So, while the Long Tail is all abuzz in the buzz-word index, you need to start traveling down what I call the Long Road: putting in the time and commitment to create compelling content and engaging your consumer in a unique experience.

One of the best ways to walk that first mile on the Long Road is to use your news reader to really home in on the two to three blogs or online communities that speak to your target market. Hang back and follow the flow of content—everything from the frequency to which types of content spur the most reaction. Within a couple of days you should be able to catch the flow. You'll recognize some of the people who add their voices to the community and, if you're keeping your head in the game, you should be able to spot some opportunities for you to join in and add your voice, your opinion.

The key is always to add value and push the conversation forward. Nobody likes someone who is taking part with the sole intent of pimping their own agenda. Approach the Long Road with authenticity and sincerity and you'll flourish. Taking part in the myriad conversations also adds to your legacy of content. Plus, should you decide to start your own blog, online social network, or the like, you'll now be a "known" throughout the more highly trafficked properties because you've been a contributor and a valued community member.

C2C: CONSUMER TO CONSUMER

In 2004, George Masters spent five months creating a home-brewed commercial for the Apple iPod mini in his spare time. He posted it to his website to get some feedback from his community. This one piece of sixty-second video to the tune of "Tiny Machine" by the 1980s pop group the Darling Buds took off like a brushfire. This was B.Y. (Before YouTube), the good ol' days (five years ago), when someone would attach a video file in an e-mail and send it off to their contact list. Getting your message noticed and appreciated back then was a lot more difficult. Now, with online video-sharing sites like YouTube, anyone can post a piece of video and drive links to it.

Masters was a thirty-six-year-old high school teacher who created a full-on ad for Apple because he really liked his iPod mini. "I did it for fun," he said in an article entitled "Home-Brew iPod Ad Opens Eyes," on Wired.com (December 13, 2004). "I love motion graphics. I like creating visuals. . . . It's off-brand but that's the point. That's the fun of being one guy. You're not limited by a style guide or a creative director. You can branch out and think different."

An entrepreneur might read the Masters story and think, *Aha! I get it—I can save money by having my consumers create the ads.*

Wrong.

Consumers make and create ads for themselves. They exchange, debate, and share them with others because it gives them status and a sense of personal pride and accomplishment. They are actually building their personal brands as much as (if not more than) yours. This is not the type of marketing we have become accustomed to.

Traditionally you were engaged in either business-to-consumer marketing (B2C) or business-to-business marketing (B2B), meaning you were either putting your messages out there for the mass consumer to pick up (individuals) or you were selling your wares to companies. In their seminal marketing book, *The One to One Future*, Don Peppers and Martha Rogers looked at a future where both B2B and B2C companies would be able to harvest their client databases and create, execute, and test marketing messages that were specifically customized to the individual and where he or she was in the buying cycle. It's a promise many hoped would be fulfilled by e-mail marketing, but alas, the technology still eludes us. Slicing and dicing the data is complex, time consuming, and expensive. We're getting closer with much more in-depth segmentation and customization, but we're not quite close to the one-to-one channel that Peppers and Rogers defined.

Somewhat ironically, the consumer-to-consumer channel is quickly becoming one of the most powerful ways to build sales and increase your brand visibility. So how do you get consumers to market your goods and services to one another? By letting them share their reviews of your products—especially their negative reviews.

Brett Hurt is the co-founder and CEO of the Austin, Texas–based company Bazaarvoice. Bazaarvoice provides applications to people who sell online, but one of their core products is third-party audited consumer reviews. In September 2008, Rubicon Consulting released a study entitled "Online Communities and Their Impact on Business: Ignore at Your Peril," which demonstrated that online reviews and comments written by consumers are hugely influential to buying decisions. In fact, the study showed that reviews and comments are second only to personal word-of-mouth referrals. In other words, we trust what others who have bought before us think. Bazaarvoice audits these reviews for website owners to ensure that the reviewer is actually a real human being (and also not an employee or relative of the company), plus they also ensure that the content does not use profanity or is not unsuitable in other ways. They have already served over 10 billion user-generated reviews to shoppers worldwide.

A conversation with Hurt (who, prior to Bazaarvoice, was the founder of the Web analytics company Coremetrics) on episode #99 of "Six Pixels of Separation—The Twist Image Podcast" brought forward two key stats that should shock you:

1. A negative review actually converts to a sale more effectively than a positive review.
2. The average consumer review is a 4.5-plus out of five.

These provide massive insights into the power of harnessing consumer-to-consumer marketing and why you, as a business owner, need to encourage and provide the platform for individuals to share their thoughts. You might expect that only the people who don't like your product or service will review it, and if they see something negative about your products, they'll leave without buying anything. Clearly this is not the case. What we're seeing is that people who love your product are much more inclined to let other people know about it, and a consumer who reads a negative review will feel that you are being honest, and will still buy from you (trust is a big thing). It also demonstrates that some reviews don't really impact a consumer if they don't share similar values. There's hope for humanity yet.

Here are some additional powerful statistics, as reported by Bazaarvoice:

- Consumer recommendations are the most trusted form of advertising (78% versus 34% for search engine ads) (citing Nielsen Media Research, 2007).

- 82% of consumers who read reviews said that their purchasing decisions have been directly influenced by those reviews (citing Deloitte, October 2007).
- 90% of reviewers report that they write reviews in order to help others make better buying decisions—and 66% are writing online reviews of offline purchases (citing Keller Fay Group & Bazaarvoice, November 2007).
- 8 out of 10 consumers trust brands that offer reviews (citing Vizu & Bazaarvoice, August 2007).

Consumer-to-consumer marketing is replacing the old feedback forms and, even better, everything is public. Everything is open for everyone to see, comment on, tag, share, and pass along. The kooks and haters have the same volume of voice as the lovers and brand evangelists. Plus, everything that's recorded serves as a permanent record in the Long Tail that is a search result. It's hard to make heads or tails of who the detractors are and, for the general public, there's also little indication whether the negative is a legitimate source or just someone with a bone to pick.

In truth, most companies should embrace this type of open forum and conversation, but, sadly, there are some who simply don't have the thick skin or bandwidth to handle and respond to everything that comes in. Ignoring what people are saying about you online is not an option anymore. The search results that are returned to users who are looking for your goods and services will be tainted with everything but your own perspective.

In the end, these digital channels may not be for you, but you really can't afford to ignore them. It's quite possible that the one person out of one hundred with something negative to say will detract from the five-star-plus rating you are getting from the majority, but that, too, is not a reason to dismiss it. We are getting to the point in time where entrepreneurs have to suck it up and set up some Google Alerts and a Technorati Watchlist to hear these voices—whether you like it or not.

PARTICIPATION = LEADERSHIP

It is one thing to participate; it's another to become a leader. All entrepreneurs are leaders and, without exception, one of the easiest ways to gain traction in any endeavor is to take on that leadership role. If you're going to participate (and by this point you'd better), why not lead from the front?

The digital world swirls with ways to advertise, monetize, or build sponsorships for these online social channels. Whether you call it Web 2.0, social media, or the live Web, entrepreneurs still struggle to figure out how to maximize these channels.

Every initiative you embrace should have your leadership vision focused on how to grow the audience and your community. These online channels are a great way to build your personal brand and to establish yourself (and your company) as a recognized authority. In the interest of bringing out the leader in you, here is a list of things you can do to help grow any online community—either your own or that of someone else you admire. At the same time, the tactics below will also get your own name "out there" if you choose not to maintain a media channel of your own.

- Add your comments and insights to a blog. It's probably one of the easiest and fastest ways to get involved without really having to do very much. Every blog has a place for anybody to add a comment. Go ahead, push the conversation forward.
- Head over to Technorati, find a blog you like, and "favorite" it. It's always good to see which people like a particu-

lar blog. Acknowledging it by clicking that little pink icon puts you in front of the medium owner.

- If you are mentioning anyone personally in anything, use their full name in a tag (e.g., "Mitch Joel"). As you can well imagine, there are not as many Mitch Joels as there are Mitches, and nothing is more beautiful than the sound of one's own name. People love to see everything from video, images, text, and audio they are mentioned in. Plus, it puts you on other people's radar.

- Connect on LinkedIn. Most businesspeople use this professional online social network and are happy to extend and connect into your network. Make sure your profile is fully updated as well (it takes time, but it is well worth the effort).

- If you see someone you know on LinkedIn and you're so inclined, write up a recommendation for them (you never know what might come back your way).

- Head over to Facebook (or any popular online social network) and add your business associates as friends.

- If you see a group or page on Facebook that is of interest to you, join and connect to others. Even better, start your own (remember, be the Leader).

- If you've been listening to podcasts that you like, write a review for them in iTunes. This is something that is hardly mentioned, but apparently, iTunes does look at this information and ranks podcasts accordingly.

- Get a business colleague, client, or friend (or fifty friends) to subscribe to a blog or podcast that you have been following. If you love someone's content, let other people know about it. The only way you're going to grow the community is by referring people to the stuff that inspires you.

- Speak at your industry's association or a local business

meet-up. You don't need professional representation from a speakers bureau to make an impact. Almost all community and business development groups hold regular events and are in constant need of quality content.

- Share. Share what you're doing. This is all about sharing, connecting, and conversations.

The best way to monetize these channels is to grow the community, which will grow everyone's business (including your own) in turn. A basic theory on community: You can't have a strong business without a strong community. Everything we just discussed in this chapter is all about building a strong community.

And we're just getting started.

Broadband penetration is still an issue in many parts of the world, and mobile devices trump Internet access as the primary way individuals connect in many countries. Whatever the platform of choice may be, we are seeing the formulation and initiation of powerful and very real online communities—and this is just the beginning. The formation of these online social networks is enabling and empowering individuals to build their own businesses, develop strong personal brands, create online environments, and connect in ways that are catapulting them to levels of fame, wealth, and stardom we've never seen before.

If you do one thing after reading this chapter, make it a commitment to pull your team together and discuss the strategy and tactics you are comfortable with to develop your community. Remember that your community is not just about what is happening on the properties you are running. A healthy online community is on many properties. Figure out multiple ways to be engaged and connected here, there, and everywhere.

CHAPTER 5

Know Control

A TALE OF TWO CITIES—IN A COUPLE OF YEARS

The Old City: My Kingdom for a Bic Pen!

Chris Brennan was a network security consultant and a bike enthusiast. One Sunday afternoon in 2004, he popped the top off of a Bic pen and jiggled it into the lock cylinder of an expensive Kryptonite bike lock. With just a few twists, the lock Kryptonite described as "perfect for high crime areas" was opened.

As the video clip Brennan created made the rounds over the Internet (the incident also happened B.Y.—Before YouTube), Kryptonite assured the public that their lock (and technology) was solid. The result was a publicity disaster for Kryptonite, damages totaling over $10 million, a harsh beating to the brand, and, subsequently, a Long Tail of search results that will make it very hard to convince a potential new customer to choose Kryptonite for bike safety.

When asked what Brennan thought about Kryptonite's response (the company said it would be putting into market a newer locking technology), he stated:

"They're worthless. . . . I don't trust them anymore."

The barrage of online chatter was supplanted by major mass

media attention, including an article in the *New York Times* entitled "The Pen Is Mightier than the Lock." Eventually, Kryptonite changed their tune and offered free upgrades for their easily picked bike locks. A quick search on Google for the term "kryptonite bike lock" in 2009 returned over 50 percent of the results on the first page with mentions of the Bic pen incident.

So, while the issue may seem like old news to you, it's as fresh as a daisy in one of the first places consumers go right now to check out what would be the perfect bike lock: a search engine.

One additional comment and question: If Kryptonite had seen the blog posting on the very well-known tech and gadget blog "Engadget," how long should it have taken for them to put a banner on every page of their website that said: "We are very concerned with a video that is making its way around the Internet (you can view it here). As we establish the best course of action, please let us know if you own a Kryptonite bike lock and we will notify you promptly (and first) with the best course of action"?

Instead, here is the copy of the product page for the specific Kryptonite lock that was picked:

- Our toughest bicycle security for moderate to high crime areas.
- 1/2" (13 mm) Through-hardened Kryptonium™ Steel shackle resists bolt cutters and leverage attacks.
- Patented deadbolt locking mechanism for extensive holding power.
- Pik-Safe™ disc-style cylinder with a disc-style key.

Nobody likes to deal with a crisis, but the Web was the one (and probably the best) place Kryptonite could have responded (or at least acknowledged the issue) in a matter of minutes—and they did not until many felt it was too late and that the damage was done.

The New City: An Apple a Day

Fast-forward: In May 2007 "Engadget" reported that it had received an internal e-mail memo that was leaked from Apple stating that the initial debut of the iPhone, along with the launch of their new operating system, Leopard, would both be delayed. "Engadget" is regarded as one of the highest-trafficked blogs in the world and has the attention of many mainstream media folk. This blog post got passed around to the mass media and sent Apple's stock into a downward tumble that resulted in a loss of over $100 million in market value.

Once "Engadget" was informed that the internal memo (which was legit) was retracted shortly thereafter and that there was no delay for Apple's products, the blog issued a posting titled "False Alarm: iPhone NOT Delayed until October, Leopard NOT Delayed Again until January." Apple's stock bounced back within twenty-four hours.

The Moral of the Story

The Internet used to have brushfires that did not cross over into the real world. Even if bad things were being said, you could dismiss them as coming from those "crazy people on the Internet." But life on the Internet has changed in a very short number of years. Had Apple not reacted and moved on this blog news, who knows how bad and prolonged the damage could have been? Most companies are doing everything they can to monitor and react to whatever is happening online. A simple glance at those two well-known and played-out stories demonstrates why it is increasingly important for your business to be paying attention to online channels and even more important to respond when something does flare up. Even the speed at which companies should respond is evolving as the channels evolve.

The common battle cry that "things are moving really fast!" is usually tempered with "People have always said that things are moving fast, but it's always the same—things have not changed all that much." The truth is that things are moving faster than ever before, and this is changing the way you do business. Major or minor issues have a tendency to "flare up," and these digital channels demonstrate that things have, without a doubt, been sped up to a much faster click. Publishing is cheap or free, and fast. In 2004, Kryptonite took its time, went through legal channels, and issued traditional press releases. Some would even say they were not paying close enough attention at the first stages to the video's viral effect because it was "only online" (back then, few businesses really took the online channel all that seriously). In 2007, Apple was rectifying the blog posting within a couple of hours (if not minutes).

What Changed in Those Very Few Years?

For one thing, the concept of blogs as a real media channel was validated. When blogging first made its debut (around 2000), most journalists and mass media people denounced it, conveying that bloggers were people who sit in the dark recesses of their basements typing about their cats. It was only being done by the lunatic fringe. There was no way for a blogger to be seen as comparable to a journalist. They were not accredited, and how could they be trusted to be "fair and balanced"? As the years rolled on (around 2004), more and more newspapers began quoting bloggers as subject-matter experts. From there, some journalists began writing their own blogs and, suddenly, the words of bloggers carried as much weight as (and sometimes more than) those of the mainstream media. There is still a dark side to blogging. Bloggers can be cruel and vindictive. As with all media, you must proceed with caution.

There was one specific tipping point. During the 2004 United States presidential elections, CNN was running its editorial coverage of the comings and goings of the political appetite in the U.S., and would on occasion shift to two young women (who looked more like sorority friends than news anchors) who were reading off of political blogs to add some additional commentary. In a short while, we went from "Who are these amateur bloggers?" to "Let's go see what the bloggers have to say about this issue."

Vindication and validation.

As for "fair and balanced," with the millions of political and news blogs floating around and gaining traction, how could those varied opinions not provide a deep level of fair and balanced perspectives when combined? This is an interesting and relevant concept for your business. The multiplication of the individual voices creates some kind of mass attention. It's no longer one channel blasting its message to the masses. The question becomes: Can you get many people talking about you or are you still trying to send your one message out to many people?

I'LL HUFF AND I'LL PUFF AND I'LL BLOW YOUR MEDIA HOUSE DOWN

The "Huffington Post" is the creation of both Arianna Huffington and Kenneth Lerer. It's a liberal news blog that focuses on a wide range of topics from politics, entertainment, and the media to business and the environment. Launched on May 9, 2005, as a commentary outlet for Huffington and her well-known friends, the "Huffington Post" is one of the most trafficked websites on the Internet.

Prior to the "Huffington Post," Arianna was a well-known journalist working on many media platforms—newspapers, magazines, television—but once she discovered the freedom to publish her own beliefs and the opinions of her like-minded friends, she left the mainstream media to develop her own new media channel based on a blogging style, format, and platform.

Her success speaks to the changing landscape of business. If you thought things were ugly for the print media industry before the economic meltdown, it's getting increasingly hard now to turn your head and not hear the woes of traditional newspapers and magazines.

On December 2, 2008, *Advertising Age* reported that newspaper ad revenue in the U.S. had fallen by nearly $2 billion. It was a record 18.1 percent decline in the third quarter, based on news from the Newspaper Association of America. Ironically, the day before this news broke, the "Huffington Post" announced $25 million in funding that set a $100 million valuation for the company:

> The funding means Arianna Huffington's news blog is now considered more valuable by its backers than quite a few publicly traded newspaper companies, such as Lee Enterprises [LEE], owner of the *St. Louis Post-Dispatch* and 52 other papers (market cap: $36 million), A.H. Belo [AHC], owner of the *Dallas Morning News* and the *Providence Journal* (market cap: $35 million), and Media General [MEG], owner of the *Tampa Tribune* and *Richmond Times-Dispatch* (market cap: $34.6 million).
>
> It puts Huffington Post in the same league as McClatchy Corp. [MNI], owner of the *Sacramento Bee*, *Miami Herald* and 28 other dailies (market cap: $150 million),

according to Michael Learmonth, author of the *Advertising Age* article "Huffington Post More Valuable than Some Newspaper Companies," December 1, 2008.

It's a question of culture and a shift in our society.

Huffington not only provides a great example of the massive shift in communications that has taken place, she's also a poster child for the ideology set forth in this book. She has used these new channels not only to connect and get her voice out to the masses, but also to build a substantive media channel that generates significant revenues and trounces the online audience of massive media properties like the *New York Times* and the *Washington Post* (combined).

Your role is to look at why some of these blog crossovers gain so much traction. How can you create content so compelling that it becomes "must-read" or "must-see"? What is it about the way the content flows on the "Huffington Post" and why do so many contributors take part without ever being paid?

A QUESTION OF SPEED

Your company's newest challenge is speed—how fast do you move? We can't blame big corporations for not moving fast enough; they're bloated with layers of hierarchy that were established within the same mind-set of the industrial revolution way of factory thinking. They want all of the facts and the time to strategize on the best course of action (and one that won't rock the board of directors' and stakeholders' boat too much). In a world of publishing platforms like YouTube and Twitter where the consumer is in (and sometimes out of) control of creating content, that's getting harder and harder to do.

Here's the bigger question: *Have companies lost complete control of their brands?*

Marketing magazine (April 30, 2007) had a cover story entitled "Marketing 2.0," and it started off as follows:

> You're no longer in control of your marketing messages. Your customer is more than just a target. The old ways you design and

advertise products just don't work anymore. Welcome to life in Marketing 2.0.

The idea that the consumer is now not in control is anathema to what most people think. The general drum-beating is that the consumer is in control, not the company. But it's not true.

Businesses still decide which brands to put into the market, the message, and the channels they will use to get the word out. Nothing has changed on that end. The consumer still controls whether or not he will buy what you are selling and whether or not he will tell everybody he knows how he feels about the brand experience. It's not a question of control at all. Consumers simply have access to some of the same global distribution channels and equal capability to have their voices heard in those specific channels. Consumers now have volume.

It's a big deal, but it's *not* the whole deal, and that about sums it up.

Consumers are not creating TV spots and running them on mainstream media. They're not booking out-of-home media properties and populating them, and they're certainly not running print ads for your brand.

They're also not buying pay-per-click campaigns through Google, sending out mass e-mails, or designing banner ads and running campaigns for you on Yahoo!

So what are they doing?

They're watching you. They're talking with you. They're sharing what they like (and dislike) with a community of people who are like-minded. They're taking the material we have given them and are mashing it up (a mash-up is when you take two or more unique pieces of content and bring them together to form something original). They're either having fun with your brand or making fun of it, but they are not in control of it.

PASSIONATE PEOPLE DO PASSIONATE THINGS

George Masters was a teacher on the West Coast of the United States. A regular guy. A regular guy who loved his iPod mini so much that he took six months to create his own iPod mini commercial using his Mac and motion graphics in his spare time. He did not ask Steve Jobs for permission to create this now-famous online ad. He created it, he published it to the Web, and he watched it spread. If you watch the video closely enough, you'll note the integrity of the brand—from the Apple logo to how the iPod mini looks. It's all intact. When that video got passed around, many consumers thought it was a legitimate iPod mini ad.

This does not put Masters in control of the Apple or the iPod brands. He used them (and their likeness) to create his own message. What, exactly, was Masters controlling here? Apple controlled the brand and the message while Masters controlled his creative expression and his newfound ability to share his creativeness with the world by uploading it to the Web.

Let's stop worrying about who is in control of our messages and start worrying about how great and innovative the brands truly are in the marketplace. If we focus on producing great brands with great messages that resonate with consumers, we'll worry a whole lot less about what "control" is, because we'll all be too busy connecting to our consumers and creating more engaging brand experiences. Great brands provoke people.

Is it "no control" or "know control"?

KNOW CONTROL

Get comfortable with being a little uncomfortable. The new business game is not about control. It's about the volume of voices. Now, all individuals (and this includes you) have the ability not only to get their messages out to the rest of the world, but to do it with the same volume of voice that the major corporations controlled for years. Here's the difference: *Money does not equal volume of voice.*

But it used to.

That was the big game of mass media. The more money a company spent, the more present they were, the more volume they had in the marketplace. The Internet has changed this. Individuals don't suddenly have control; they suddenly have a Marshall stack amplifier, and if you've seen the movie *This is Spinal Tap*, you already know that it goes to eleven.

Think of it this way: Let's say you own a small café and you decided to start a blog today about the lifestyles of the hyper-caffeinated. And, on that exact same day, Starbucks decided to start a blog about the world flavors of coffee. Both you and Starbucks have access to the exact same audience. Granted, Starbucks could outspend you on mass media to build awareness, but all things being equal—both companies start a blog on the same day—your opportunities to reach an audience are pretty much the same.

There has been a democratization of the media in the online channels, and the mass media have been disintermediated; businesses no longer need them to get their messages out to the masses.

Big companies fear this shift because it forces them to change their "business as usual" paradigm. Entrepreneurs should embrace it. We live in a world where you can create an audio program with a $30 headset and free software on a laptop, and where you can publish your thoughts for free. You can create compelling video content with a cheap video camera and some basic editing software and skills.

HOW LONG HAS USER-GENERATED CONTENT BEEN AROUND?

When people think about user-generated content, they tend to think of a sixteen-year-old kid getting his cubes slammed in a random skateboarding incident gone wrong, but this is simply not the case. More than half of YouTube's audience is over the age of thirty-five. And, at last glance, if the numbers are accurate, every sixty seconds more than eight hours of new video content is being uploaded to YouTube. That's about 11,500 hours of new video content every day.

The other thought to consider is that user-generated content is not new. Think back to paintings on cave walls. We've been generating content since we first bashed rocks with sticks. The major difference—and this falls directly into the "know control" bucket—is that now we've been given an amazing (and mostly free) publishing platform to share our ideas with the world—and we're doing it in droves. The content we're generating can now be published and shared with all. It no longer dies when the fire fades on those cold cave walls.

Here's what you can't control: *You can't control the conversation*. You can't control whether there will be user-generated content created around your brand. You can't control how a user-generated message is placed and ranked in the search engines.

Here's what you can control: *You can control whether or not you take part*. You can control whether you will encourage your consumers to be so passionate that they actually start marketing your company *for you*. You can control whether you will be present and available should things go wrong. You can control how available you will be to fix whatever people say is broken.

Think differently about "control." Think differently about your business.

RESIGN YOUR PRIVACY

Yes, you're naked on the Internet. You may think you can hide behind an anonymous user name. You may think you can pretend to be somebody else and no one will know. You may think that when you're surfing for porn at home no one else knows.

You may think all of that—and you would be wrong.

Everything is being tracked and individuals are getting better and better at identifying just who is behind the user name "freakyboy_17." It's not all that complicated and it's not as clandestine as some might think.

The truth is, the majority of people on the Internet are just like you—trying to figure the space out, connect with more like-minded individuals, have some fun, and grow their business. Yes, you do need to be very self-aware. We've all heard that the Internet is just one big place for porn and gambling, but the truth is, if you don't go to those sites, you'll never see them. You need to be playing in the right sandboxes and guiding yourself with an overriding philosophy that someone is recording you at every twist and turn and that everything you say can—and will—be used against you in the court of public opinion.

Female readers might be thinking, *That's easy for you to say; it's different for women.* It might be (the online channel is very representative of the real world), and in the interest of covering all of your bases, the standard recommendation is that you take part in only as much as you are comfortable with. You may have to deal with nasty comments, and there have been instances where individuals have actually stopped blogging and completely disconnected due to harassment. It's sad, but there is a small percentage of people who are evil. The general rules of thumb are: Be smart, be very self-aware, and always think about the content you are creating and putting out there as a lasting record of yourself.

The other side is this: The older generation (people over the age of twenty-five) sees what the younger generation is posting online, and we shudder. Does anybody really believe you will be employable if the HR department hops onto Facebook and comes across photos from last week's frosh party and sees you (and your friends) out on a bender?

"As younger people reveal their private lives on the Internet, the older generation looks on with alarm and misapprehension not seen since the early days of rock and roll. The future belongs to the uninhibited," reads the first paragraph of an article, "Say Everything," by Emily Nussbaum for *New York* magazine (published February 12, 2007).

That article could well be one of the best articles on Internet culture and privacy. It cuts right through the topical issues and lands in a very murky arena: it's the place where our old value systems clash and conflict with something so new. The very idea of privacy is changing beneath our feet. What happens to individuals in a world where producing content and distributing it to the world is as easy as making a phone call? The answer is, everyone starts doing it. If everyone starts doing it, the ramifications start becoming even more intense because everything, all of the time, is being recorded. We're exposing ourselves more and more.

The sum of the message is that while we tend to cringe at some of those quirky photos of ourselves that made their way onto MySpace, the shift is real, and as more and more people mature and enter the workforce, we won't be able to judge the person who has those wild party pictures posted on Flickr negatively because everybody will have them—including you (and then who will you hire?).

Numerous books have already been written about privacy and the Internet. When it comes to being a business owner, the best thing you can do is resign your privacy (maybe just a little). Don

Tapscott, author of several books on the Internet, culture, and business (including the most excellent *Wikinomics*), says we all need to be more comfortable with being naked, but "if you're going to be naked, you better be buff."

Being "buff" (as Tapscott defines it) for entrepreneurs means making sure that whatever you put out there is real, that you are not making false claims and that you are doing it with the intent of adding value to the community. At the same time, being buff also means being smart. Make sure you are monitoring what is being said about you outside of your own properties. Be sure you either respond or comment when appropriate. Being buff is about being smart and sharp.

LET THE COMMUNITY PLAY WITH YOUR BRAND

You probably have a very real fear about embracing the idea that your customers can now do whatever they want with your brand. But here's the ultimate question: Do you think that by imposing levels of control you are really going to be able to stop them or encourage them not to do something?

How about a deeper question: If this is the current way of the world and everybody's reality, is imposing control on your materials going to turn them toward another brand or competitor?

George Lucas can be pretty controlling with the many assets he manages for the *Star Wars* franchise. Yet, not too long ago, he placed several movie clips from the *Star Wars* saga online for the hard-core fans who wanted to create their own scenes, extend them, tell another story, or the like. Did you even hear about this? Unless you're obsessed with *Star Wars*, Lucas's action probably didn't even hit your radar. With so much media choice now, consider the concept that there is so much content now available that someone doing something with your brand will probably have a limited audience.

Use the information.

Be smart. Do your own marketing research on your own company. Instead of complaining that someone took your brand and created a *Saturday Night Live*–type parody with it, why not learn from it? See how many people viewed it on YouTube. How did it rate? How many comments are there? Good, bad, or neutral? What can you learn about how the general public perceives your brand? On average, how many people are viewing this every day? Do you notice any spikes? Take the link of the posted video and type it into a search engine—who else found it interesting enough to talk about it and share it? Did you know about those spaces? Can the owners of those communities become friends? Did anyone take that video and mash it up into something else?

Never fail to remember that the Internet is, without question, the most powerful and real focus group of all time. If a campaign fails (or works) you will know exactly why—in real time.

GIVE THE COMMUNITY THE TOOLS THEY NEED TO CHANGE YOUR BRAND

Instead of complaining about how the consumers are now in control online (remember, they're not), why not stop worrying about what's being done to your brand? Just let it all go and give them what they want.

Allowing your consumers to play with your brand is one of the best ways for you to figure out how to improve it, make it more relevant, and connect more with others.

Give them the assets.

More and more companies are looking for ways to get their consumers to create user-generated content. The easiest way to encourage them (beyond running a contest and offering up cash and prizes) is to empower them by creating a digital space where they can pull whatever they might want (logos, colors, text, audio, video). Letting people know that you stand behind your brand—and encouraging people to create whatever they perceive your brand to be—is a great first step in joining the communities and taking part.

Don't forget to track everything. As you give them the tools and as they start creating content, it is critical for you to be involved and let them know you are present. Some might argue that it's better to be a lurker—to be around and watching but never saying anything about who you are—but it's better to be transparent. There might be instances when lurking is better than saying, "Here I am—how can I help you?" but for the most part, the creators of the content will feel vindicated and happy to see that those they are honoring (or making fun of) are watching. Why do you think they create that content in the first place?

Don't be afraid to be more like George Lucas. It worked for him. Let it work for you.

It is not uncommon to be a little bit uncomfortable with this line of thinking. It is a different way to act, and it forces you and your brand to be open. Always remember that when you open yourself up to feedback, you have to be prepared. Most companies that have gone down this route were quick to realize that even the negative feedback made them look good. They were able to act on the information, in a very public way, and demonstrate not only that they are listening, but that they are doing something about their problems.

IT'S NOT JUST ABOUT THE INTERNET: THINK MOBILE TOO

Mobile is changing everything we know about the space as well. We're going from the real world to virtual worlds to that mobile device in your pocket. There are all sorts of new mobile devices in the marketplace, and all of them are promising the ability to stay connected to friends and loved ones.

When looking at what people are creating online and how letting go of your privacy is empowering you to connect at entirely new levels, be aware that the mobile device is also going to change everything.

You're sitting with your family at Sunday brunch and someone asks, "What time does the bookstore open?" Suddenly, you can do a mobile search, see how close the nearest location is, what time they open, and what other people have said about the specific book you are looking to pick up.

Our social channels are connecting closer with mobile because it is a highly personal and contextual device. Has your mobile ever been misplaced or stolen? Remember that feeling of violation? Someone knows everywhere you've been, where you're going, who your friends are, what their contact information is. It's very different from the Web experience, but the device is shifting into the most personal connection an individual has with technology.

It's going to change business, and if you can help people find you faster by being involved in the mobile space, dive on in. More and more searches are being done every day on mobile devices, and it's a space that few entrepreneurs are paying attention to.

Bottom line? Get your website into a mobile version and encourage your consumers to help you be more present in these mobile channels.

GOOGLE IS LIKE AN ELEPHANT: IT NEVER FORGETS

Everything you do, good and bad, is online forever. Even the stuff you might have done before you were ever online is there too (or will be soon enough). As the search engines try to aggregate more and more content, they are diving into everything from newspaper archives to press release archives to documenting, tagging, and indexing the knowledge of the world.

Your business has a very simple calling: *to provide new and compelling products and services that consumers want to buy.*

The message is serious: You have to decide and govern yourself based on how personal you want to be in these online channels. That's why you need to be overly self-aware about what you create (and what others are creating about you). All of the content you create is a reflection of your personal brand and, for most, the only true reflection of who you really are in everybody else's eyes—both personally and professionally.

Everything you are seeing and hearing about online is still relatively new (as old as some of it may seem). All of this content being created becomes part of your personal brand's Long Tail. It is your digital footprint. It will exist forever whenever somebody does any kind of search on you. The information and content created can be accessed by anyone at any time.

MIND YOUR TONGUE AND TYPE

A major point to bear in mind is to have a little levity and humility. Just because you have a blog with traffic does not mean you are at par with people like Malcolm Gladwell or Tom Peters. Yes, you have the same ability to reach the same audience with the same volume, but this doesn't mean you have the experience, insights, and analytical skills. You have your own perspective and they have theirs. Both are worthy and should have a public voice, but don't kid yourself into thinking you stand on the same level (yet) with the giants just because you both have a blog. Personally, I have years ahead of me in marketing before I can gain the insights, learnings, and experience of some of the greats who have been doing it for decades longer. I keep this in mind when I blog and create content, and so should you. This way you're not fooling yourself into thinking that what you say is as valuable as someone who has done it, sold it, and has the T-shirt. Be a little careful when you post and with what you post. Clients, future clients, employers, and future employers are reading. It's easy to say "I would never work for anyone who does not like what I have to blog about," but go back and look at some of the stuff you did in business five years ago. Your opinions at that moment in time may not reflect your current state of mind (we cringe just a little when we look back). People change, people grow, and people gain experience. I am of the David Weinberger (co-author of *The Cluetrain Manifesto* and author of *Everything Is Miscellaneous*) mentality that everyone should create all different kinds of content on the Internet. Everyone should share their thoughts and their insights. At the same time, be careful: Google has a mighty Long Tail.

MASS MEDIA OR MASS CONTENT

I remember listening to David Weinberger speak; he said something that changed my perspective on blogs. For a long while I was on a kick where I thought people should blog only if they have something unique to say. I don't know how the conversation came up, but David made a comment about how everybody and anybody should blog. There's no set bar, and all thoughts, ideas, and stories should be treated equally.

It was a very powerful moment, because I realized that your

stories may not be important to me, but they are important to someone (even if it's just your own small community). Blogging is a great way to put all ideas out there—and maybe all blogs and ideas are created equally. Maybe the number of readers, comments, and links are the "old way" of measuring success.

Maybe just sharing the blog thought is everything, and nothing else matters.

This concept reaches well beyond blogs into all of these channels. Whatever you say, do, and create online should connect with your community. *It is not about how many people see and connect to it—it's about who sees and connects to it.*

If mass media were to go away (which they won't), what's left? Everyone is able to produce, share, and distribute his or her own content. The syndication comes in the form of subscriptions, where people either sign up to receive your content or pull it from you into their readers. If things go this route—and more and more people are creating more and more content—instead of mass media, we're now stuck with mass content.

How does your business win?

Is the "win" in the fact that we choose what we want, how we want it, and control how the content flows? Is the "win" in the personalization of everything?

Take a quick glance at a Twitter feed. Once you start, you'll soon be following more people than you can name and if you step away for an hour, you can't effectively catch up. Even if you could, the conversational aspect of it has already moved on, replaced by even more tweets and content to ponder. Gut-check time: because of all these new media channels, you are more media saturated than ever before. Being ruthless with what you follow won't seem like a viable option, either. There are just too many smart people out there whom you will become interested in following, sharing, and commenting on.

Welcome to the era of "snackable" content. The days of reading something, taking notes on it, passing it around, and pondering it are quickly dwindling. The more engaged you become with this content, the harder it will be to comment and to share as much as you would like. Get yourself very comfortable with the idea that you are now skimming, grazing, and perusing everything. Because there is so much mass content, you will quickly begin to feel like you're not even able to give the truly great stuff the time it well deserves—because you simply can't.

The lesson is to remember that people feel the same way about the content you are creating. *Keep it short, punchy, memorable, fun—and, most importantly, simple.*

We're stuck in the middle of this battle for content and audience. It's either too much of the same thing from a select few (think about the television companies) or it is too much of very specific things from a mass number of individuals. It can all be a little overwhelming, and in reviewing how this fits into your business, think about how the generic television broadcasting companies are moving more toward specialty TV. The shift is afoot, and in order to be effective as a business, it's going to take a full-court press toward resigning some of your privacy online, embracing the idea of consumer-generated content, and maybe even partaking in the creation of some killer content as well.

CHAPTER 6

The Real World

TURNING ONLINE RELATIONSHIPS INTO REAL-WORLD MEET-UPS

It seemed like any other conference any one of us had ever attended over the years. But this one was a little bit different.

I woke up early and made the five-hour drive from Montreal south into Massachusetts. My final destination was Bunker Hill Community College. As I crossed into Boston, I had a sudden, sinking feeling in my stomach. *What if no one shows up, and I am the only one there?*

In any "normal" conference scenario, this could never be the case. Most conferences are produced by a company or an association and are heavily marketed, using tools like direct mail pieces, full-page ads in industry trade publications, and getting their keynote speakers featured in the local media. Ticket sales are done way in advance, sponsorships are made available—you know the drill.

But there is now a new kind of conference. They're being created by people who are organizing online but meeting up in the real world. These are not your typical conferences. These are called "unconferences."

PodCamp Boston was held on September 9–10, 2006, at Bunker

Hill Community College (the exact location where Robin Williams treated Matt Damon in the Academy Award–winning film *Good Will Hunting*). According to Wikipedia, an unconference is "a facilitated participant-driven face-to-face conference around a theme or purpose. The term unconference has been applied, often self-applied, to a wide range of gatherings that try to avoid one or more aspects of a conventional conference such as high fees and sponsored presentations." That's nice, but here's what really happens:

Someone takes the initiative to choose a topic, sets up a wiki (a Web page that anyone can edit), maybe even finds someone to sponsor a venue or supply the audiovisual equipment, and then the community takes over. These unconferences are fully self-organizing, meaning that attendees must sign themselves up on the wiki, and all attendees are encouraged to present and to help keep the day and the venue flowing efficiently. An additional wiki page is set up for the schedule and program of the day, and individuals can post the topics they wish to present on their own.

There is something extremely fascinating and compelling about this unconference movement. The general sentiment people have about anything "online" or "digital" is that the people who are taking part are lonely. They sit in their basements on their computers and pluck away at the keyboard while the "real world" passes them by. Nothing could be further from the truth. The bottom line is that these online channels are leading to real-world meetings, and that's key.

Do a quick search on the city where you live and you'll see a plethora of meet-ups, get-togethers, unconferences, and more. In a time of economic concern, why spend thousands on connecting like-minded people when you can organize and meet up for free?

CREATE A LOCAL UNCONFERENCE AND CHANGE YOUR BUSINESS LANDSCAPE

In a post–9/11 world, travel has become complicated, expensive, and time consuming. Also, with the advent of the Internet and new communications technology, finding out about the latest and greatest in your industry is no longer just that once-a-year junket to Las Vegas to walk the conference floor and soak in the glory of your competitors' brochures, knickknacks, and breath mints. Unconferences were created with the sole vision to make meeting up in the real world a valuable networking, learning, and sharing experience combined.

One of the first kinds of unconferences was called BarCamp, where people in Silicon Valley decided to come together to discuss technology. This happened back in 2005 and attracted close to 200 people. Since then, BarCamps have been held in over 350 cities all over the world (some unconferences have had close to 1,000 participants) and the concept has expanded beyond the topic of technology—well beyond. There have been unconferences focused on marketing, entrepreneurship, the environment, the banking industry, and many more subjects. For the hobbyists out there, they've even had WineCamp (nothing like sipping some Cabernet Sauvignon and discussing your favorite online social network under the stars of the Napa Valley).

Unconferences are not just about attending. Everyone knows that the person speaking gets all the attention, and an unconference is a great place for you to teach the community or to share a case study. *Be forewarned: If you intend to do any kind of sales pitch or self-promotional type of presentations, you will be booted off the stage.* The unconference movement is ruled by the "Law of Two Feet," which states: "If at any time you feel you're not learning or not contributing, you can use your own two feet to go somewhere else"—and people do. This is the primary reason why the content is so compelling. All presenters know that if they don't bring their "A" game, people will leave (in droves). Think of an unconference as a public meeting: anyone and everyone is welcome to attend and encouraged to participate.

How do you become a presenter at an unconference? Simple: add the topic and description on the wiki in the time that suits you best.

Another way to show support is with money. Sponsoring an unconference is a cheap and meaningful way to help the community come together. All too often entrepreneurs are shut out of good sponsoring opportunities because the costs are prohibitive. Look to see what the sponsorship levels are at an upcoming unconference and see if it makes financial sense for you to take part. Another option might be to barter. Because these unconferences are predominately self-organizing, people are constantly looking for solutions. A good barter demonstrates your support for the event and typically does include serious recognition and acknowledgment at the event.

Getting a little creative, you might want to consider sponsoring a meal or the drinks tab at the evening events, or even come up with something more unique.

The point is that no one ever just "attends" an unconference. The spirit of it is that we are all equal, able to share our knowledge or help in any way we feel will best serve the community.

You might be shaking your head at this point, thinking this is all a little too much "kumbaya" for your liking, but trust me: unconferences will change the way you think about business.

BACK TO PODCAMP BOSTON

According to the wiki, over 300 people were supposed to be converging at Bunker Hill Community College for this unconference. But what if nobody showed? I hadn't bought a ticket, and there was nobody to call if there was a problem.

But sure enough, almost everybody who registered showed up and the sessions were extraordinary. They had titles like: "Inside a Pre-Launch Startup New Media Company," "Hollywood 3.0: The Challenge of Video-Podcasting," "The Advertising/Marketing World and Video Social Media: What We've Learned So Far," and so on.

It was three rooms, two days, and more information overload than I've experienced at big conferences I've paid thousands of dollars to attend. Lifetime friendships and business opportunities were forged. To me, the reason why unconferences work is because everyone who attends truly wants the same outcome: to learn more and to share with their peers.

IF IT CAN WORK FOR SOMEONE WHO SELLS STUDENT LOANS, IT CAN WORK FOR YOU

Christopher S. Penn was one of a handful of organizers behind PodCamp Boston. By day, Chris is the chief technology officer of the Student Loan Network. Don't be fooled by the title or the type of business Penn is in: Chris is a living and breathing model of how anyone can leverage these new channels to grow their business. The competition to buy online advertising in the field of student loans is fierce and expensive. Penn thought about the many ways he could rise above the competition, and quickly realized that his passion for media would be one of the keys. He delivers a daily podcast called "Financial Aid Podcast." With well over 900 episodes, it has become the choice audio program for people of all walks of life because it is interesting and not just geared toward college students. He features great new music, gives reviews on the state of the economy, and even interviews some fascinating people.

His passion for the "Financial Aid Podcast" led him to meet other highly regarded new media types in the New England area. They saw what was happening on the West Coast (with the Bar-Camp and unconference movement) and decided the time was right to try a similar model but focusing more on podcasting and new media instead of technology. Being a founder of PodCamp has established Chris as a visionary in new media, and he has been called upon for expert information by researchers for the Congressional Advisory Committee on Student Financial Aid, the Federal Bureau of Investigation, and the U.S. Department of Health and Human Services, as well as having been sought after for conferences and private intensive seminars.

This has led Chris to many speaking gigs ranging from executives of major venture capital firms to multiple state and federal agencies to aspiring college students looking to make their mark on the world. As his personal stock continued to rise, Penn started another podcast focused on marketing called "Marketing Over Coffee" (which is co-hosted by John Wall of the podcast "The M Show"). Leveraging these new media channels has changed everything Penn thought he knew about growing a business. The connections and audiences his blogs and podcasts generate have established him as a trusted resource and as the guy that many college students turn to with questions about student loans. Right after the U.S. economic crisis took hold, Penn continued to soldier on by spreading information about the economy throughout his blogs, his podcasts, and his presence in a multitude of online social networks. (This included a free forty-seven-page eBook entitled "2009–2010 FAFSA

Guide," which takes interested parties through the FAFSA financial aid application process line-by-line and offers tips geared specifically to families being pinched by the economy.)

Beyond the millions of dollars that have been generated in student loans for the Student Loan Network, Penn has become an industry evangelist, taking his message well beyond the intended audience (look, we're even talking about him in this book). His online social networking success has led to his being featured in many books and newspapers such as the *Wall Street Journal,* the *Washington Post*, and the *New York Times*, and magazines such as *BusinessWeek* and *U.S. News & World Report*. He's been on PBS, CNN, ABC News, and more. He's taken his passion for the industry he serves and mixed it with his interest in new media and expanded his own job. Not only is Chris a prime example of what it means to be the consummate entrepreneur within an organization, but his passion to drive the success of the company has made him an online celebrity and a sought-after resource.

Ultimately, unconferences empower individuals to build their businesses by blurring the lines between online social networks and real-world meet-ups. These next-generation Tupperware parties build loyalty and establish expertise beyond reason. The other benefit is that these types of meetings in person are still very new. They're constantly evolving and organizers are looking for more and more people to take part. Also, there are tons of industries that have never even heard of these meetings, so the opportunity for you to lead one is out there right now.

HOW DO YOU EVEN FIND OUT IF THESE TYPES OF MEETINGS ARE TAKING PLACE IN YOUR TOWN?

Your most powerful tool to find out about which unconferences are taking place (and where) is to use any major search engine

(Google knows all). The reality is that if you are already following the key blogs and podcasts in your industry, you should come across the promotion of these events there as well (doing a search on Technorati or setting up a Watchlist there is a good idea, too, as bloggers tend to be the first people to announce an unconference).

You should also set up a News Alert for the word "unconference" or for the city you are in. Yes, there will be plenty of alerts sent your way that have little to no value, but when there is one of relevance, you'll be happy you took the time to set it up (you may also want to adjust your settings so that you're notified only once a week).

On a past trip I realized that I had one free night, and it just so happened that a marketing-related unconference (called Case-Camp—where marketers present and share real case studies with real results) was taking place. I wound up not only learning but connecting and networking on what otherwise would have been another night of room service and YouTube.

There are also many websites geared specifically toward the listing of events. They include sites like Upcoming.org and the like. Through the magic of RSS, you can select your city of choice and grab the feed from it (placing it in your news reader); in this way you'll not only see the many cultural event listings, but also when unconferences and meet-ups are happening.

DON'T JUST SHOW UP; BECOME A PRESENTER

You know the old saying that people fear public speaking more than they fear death. Fair enough. To paraphrase Jerry Seinfeld, the average person would rather die than have to give a eulogy. Keep in mind that you're not "average." You're an entrepreneur and you've done way crazier things than get up in front of a group of your peers to talk (like, for instance, starting your own business).

Presenting at an unconference is not the same as speaking at the opening night of the Democratic National Convention. At an unconference you can use slides or you can just as easily have people huddle around in a circle and guide a conversation with a couple of speaking points. An unconference can also be the best place to test-drive some of the stuff you've been thinking about in terms of where your industry is, where it's going, and, most importantly, where you think it should be going.

The best advice is to put yourself out there. Choose a topic, challenge yourself, invite people to take part and add their thoughts. Create a scenario where you are contributing to the community and take a leadership role. Unconferences have hosted presentations that have leveraged the latest and greatest in multimedia and some have just been a person with a bunch of notes in a Moleskine notebook. PodCamp Ottawa is a tiny meeting (with a maximum of eighty people), and those who come sit in a circle on the floor and are asked to leave their technology at home. The meeting is about sharing experiences, telling stories, and not fussing over any technology. The event is a Wi-Fi-free zone.

BECOME A LEADER

Offer to help organize an unconference. It sounds like a tall order, but it's not. All communities are looking for the "next generation" of industry leaders. If you're going to attend an event, why not call up the organizers and see if you can volunteer or lead a certain sub-committee or an important function? If that fails, why not start your own? A bunch of cool Montreal social media types decided they wanted to host a PodCamp. They quickly self-organized and led an event that saw close to four hundred people attending. All eyes were on this small group of people who took the time and effort to make the event happen (full disclosure: I was one of the organizers of PodCamp Montreal). What do you think it says about them to their staff, potential and existing clients, or the business community at large? Leadership is one of the hardest skills to foster in business. Demonstrating it not only adds value to your business, but it takes you several notches above your peers and builds your community.

There are some strategic by-products that come from taking a leadership role. It should be noted that you should not take a leadership role for these reasons, but interesting things do happen to those who dare to lead. Leaders tend to get some of the attention from the media surrounding the event. Leaders tend to get business leads or make solid business connections because it's human nature for people to work with other people who are perceived to be taking the lead (whether real or not). Don't do it for these reasons, but understand that the benefits of being a leader far outweigh the extra time you're putting into the event on top of simply attending.

Christopher S. Penn didn't ask for anyone's permission. He acted like a leader and simply mobilized an entire community that has now expanded well beyond the borders of New England to a global base. Those not even interested in student loans are interested in Penn. There's a definite addition of time responsibility that comes with being a leader, but once you're planning to make the most of these events, why not be one of the people who effects real change? If you thought, *What do student loans have to do with podcasting?*, now you know. It's all about growing the community, and through this strong community Chris is now growing his business (rapidly). He is a leader, and you should lead your industry too.

USE EVERY CHANNEL POSSIBLE TO CONNECT

Don't be a pest would be the first rule, but keep in mind that most of these events do have multiple online locations that enable and engender some kind of online social interaction before, during, and after the real-world meeting. From a Facebook group to the wiki, most people willingly put their information forward in hopes that others will connect.

One of the more powerful aspects of the unconference is everyone's desire to connect—not just at the event, but prior to it (and afterwards). Make sure to join any and all related groups. Also, if you are creating any kind of content for the event (blogging about it, taking pictures, shooting videos, etc.) make sure to tag your content appropriately (a tag is simply one or several words that the group agrees to use so that all of the content—images, audio, text, and video—is more easily findable online). The organizers of the event will typically list on the website which tags they will be using. This way, all content created will be found by everyone who is looking for it. It's a great way to e-meet someone prior to an event, and an even better way to stay connected once the event is over.

In helping to organize PodCamp Montreal, the Facebook group became an integral place to see who was going to attend and what they were all about. Everyone was also able to create connections with many people they were not directly connected to but were interested in meeting live at the event. Along with sending a friend-invite to people you really don't know, common courtesy would be to leave a little note saying where you found them and why you're looking to connect to them. In most scenarios you should be able to meet new people online prior to these live meet-ups, which makes it even easier to connect in real life.

As the weekend of events unfolds, many of the people you will have connected with online will come over to say hi and thank you for adding them. These blurring online relationships and real-world connections make it easier for all of us to come to an event because we actually had some form of introduction prior to being there in person (even if it was only in our digital formats).

ACT AS A CITY HOST

As popular as this movement has become, the truth is that, more often than not, there won't be an unconference happening in your neck of the woods. So instead of waiting for one to be scheduled, become that leader. Be the person to start the idea of creating an unconference in your community.

The first step you should take is to try to create an organizing committee. As relaxed and self-organizing as these events are, there will still be logistics, questions, media inquiries, and a variety of other details that need to be addressed (like making sure no one is ruining or spamming the wiki). Put some feelers out for other people in your industry who would be into making this local event happen.

Once you've settled on a topic and a date, shoot a message out to some of the influential people in your industry to get a feel for whether or not they would put their stamp of approval on it. Maybe even ask one or two of them to be a guest speaker. Odds are that once these players start talking about the event, word of mouth alone will be enough to get things rolling along. You'll also be surprised at how interested the local media will be in an event of this nature. A quick press release or e-mail to some of the local business editors will strum up some event recognition and get registration numbers pouring in.

Try to find a local company, community center, or school that will donate the venue. Doing it at a local college or university is ideal. They typically have all the facilities you'll need (and this includes the technology: Wi-Fi, projectors, screens, white-boards, etc.).

If the idea of acting as a city host for an unconference is something that sparks an interest in you, head over to Kaliya Hamlin's blog entitled "Unconference" and read her post, "How to DIY Un-conference" (http://kaliyasblogs.net/unconference/?p=21). It's a step-by-step walk-through of how to organize and run an unconference, with all of the nitty-gritty details. Upon running through her blog post, you will be able to note some key reasons why some unconferences have been more successful than others. Her pointers and lists also provide an uncensored look into what participants can expect to get out of an event of this nature.

While it may seem like a lot of busywork, helping to organize a specific type of unconference really is a huge community and business builder. My company, Twist Image, looks upon taking a leadership role in both organizing and sponsoring these events as key to our visibility and growth within the community and the industry we serve.

IT'S JUST DINNER

While it sounds geekier than it is, events like Geek Dinners are another simple way to build, maintain, and encourage more real-life interactions.

A Geek Dinner is just another kind of simple and quick informal meet-up. I travel a lot and very often have an opening during dinnertime (no one likes to eat alone). At one point, a colleague (Michael Seaton of "The Client Side Blog") asked if we could meet up for dinner, and I thought it might be fun to open it up to the public. I posted on my blog that I would be in Toronto and was interested in meeting others in the marketing space for dinner.

Nearly twenty people showed up, all representing major marketing and communications agencies, along with brand marketers. It was a great night and involved no real work or logistics beyond finding a restaurant that could accommodate the group (and on a weeknight, they were more than happy to accommodate).

We made it very clear that there would be separate bills (each individual would be responsible for his or her own food and drinks) and that the evening would have no format or agenda: it simply would be an excuse to get together, talk shop, and enjoy dinner and drinks and each other's company.

From that one dinner, I've held Geek Dinners during additional trips to Toronto, and we've done them in other cities as well (there was one that had close to fifty people). They have been extended to include breakfast meet-ups, and some people even hold "Tweet-ups." People leverage the micro-blogging platform Twitter to leave messages like "Tweet-up at the Starbucks on the corner of Broadway and Reade at 4:00 pm," and sure enough, a meet-up is formed. What will immediately blow you away is the camaraderie everyone feels regarding where your industry is and where it's going. You'll also have the pleasure of meeting people in person. It is likely that people who see your comments online or follow you will be interested in a real-world get-together. At one of the dinners, it was a huge pleasure for me finally to meet one of the co-hosts of the "Inside PR" podcast, Terry Fallis. Terry summed up these real-world meet-ups best; right before he left for the evening, he said, "I would say it was a pleasure to meet you, but I really feel like we already know each other, so it was great seeing you."

At that moment we both just laughed. But as I thought about it further, I suddenly realized that the content we are creating online has real-world implications. Meeting people in person is not something you can just hide behind and pretend it is "other" than what you are doing to build your business on a day-to-day basis. These new digital channels truly do bind people together. The idea of Six Pixels of Separation is only real when your on-line community and your real-world community become, simply, community.

All of these types of events are fun and easy ways to host people and to fill a room with smart folks.

An additional way to make a Geek Dinner work in your own city is to look at the industry conferences and events that are com-ing through your town. When you see an event with a keynote speaker you would love to meet, drop him an e-mail and ask if he would be interested in taking part in a Geek Dinner (always make sure to treat him if he agrees). I've done this on numerous occa-sions and they have always been super-successful. Shel Holtz is a widely respected communications expert (he also happens to be the co-host, along with Neville Hobson, of one of the better audio podcasts for communications professionals called "For Immedi-ate Release: The Hobson and Holtz Report" and the co-author of the book *Tactical Transparency*). When I saw that he was giving a keynote presentation for a local conference, I asked if he would like to attend a Geek Dinner. We wound up having over twenty people come for drinks and dinner. Shel got the chance to hang out and schmooze with some of his peers and we all got a chance to get to know Shel in a much more private and social setting. In short, we connected.

Geek Dinners are pretty simple to set up, and they enable me not to worry about whom I am going to meet and with whom I am going to speak, because all of the people attending RSVP'd through me. All you really have to do is put the word out, track your RSVPs, and make the reservation. The only caveat is to make sure that if people are not going to show up that they notify you in ample time so you don't look like a jerk to the people who run the restaurant.

BE A GOOD CITIZEN: BUILD YOUR COMMUNITY AND WATCH YOUR BUSINESS GROW

In-person meet-ups, be they unconferences, Geek Dinners, or Tweet-ups, are an excellent way to build your company brand and become a valuable member of the community, and they will, without question, build your business. The spirit of doing these types of events is to encourage learning and the connecting of your peers in a real-world setting; it is not to push a sale down someone's throat. *If you build trust and community by providing value to others, good things (like more business) do happen.*

CHAPTER 7

You Are Media

EVERYBODY LOVES CHRIS

It felt like the final car chase scene from *The Bourne Identity*, but we were in Boston (not Paris) and the car was not zipping down staircases, but trying to figure out the many roundabouts and one-way streets that would eventually get us to the night festivities of the second PodCamp Boston. I had thought the driver of the car, Chris Brogan, would know where we were going. After all, he was from these parts and had offered to give me a ride. But after a couple of minutes of Brogan's making U-turns and paying much more attention to the street signs than to the other cars, it became apparent that we were lost. With one hand on the steering wheel and the other on his mobile device, Brogan hopped onto Twitter and posted this message: "Help! Lost! Call my mobile." Before the next intersection, his phone was ringing off the hook.

We got back on track with the help of someone who doesn't even live in Boston but was following Brogan and was able to guide us over the phone using Google Maps. That's the kind of response you can get when you have over 80,000 people following you.

Chris Brogan is a very special individual, but he is not an

anomaly. A technology guy and a man who saw the power of the online social channels from the early days, Brogan is widely known as "The Guy" when it comes to building online communities. Along with being one of the co-founders of the PodCamp movement, Brogan has led an interesting career, including working for technology and telecommunications start-ups, but his real passion seems to be connecting.

His eponymous blog sits on the exclusive Top 100 of Technorati and is updated multiple times a day. It is not uncommon for some of his blog postings to get upwards of 100 comments, and the same type of traffic is replicated in the many social channels he plays in, from Facebook and FriendFeed to Twitter and anything else he touches. People want to be connected to him. People want to be him. By being open, available, quick, and responsive in all of the spaces he occupies, Brogan has become a much-sought-after new-media and community consultant, author, and speaker. He is another prime example of a person who has seen a total shift in his professional and personal life through using online communities to share his ideas and insights and has turned that into real-world benefit.

But Brogan has done much more than that. In the online channels, the Chris Brogan brand is as well known and as respected as corporate brands like Dell and Starbucks (some might argue that Brogan's brand is even more respected than the corporate ones). What has happened to Brogan is happening to more and more people who create compelling content in the online channels. While some might simply dismiss it as a common case of "micro-celebrity" or link it back to Andy Warhol's fifteen minutes of fame, there are deep ramifications to what this means to any and all businesses looking at exploring these digital channels.

To start, Brogan can't lie or deceive this audience. If a brand is about trust, a personal brand is like the deeper trust we extend to our immediate family. If, for example, Chris wrote a blog posting tomorrow telling his community how much he loves a certain movie, but took money from the movie studio and didn't disclose to his audience that he was being paid to write the endorsement, his entire following would disappear before you could say "payola." Unlike with corporate brands, which can do harm to the environment or have an internal meltdown and still beat the street, online digital channels are all about transparency and trust, and Chris's network and his ability to connect with it is a very fragile relationship.

Chris Brogan manages and develops a very personal brand that has a huge audience—one not seen by many big corporations—and the lesson here is clear: In a world of Six Pixels of Separation, it is not about how your business connects and communicates in online channels, it's about how you (or your employees) as an individual build, nurture, and share personal brands. A company is no longer made up of anonymous people building one brand; rather, it is made up of many personal brands that are telling your one corporate-brand story in their own, personal, ways.

THE RISE OF THE PERSONAL BRAND

"Big companies understand the importance of brands. Today, in the Age of the Individual, you have to be your own brand. Here's what it takes to be the CEO of Me Inc." With those words, management guru and best-selling business book author Tom Peters launched the concept of personal branding with the cover story for *Fast Company* magazine, nearly ten years ago.

Through the years since Peters first brought the concept forward, many image consultants, HR professionals, and sales trainers have encouraged their clients (and anyone else who would listen) to think about themselves as personal brands as they grow their entrepreneurial endeavors. In most cases, this involved tips, tricks, and tactics to get other people to simply "like you." Effective? Maybe, but it was never a great long-term strategy.

On top of sales-like tactics to get people to buy from you, personal branding takes on an ever more important part in your life in this era of digital footprints. Because you are publishing content and building community in this very personal channel, it's not just about what it does for your business, but what it will do for you, personally. One of the major discoveries you will make is that, like any of the major brands out on the market, your personal brand is also going to rise and become publicly known. The true power of Six Pixels of Separation comes from understanding how your personal brand is developed and nurtured, and in making sure it connects effectively in these digital channels. This is a whole new way of doing business. Now, with a simple search, your personal brand lives, breathes, and is the overall perception people have of you (and your company).

Now, more than ever, our personal brand is something all of us need to pay a lot more attention to. *In this digital age, your personal brand will be your most powerful ally (or enemy).*

There's no trick to nurturing and developing your personal brand. Be yourself. It's not about being fake. Use these channels to align yourself with others who are similar or complementary to you. If we've learned anything so far, it's that you have to be able to find that specific online niche that will be the perfect place for you to be you and grow your business accordingly.

My job, on a day-to-day basis, is to help people navigate the complex world of new marketing. Our company, Twist Image, helps world-class brands bridge the present to the future by understanding the new conversations consumers are creating and engaging in. It's as bleeding-edge as you can get when it comes to marketing, communications, and branding. I'm playing in spaces like blogs, podcasts, wikis, and online social networks. In my day job, personal brands are created every day by individuals who are changing for the better. Every day, a huge company is trying to understand their brand better and bring that concept forward to their customers. Every day, those exact same companies are realizing that it's going to take a very human voice with some very active and real people to truly deliver on that promise.

In the end, what we're learning is that the brand comes from within. A strong brand shines when the core values and belief systems of why it was created are as obvious as the logo, packaging, website, and supporting marketing materials.

People are confused about the meaning of the word "branding." Branding is not the logo, the brochure, or the e-mail. Branding is the heart and soul of a business—and of the people who make up that business. Branding is what the company (or person) "is." It gets ever more complex in a world where individuals are becoming recognized brands as well. The truth is that branding can't be defined in a few paragraphs. Volumes have been written about it.

That being said, brands rise (and fall) every day because each and every one of us is making decisions about that brand based on our own values and beliefs. From there we decide if the product or service "fits" who we are—or who we want to be. We are either investing in that brand or divesting ourselves from it.

How do you evaluate your personal brand and your ability to communicate it in a digital world? Here's a personal brand questionnaire I have created for you to work on. For optimal results, put aside the time required to really go through these questions. The result should be a road map for you to apply to the digital channels that will suit you best.

YOUR PERSONAL BRAND QUESTIONNAIRE

- What do people "feel" when they think of you?
- What does your brand do for people—are they excited? Do they want to tell everybody?
- How would you feel if someone gave you your own business card? Does it impress you?
- What does a corporate or marketing kit from you say about your personal brand?
- How do people find out about you?
- How much marketing are you doing to make people know about you?
- How much money will you spend to attend trade shows, conferences, and networking events?
- How often are you speaking at events?
- How often are you involved with organizing those events?
- What are the many cost-effective ways you can better market yourself?
- How comfortable are you with the new digital channels?
- What kind of relationships are you forming in your business? Are you a trusted adviser, an appreciated ally, or just another supplier?
- How many websites, blogs, books, magazines, etc., that cover your trade are you currently reading (and have you thought about writing for them)?
- What untold stories unfold every day in your company and how are your employees, customers, and the general public informed of these successes?
- What is your unique promise?

Once you have dug down deep into those questions, you'll begin to see how closely intertwined the digital channels are with your personal brand and how it connects to your business and your future. The irony? So many people thought that the advent of the Internet was going to remove the entire "human" aspect from communications. In turn, we've seen the complete opposite. More than anything, your success in these channels will be directly related to how well you understand and connect your personal brand.

YOU CAN'T FAKE SINCERITY

In his excellent book *A Whole New Mind*, Dan Pink writes about some testing that was done on the human face and the muscles we use to control our emotions. It turns out that when we smile out of true happiness, certain muscles are activated that can't be controlled. That means that when we fake a smile versus making a genuine smile, our faces actually look different. Don't believe me? Take a look at photos of yourself where you are "caught" smiling in a candid shot and compare that to a photo where somebody uttered "Say 'cheese!'" The differences are disarming.

One message you will hear consistently in this book is that you can't fake passion. You also can't fake your personal brand. Ultimately, to paraphrase Dale Carnegie, you can learn how to win friends and influence people, but if it does not align with who you really are, those relationships won't last. Digital or otherwise.

How can you live your brand every day? It's not something you will find in a book like this. The real truth of living your brand comes from acknowledging that your brand is not for everyone. Don't focus on everyone. Focus on connecting to like-minded people. Make those real connections really count.

It's a tough concept to swallow.

As we build our personal brands through the digital channels, it is incumbent on us to know the types of people who fit with our brand and what we are doing and, on a daily basis, to engage with those types of people.

Just like in marketing, it takes a certain type of person to drive a BMW, and that may not be the same kind of person who likes retro country funk music. The point is not to try to be all things to all people. Be true to the people who appreciate what you stand for and believe in, and find others who are like-minded. These are the people you need on your team. These are the people who allow you to live your personal brand. These are the people who will be the best customers for your business.

What's the first step? Live your brand every day by focusing on what you bring to the lives of others, from co-workers and community to clients and customers. That is the culmination of a personal brand, and that is what people feel, think, and say about you when others ask. It is also what they will receive when they look you up online or see what you have created.

Your personal brand is unique to you. It is your internal fingerprint and your digital footprint.

EMBRACE YOUR DIGITAL FOOTPRINT

Your digital footprint offers a whole new world of opportunity and business growth. We're not only surfing, but millions of us are creating tons of content in online channels. And, if you're not, now is a good time to start. We're blogging, podcasting, sharing files, and watching lots of streaming video content of one another. The Web is connecting millions of us to each other, and within these connections people are forming communities around varied (and specific) interests; the spirit of Six Pixels of Separation continues to grow.

By keeping yourself in the digital loop through reviewing a handful of websites, blogs, and podcasts that speak directly on the subjects that interest you, you become empowered, known, and a part of these communities. It is amazingly powerful when you think about it: Individuals, like you and me, can now create our own "programming schedule" that is 100 percent catered to our personal needs and preferences. There are two big bonuses to this.

First is the concept of "time-shifting." We can now read, listen to, or watch all of this preferred content when it's best for us. It can be early in the morning or late at night. It's always there. The second big bonus is that we can create the content by either adding in comments or sharing the information with our peers. As a business owner, start thinking about what you can create to deepen the impact of your personal brand online.

WHAT DOES ALL OF THIS HAVE TO DO WITH BUILDING A BUSINESS?

Everything.

Because of the power of the Internet and how connected we all are, the Web has become a fertile ground for individuals to build their personal brands. There are three main reasons why all of us need to nurture our personal brands:

1. To add more value to our lives
2. To make more connections and build our personal network and community
3. To increase our business opportunities

Right now, each and every one of us has an opportunity to be a part of a conversation with millions of people online. The days of building our personal brand through a chamber of commerce event or by speaking up at our local PTA meeting are now being trumped by the online world.

ONE PAPER CLIP CAN MAKE ALL THE DIFFERENCE TO YOUR PERSONAL BRAND AND YOUR BUSINESS

Kyle MacDonald had a simple idea. As he was sitting staring at his computer screen in his apartment, Kyle wondered how he would, someday, be able to afford a new house. His attention moved from his screen to his desk, where he saw one red paper clip. Kyle had what inventors call an "aha!" moment. He decided to build a simple website and see if, through a series of successive trades, he could upgrade his paper clip to a free house. His simple idea quickly became a big idea.

You've heard the story, but frame it now in terms of how Kyle built his personal brand. Word of mouth spreads much faster online than it does in the real world, and people all over began writing articles and chatting about this one guy who was trying to trade one red paper clip for a free house. Kyle's adventure was documented on his website/blog (www.OneRedPaperClip.com). In less than one year, Kyle managed, through a series of fifteen trades, to go from one red paper clip to a new house.

In the process, he also managed to travel all over the world and appear on CNN, BBC, MSNBC, and every other major news outlet. He's since released a book telling his story and is in the process of producing a movie about it as well.

By not being afraid of technology and by using it to his advantage—in a very simple way—Kyle not only got the house, but he was able to build a tremendous personal brand.

Kyle's story is not unique; we all have this potential within us. Think about how you communicate your business and your personal brand to the digital world. Think about new ways to engage in dynamic conversations that will change the course of your business in a positive direction. Allow these channels to open the doors of the world for your business.

BUILD A 3D PERSONAL BRAND

Full disclosure: I stole this concept from Anna Farmery (who has a great blog and podcast called "The Engaging Brand"). In early 2007 she had a blog post entitled "3D Is the Place to Be!" The post was inspired by a conversation (and podcast) she conducted with Jason Alba of "Jibber Jobber," a blog about building your career. Their discussion revolved around the idea of giving both personal and corporate brands a more "three-dimensional feel." The concept of a 3D personal brand makes perfect sense as we watch real and digital combine to become one and the same.

Personal branding is not about what you want your brand to be, but rather it is about defining what your personal brand already is (and making sure that you are able to communicate that core effectively). This is the paradox of personal branding. All too often we read materials that give us great tips and tricks on how to do things differently—to make a bigger splash. That should not be of interest to you. If you have to do things differently, then clearly this is not who you are or what your personal brand truly "is." That being said, we all must be able to take this excellent information and modulate it so that it fits with our own, unique, personal brand.

As for the three-dimensional aspect, how do you make a personal (or corporate) brand resonate over and above a résumé, advertisement, or article about you? How do you make a personal brand come to life?

A three-dimensional personal brand has three parts:

1. Give Abundantly: The best way to build a personal brand is to give your knowledge away. It's the ability to go for a new customer and not worry about what he can do for you, but, rather, doing your homework and research and knowing what you can do for him. Imagine going for a new client and later realizing that the client is not the perfect fit for you, then referring him to someone you think would be perfect. That's investing in your personal brand.

2. Help Others: When you go to a networking event and you start meeting a variety of people, stop worrying about how they can help you and start thinking about who in your network can help them. Listen for their areas of pain. If you happen to come across a website or blog that speaks to them, let them know. Stay in their loop (this keeps them in your loop as well).

3. Build Relationships: We all know how important the idea of "conversation" is in this digital revolution, but it's all about creating real relationships. Conversations are important, but if you don't nurture a true relationship, it's just a bunch of digital gums flapping. Build your personal brand by building strong relationships in the online channels.

YOUR PERSONAL BRAND IS ALL ABOUT STRATEGY, NOT TACTICS

The words you say are a small fraction of the communications game. There's that old saying that words account for only 7 percent of the communication you have with somebody. That translates as: "Your personal brand is screaming so loudly I can hardly hear a word you are saying."

How can you build a better three-dimensional personal brand? Understand who you are. Know what you stand for. Do something every day to make sure your actions (and words) speak as loud as your personal brand already does.

YOU ARE MEDIA

Robert Scoble is like Chris Brogan. Scoble is the former technology evangelist for Microsoft, co-author of *Naked Conversations: How Blogs Are Changing the Way Businesses Talk with Customers* with Shel Israel, and a highly regarded blogger and online social networker. Sebastien Provencher from "The Praized Blog" had a great post about Robert Scoble entitled "Robert Scoble Is Media."

Here's a snippet:

> It made me wonder: why would Robert Scoble accept a "friends" invitation from people he does not know? Why do you want to be connected to people you don't know and alert them to stuff you're doing? And then it hit me! Robert Scoble is media. He's building his own broadcast network. He understands that media is completely fragmented and, by participating in all these new social communication vehicles (blogging, Twitter, Pownce, Facebook), he's aggregating readers and viewers, thereby increasing his penetration and his worth as a media. I'm convinced Robert reaches close to 100% of all early adopters in Silicon Valley (and a good chunk in North America). He now has tremendous influence on "influencers."

Shortly thereafter, Robert Scoble posted this: "My Facebook Secret Is Out." Part of it read:

> Facebook makes my blog seem very one-way. I can't see anytime one of you writes something, or puts some media up, even when you do it on your own blogs. Facebook makes our media a lot more two-way.

This is where the learning and marketing kick in. Here are two major concepts for you to embrace:

1. **Content Is Media:** Scoble, Provencher, Brogan, you, me, and anyone else who creates content is creating media. That is the advertising. Everyone keeps searching for the ad model in blogs and podcasts ("How do I monetize all of this digital activity?"), not realizing that the content and the individual producing it are the media. People see you as an expert and want to work with that expert.

2. **Personal Brand:** Steve Rubel over at "Micro Persuasion" (by day, Steve works at Edelman Digital) posted a killer blog entry entitled "The Golden Age of Individualism" where he states: "Individualism is as old as American ideals, though it's certainly not a global phenomenon. However with the Net Gen taking over the workforce, the value of personal brands will continue to rise and perhaps be a prickly force to be reckoned with. This means big changes in the workplace and a critical importance for everyone to be team players even as their stars rise online. It also means that personal brands will become unofficial spokespeople at times (perhaps involuntarily)."

These concepts are real and have come full circle. Individuals are creating content; the individuals are the media. The media they are creating are also a form of advertising. What is the advertising selling? Their personal brand and their company. Who's buying their personal brand? Lots of people who, prior to tools like Facebook, Twitter, and podcasting, were relegated to trying to find people in their city whom they hoped had similar interests.

MAKE PERSONAL BRANDING PERSONAL IN A DIGITAL WORLD

On May 19, 2008, there was an article in the *Wall Street Journal* entitled "The Next American Frontier." It was written by Michael S. Malone (author of the book *The Protean Corporation*). Mr. Malone wrote:

> Newspapers are dying, networks are dying, and if teenage boys playing GTA 4 and World of Warcraft have any say about it, so is television. More than 200 million people now belong to just two social networks: MySpace and Facebook. And there are more than 80 million videos on YouTube, all put there by the same individual initiative.
>
> The most compelling statistic of all? Half of all new college graduates now believe that self-employment is more secure than a full-time job. Today, 80% of the colleges and universities in the U.S. now offer courses on entrepreneurship; 60% of Gen Y business owners consider themselves to be serial entrepreneurs, according to *Inc.* magazine. Tellingly, 18 to 24-year-olds are starting companies at a faster rate than 35 to 44-year-olds. And 70% of today's high schoolers intend to start their own company, according to a Gallup poll.

All good entrepreneurs are the first to admit that they are "unemployable."

New media are doing a whole lot more than giving us a bunch of new channels through which to market to people. They're doing a lot more than simply enabling us to connect like never before. What we have is a fundamental shift in how society operates—and it's shifting beneath our feet. Thankfully, there are writers like Malone to help us acknowledge these changes and the ramifications they are having on all of us and our businesses.

Here's what he's really saying:

Without noticing it, we have once again discovered, and then raced off to settle, a new frontier. Not land, not innovation, but ourselves and a growing control over our own lives and careers.

And why not? Each step in the development of American society has been towards an ever-greater level of independence, freedom and personal liberty.

There is a direct and obvious link between this type of entrepreneur and the power in understanding your personal brand and how it connects in digital channels. I believe that the rise in entrepreneurship is tightly linked to people like you and me who have begun to use online channels to connect, share, and grow. We're also seeing the pace of growth of these entrepreneurs increase because the ability to understand your personal brand and use online channels toward building a global audience is creating new business models and new marketing campaigns that are targeted and relevant, and deliver tremendous ROI.

RISE PERSONAL BRANDS, RISE

Here's the new reality check: not a day goes by that someone, somewhere, is not checking out who you are, what you're about, and whether or not they are willing to invest (or divest) in you through a quick search.

Here's how you can do your own personal brand audit in the online world:

1. Blog: Do your best to answer and update all comments. If someone has taken the time to post a comment, make sure you do your best to respond or acknowledge it.

2. Website Stats: Be vigilant about checking the statistics for websites. The main areas to look at are how many unique visitors you're getting, what links brought them to the community, and which keywords triggered people to check out what you're about.

3. Technorati: Do some top-level searches (which you can aggregate into a simple Watchlist) on keywords like: your name, your company, the brands you sell. From there, feel free to comment on postings with mentions of you.

4. Facebook: Here's a three-step process for Facebook (granted, you can use this for any and all online social networks). First, check to see all friend and group requests. Second, review the groups or pages you administer (if you don't have any groups or pages, consider starting one to build community within Facebook). Last, do a quick scan on your public profile to see if there are any new updates. You should be looking for growth (how many new people have joined a group or how closely you're linked to people of importance to you). Facebook has grown so quickly, and online social networks are one of the key drivers for personal brand success. That being said, there were online social networks before Facebook and there will be newer ones. Keep your eyes open for the newer ones.

5. LinkedIn: This is a great resource, as this online social network is strictly focused on business and professionals. Do a general walk-through of all the features and news. Look to see if any one of your connections has changed titles or added more connections. LinkedIn is the dark horse of online social networks for professionals. It is amazing and, with some simple tweaks, you'll be shocked at how quickly it can grow your digital footprint.

6. Google: Do a quick search on your main keywords (your name, your company, the brands you sell). You need to be looking at how many results these keywords pull. As the months progress, if you are doing your job, that number should increase. This is your barometer for depth. How deeply have your personal brand and business penetrated the online space?

7. Google Alerts: This is a constant effort. As we've already discussed, sign up for all of your major keywords and constantly monitor where (and in what context) your personal brand is being mentioned.

It may seem like an exhaustive and time-consuming list, but your personal brand audit should only take a few minutes. If you don't have a blog, podcast, or Facebook groups to administer, you can probably perform a personal brand audit in a flash.

While there is a vanity component to this (it's nice to know that people are talking about you), the main point here is to stay focused on whether what your personal brand "is" is properly being maintained in the online channels and how it is connecting to your business. It's not a question of defending against those who think differently; it's a personal brand audit to ensure that who you really are is coming through—loud and clear—in the online channels where individuals do have equal stage with multinational corporations.

The impact of personal brands on business and society is huge. It should not be dismissed or diminished. We are just at the start of the paradigm shift where individuals who, traditionally, have been told to keep their names and identities private in the online space are now being public about who they are and what they are thinking in a bid to grow their personal brands and their business. Not only is this a shift in how we traditionally looked at the Web, but it's a new way to look at how we see one another. This poses a new and exciting opportunity for business in a world where individuals are creating their own personal brands and have the ability to connect with communities and consumers in ways we have never seen before.

CHAPTER 8

From Mass Media to Mass Content

Let's also define what "you" means. If you're not going to be the one creating the content, make sure you work with someone who understands the space and everything it entails. Hiring someone as a ghostwriter could pose problems in a world where authenticity and transparency are the currency. More often than not, you should be looking for someone from within the organization who has a passion for the types of content we're going to discuss.

There are really only four types of content you can create:

1. Text

Be it writing a blog of your own, commenting on other blogs that are popular in your industry, writing articles for websites, associations, or multi-authored blogs, or becoming known for creating amazing reviews, writing text is one of the better ways to get your message, name, and brand "out there." The primary reason why text is the default content creation favorite of the Web is because text is how we search and find content.

The technology will advance, but right now the Internet is primarily a text-based channel. Yes, it's moving fast and more and more people are watching videos and listening to audio online, but the reality is that most of those resources are not effectively searchable quite yet.

Search engines are doing everything they can to index video and audio better, but those days are still ahead of us. By creating a small amount of text-based content, you're instantly making everything you do that much more accessible.

2. Images

We all know a picture is worth a thousand words, and to that end, images are a highly sought after resource online. We all love looking at pictures. Be it a TMZ paparazzi shot of Lady GaGa, some product shots of the latest Apple MacBook Pro, or pictures of someone we knew in high school on Facebook, we love "seeing" everything we can (especially before we buy).

The trick to creating compelling images is that you have to have a product for which pictures really do tell the story better than any number of words, plus you need to have a level of proficiency with photography or other image creation. It's also important to note that you could very well make your splash in the world of images and their social life, but of the four pillars of content noted here, photos tend to be the least popular (in terms of building community), and yet they are highly critical to your overall success (even text-based blogs use the power of good photography to drive traffic and readership).

3. Audio

The iPod has quickly become the biggest-selling electronic device of all time. Early last year, the iTunes Store became the largest retailer of music in the world (beating out Wal-Mart). So even with the illegal downloading of music versus the purchasing of it at a 40:1 ratio, audio is hotter than ever. People love music.

As a result, podcasting, streaming audio online, or making audio files available for download are great ways to connect your company to customers. A compelling audio program can be five to eight minutes or a weekly half-hour show. Setting the format, style, and recording quality can be as low-tech as a headset with a microphone built in or as high-tech as renting a professional studio.

If you're an audiophile or ever DJ'd in college, audio could be one of the more effective ways to build your business. Hop over to iTunes, click on "Podcasts" and check out the plethora of compelling audio content available to grab—100 percent free.

4. Video

The cost of recording, producing, and publishing video continues to drop, and the allure of becoming the next YouTube celebrity is enchanting.

There are many people who actually use YouTube (and other online video-sharing sites) as their broadcast media channel to the world—with millions of viewers (you read that right: millions of viewers).

Example: Blendtec sells blenders. Nothing too exciting there, but Tom Dickson, the company founder, enjoys getting the word out. A few years back he started producing videos and posting them on YouTube under the show title, "Will It Blend?" In short segments he takes everyday objects, dumps them into his Blendtec blender, and answers the question, "Will it blend?" Knowing the target audience of the online video community, Blendtec has created a powerful viral video success that drives significant sales. One episode, where Dickson actually blended an iPhone, received more than 6.5 million views on YouTube alone. The company has produced over seventy videos (some serious, some funny) and ranks as one of the "most subscribed to" channels on YouTube.

Admit it: you're dying to know if a Rubik's Cube, a Wii Remote, and a golf club will blend—aren't you?

The truth is that producing videos, which are probably the most popular type of online content you can create, is a lot of fun, but it is also a lot of work. You need a semi-decent camera, microphones, and some decent production to really build traction. To actually produce the piece, with proper audio, editing is very time intensive. The payout, in terms of building audience and sales, can be there if the idea is sharp, crisp, and—most importantly—relevant. While some have been able to build audience with serious content, the videos that really hit the multi-million viewership levels are the ones that are somewhat provocative, either through humor or through innuendo and parody.

SO WHERE DO YOU NET OUT WITH ALL OF THIS CONTENT?

Are you going to create a blog, share photography, a video, or an audio podcast? Are you going to join the latest and hottest online social networks? Are you going to create your own personal profile and/or make a page or a group around your business and brands? *Whatever choice you make, focus, initially, on where your passion truly lies.* If you love writing or have a knack for words, consider a blog, Twitter, or writing peer reviews. If you love taking pictures, shooting video, or creating audio, you now know where you can start planting some seeds. Also, don't focus too much on what others have done or have not done. This space is still relatively new (you will be hard-pressed to find many industry-specific best practices, and even if you do, following in those similar footsteps won't get you where you need to go).

It's also one thing to talk about what you should be doing, and another to do a walk-through. In the spirit of "doing" over "talking," let's take a business you probably wouldn't expect: selling pens. Let's agree that this business could use a blog (mostly because the owner of this boutique, which we'll call Ink Well, was a writer for the campus newspaper back in her college days and now does an occasional op-ed piece for the local community newspaper). Before we look at how Ink Well is going to develop and deploy a blog, let's also agree that this strategy can be modified and adapted to any of the other content channels we have discussed earlier. Ultimately, this is about creating a new form of communication and marketing platform that turns her business of selling pens into a real, living, and breathing conversation.

BUILD AN OVERARCHING STRATEGY FIRST

Ink Well sells pens, writing products, and related items. It pulls in decent revenues and has recently launched an e-commerce platform to start selling beyond its physical retail outlet. Because the owner enjoys writing, she has decided that a blog might be the best way to spread the word about her store and its products. She has also decided that she will post a new entry every other day. But the big question remains: What should the Ink Well blog be about? Are people really interested in news about the pen business, which paper products are on sale, or her top-level thoughts on how the industry has changed over the years? Strategically, it would seem that she's going to need to cast the net a little wider.

In this instance, let's agree that Ink Well's owner is not going to blog about pens, but, to expand her audience, she's going to create a blog around "the passion of writing." This way, the blog's potential audience can be everyone from professional writers down to the weekend writing warriors who have a dream to be published one day.

Casting the content net wider and focusing on "a love of writing" instead of "just pens" empowers Ink Well's owner to demonstrate her passion—why she does what she does and what she brings to the table that is uniquely different from her competitors.

Who would you rather buy your penmanship products from? A random big-box store, or someone who, consistently, demonstrates through her own words the same passion you have for the written word? This is how an online community begins to grow.

Also, by focusing on writing versus pens, Ink Well's owner can play around with different types of content. By tracking this content through the statistics and Web analytics on her blog, she can even refine her content for her audience. Again, it's all about reaching out and developing a following online with her customers, who then tell their friends, and on and on.

SETTING IT UP

A few years back, I was sitting on the Digital Marketing Council for the Canadian Marketing Association (CMA). Blogging was beginning to pick up steam and many members of the council thought that perhaps the CMA could get involved in blogging by creating a space where Canadian marketers (both members and non-members of the CMA) could blog about the issues that mattered most to them. In perusing the landscape, it became immediately apparent that there was no real competition for this type of content and that the CMA could play a leadership role. Yes, there already existed several marketing blogs written by Canadian marketers on various topics, but there was not a multi-authored blog focused, specifically, on the overall general subject of marketing in Canada.

You've been in meetings like this. They can get very energetic with individuals making all kinds of promises as to what they are going to contribute and how they would generate content and push the blog into a leadership position.

In this particular meeting of Canadian marketers, there were two paths that could have been pursued at that exact moment:

1. The CMA could have put out an RFP (request for proposal) to a bunch of interactive agencies and spent thousands of dollars developing the design, technology, hosting, and implementation of a fully functional blog platform.

2. Or the CMA could have hopped over to a free online blogging service (like Blogger or WordPress) and, with a little effort, have a free blog up and running in a matter of minutes.

Without a doubt, going with option number one is the more professional route to pursue. Having control over the domain name, design, hosting, customization, and overall management is a huge advantage and that's what the end-goal should be, without question.

But, curiously, the CMA chose option number two. Why? What would be the point in investing all of the money (and time) upfront to get a proprietary blog platform up and running if they were not sure who, exactly, the bloggers would be, how often they would post, and, most importantly, if they would have any readers, comments, and feedback?

Understanding that the media of the Web are fluid, fast, and organic, the CMA opted to create their Canadian marketing blog on the Blogger platform to see what type of content would be created, who the readers would be, and what the results would look like. After surveying the content and comments for a few months and seeing how active the contributions were, they switched over and hired a digital marketing agency (actually, ours) to build the blog and then took full control over their own experience.

In setting up your blog, thinking like this can save you tons of time and money. It's also worth noting that the CMA didn't wait too long to switch over to their own space. If traffic had built significantly on the Blogger platform, it would have been considerably more challenging to let readers know the CMA blog had changed homes, etc.

Setting up your blog blends into your strategy, so take the time to conduct the proper due diligence in terms of what type of platform you will use (one that is Web-based or one that is software you are running off of your own servers) and who is going to host it (if you have lots of traffic and your blog goes down, so will your readership). The point is, get some advice and help on the technical side to make sure you can support whatever traffic you plan on generating.

FINDING THE RIGHT NAME, DESIGN, AND PEOPLE

There's a lot in a name (and even more in the design).

Yes, the name and design you choose for your blog are important. A clever blog name is easy to remember and keeps the intrigue up. What do you think is cooler: "Boing Boing" or "The Technology Round-up"? Be creative and take the time to ensure that you choose not only a great name, but also one that you can grab the URL for. This is part of the reason we're seeing many of the more popular blogs that have titles like "Jaffe Juice," "Diary of a

Shameless Self-Promoter," "Presentation Zen," and "The Instigator Blog." They may "seem" like long titles, but it's increasingly difficult to secure a good, solid domain name. As a result, many of the top bloggers are getting pithy, clever, and creative with their blog names. The other side is that blogs are personal in nature, so naming it after your company can be a little cold and impersonal. When my company started blogging in 2003, we called it "The Twist Image Blog" (not very creative). But as Six Pixels of Separation started to gel over the years, we realized that it's not just a catchy line, but could be the name of the blog, the podcast, the newspaper columns, and, of course, this book. It was also something we felt we could "own." Don't believe it? Do a quick search for the words "six pixels."

In short, choose your name with the perspective that it could well become the way you are known going forward.

Design Matters

Take the time to design your blog well. Add in some good usability, navigation, and functionality. Make it easy on the eyes and enjoyable for people to read. Strong design lends credibility to your project. It's a mistake to think it's only about the content. The content is a huge part of how successful your blog will become, but a strong design will also enforce your industry leadership.

Surround Yourself with Great People

You can start a quick blog with all guns blazing and see how it goes, but when it begins to take off, you will need a small team (and budget) to help with the technology, design, and—yes—even the content. If you've been following and commenting on the other blogs in your space, these other bloggers are, in effect, part of your team, too. You can ask them for help, see what has worked, and get their feedback on everything you're doing. Don't forget that your current website visitors are also a part of this soon-to-be-great community. You consistently have to ask what they want and what they think about everything you're doing. People love to give their opinion, but, more importantly, people love to know that they have played a small role in the successful launch of something that is going to add value to their lives.

FINDING YOUR VOICE

The tone, flow, and vibe you give off in your content will reveal who the "real company" is. This is, specifically, why blogs are so popular: they're the human voice behind it all. But understand that there's no easy way to answer the question, How do I find the right voice for my blog? That being said, there are some guidelines to think about in terms of style and tone. Also worth noting is that finding your voice will take some time. It's an iterative process (in full disclosure, it's one I still massage and work on with each and every blog posting). Give yourself the freedom to explore your voice and how it connects to your community.

Online, there has been a recent uprising of voices that are more contrarian, curmudgeonly, and argumentative. It's a welcome approach (yes, it takes all kinds), but if you're a business and doing everything you can, including spending a lot of time putting your thoughts and information into a blog, be wary that your consumers, employees, and future business partners are also going to be reading and following it.

The biggest question you have to ask yourself is: What kind of storyteller do I want to be? Will you be analytical, funny, and easy to read, or complex and/or thoughtful? Do write some sample blog postings and ask friends, customers, and family members for feedback. Spend a bit of time (before hitting the publish button for the first time) getting some critical feedback on the content you are creating. *Remember: What seems funny and clever to you might be seen as insulting and sarcastic to others.*

If you're not the main blogger and have passed that responsibility on to someone else, make sure to stay in his or her loop. But this doesn't mean censoring the person or having him go through the legal and PR people in your organization before publishing. By working closely together, you'll both be able to identify the right voice for your blog.

Be it in a blog or a best-selling book, you will quickly realize that your "voice" is going to determine your level of success. If people can connect to it, they'll follow you, comment on your work, and tell everyone they know how great it is. But if your voice doesn't resonate, your blog statistics will speak volumes through their silence.

One final bit of advice: *Spelling and grammar matter.* When blogs first came onto the scene, there was a certain charm in the humanity of the mistakes. While the blogosphere is hardly a mature publishing medium, things have advanced: poor grammar, spelling mistakes, and too much slang don't earn much street cred anymore. Make sure to use a spell-checker and figure out how the grammar flows. Take the time to edit your work. Some highly trafficked blogs now use a third-party editor to review the content—not for the subject matter or what's being said, but simply to ensure that everything is readable and easy to digest.

KEEP IT GOING

On the audio podcasting front, it's known as *podfading.* Podfading is when someone starts an audio program and then, either slowly or quickly, begins running out of things to say. It's more common than you might suspect, and it's all the more reason to have respect for those national newspaper columnists or cartoonists who, day in and day out, deliver some kind of compelling content. You may be thinking, *There are a million and three things I can blog about*. So here's the challenge: make that list.

One of the easiest ways to ensure that your content stays fresh is to schedule the time to blog. Once you've blocked off the time, you need to ensure that you have enough content to spread out and share. Magazines, newspapers, and every other kind of printed publication rely on what they call their editorial calendar (ed cal for short). Make an ed cal (or as close to one as you can). Set up the topics and titles of your blog postings for the next month, but also allow yourself the freedom to be spontaneous. There might be some late-breaking news item in your industry that you might feel the need to comment on, or someone might send you something you feel would be perfect for your audience. As soon as you start to build some type of editorial calendar you'll notice that some of the topics are time sensitive and others can be published as you wish. Play with that process and let it evolve.

ALWAYS HAVE NOTEBOOKS OR ANOTHER WAY TO RECORD IDEAS NEARBY

Whether it's in a physical notebook or the note application on your iPhone, make sure to mark down your blog ideas as they happen. If you're cursed like me and you tend to get your best ideas when you're in the shower or working out, make sure to have a way of capturing that moment. Traditional publications (magazines, newspapers, and books) provide a wealth of blogging fodder. Once you have your own publishing platform, you'll be amazed at how much content and interesting inspiration you can find in the stuff you used to just consume and toss away. In my Outlook e-mail program there's even a folder entitled "Blog" where I file all news items, information my friends pass along, or articles from e-newsletters I find interesting. If you're engaged in your industry, sustaining your content should be fairly simple, as long as you're reading what's going on and have an opinion on it.

Once you've started publishing, your community of readers is likely to help you keep it going by submitting guest posts or by asking questions you can provide the answers for in a blog posting. Another great way to keep the content fresh is to buy a small audio recorder and conduct interviews with people who might be interesting to your readers. As an example, the Ink Well blog could use their space to promote new and emerging independent authors by previewing a book on one post and then conducting an interview with the author in a follow-up post (they could even turn it into a four-part interview that would run every week for a full month).

What you're starting to see is that the creativity of your blog will not rest solely on the voice you provide, the technology that is driving the platform, or the flashy design. What's really going to push the content out there, build community, and get people talking about your brand and your services is how creative you are with the structure and flow of the content. The best bloggers in the world are the ones who don't just type whatever comes to mind; rather, they are the ones who take the time to listen to what their readers like and what they like about the other blogs out there. They also spend some time checking out blogs like "Copy Blogger" and "ProBlogger" for tips and tricks on how to make their blogs more successful. You should too.

MARKETING

You know the expression "Build it and they will come"? Well, that may have been true at some point, but now it's a myth. There is simply too much content, too much to choose from, and some would even argue that any original idea you may have has already been done. In order for your blog to drive any form of ROI, you're going to have to market it, PR it, and get the word out there.

This could well be the main reason most blogs fail and why most brands have not been successful in building a strong community. Your blog is a new media channel. To build audiences and awareness, you have to market and promote it just like your products and services. Yes, this means more work. You're not going to have something "go viral" just because you posted a video on YouTube (those occurrences are few and far between).

PAID MEDIA WON'T WORK AS WELL AS EARNED MEDIA

Earn media attention and audience by doing everything we've spoken about in the previous chapters: Know the popular blogs in your field, follow them, comment on them, add value, and push those conversations forward. Become the subject matter expert, so that people coming across your comments and insights on the more highly trafficked blogs will be curious to read about what else is on your mind.

Use the popular online social networks like MySpace, Facebook, FriendFeed, and Twitter to promote your content. Granted, there are very few people who will endure staying connected to you for the sole purpose of your promoting your wares to them, but there is little wrong with posting links or informing people that you've posted something new and would like their feedback. The general rule of thumb is "one-quarter." For every four updates or posts you create in your online social circles (outside of your dedicated blog), you can let people know about something self-promotional once. Keep in mind that any form of self-promotion is seen and felt as such, so your mileage may vary.

Strategically, the easiest way to avoid being overtly self-promotional is to turn every "I" you write into a "you." Make the content about your audience. Even if you are promoting an event, make it about them. As an example: The Ink Well has an evening with author Tom Asacker. Instead of promoting it as "Tom Asacker, branding expert and author, live at the Ink Well," tweak it and focus on them: "Improve your branding and get up to speed with the latest in marketing. Come learn from Tom Asacker, live and in person at the Ink Well."

It might seem like semantics, but with so much content out there in an overwhelmingly unmanageable fashion, making your blog about your consumers is the easiest way to build community and trust. It also keeps you honest and focused on them (not you).

Once you gain some level of audience and community, feel free to push beyond your personal profiles in the online social networks and develop fan pages, groups, or even a unique My-Space page for your blog (bonus points if one of your community members takes the initiative himself because he loves what you're doing so much). Just make sure you're not biting off more than you can chew. Maintaining multiple areas in multiple online social networks takes not only time, but also lots of organization. Also, if someone else takes it on and starts it before you do, be present, active, and involved. Being high-browed in online social networks does not work. You have to be around and responsive.

Using micro-blogging platforms like Twitter, commenting and being very present on other blogs as well as adding valuable content (writing reviews and sharing information) also helps promote who you are, what you're about, and why people should care. Always take the time to look at the newer places where people are converging, but make a pact with yourself that you're not going to engage in everything. There are plenty of new and shiny objects that come around that simply don't fit with the type of content you are creating or the type of time and effort you have for the online channels. I'll tend to take a quick glance at everything I can, but will only deep-dive on a handful of channels that can really add value.

Be curious about everything, but ruthless in what you get involved with.

Those who don't blog might be equally excited about what you're doing.

"You have a blog? What are you blogging about?"

Public relations and media attention really do build traffic and get your business recognition outside of the digital channels. Promote your blog. Let people know about it by having it on your business card, putting it in your e-mail signature file, telling people on your voice-mail message to check it out, and always mentioning it in your corporate bio and when and if you get interviewed by the media. On countless occasions I've told people to check out the blog if they want to know more about how we think at Twist Image. As mainstream as blogs may seem, people still think that anyone maintaining a blog is cutting edge. Another idea to generate media attention is to follow the mainstream media that your consumers follow and blog about related content. You can always e-mail the journalist in the mainstream press and let her know you were inspired by her words and blogged about a similar topic. Tell her what you thought about her take on the subject, where your opinions might differ, or when you're seeing things eye to eye. You just may be surprised when your phone rings the next time she's looking for an expert on the topic.

Ultimately, to get mainstream publicity, you need to make sure that your blog is fully and completely up to date, fresh, and adds insightful perspective to whatever topic you are covering.

ONLINE ADVERTISING AND YOUR BLOG: WORTH DOING?

Beyond earned media attention, you can also buy advertising on the major search engines on a pay-per-click basis. For a couple hundred dollars you can just choose some of the keywords your customers would use to find your products and services and create catchy text-based ads. If you start seeing some serious traffic spikes and people are, genuinely, connecting because they are seeing your ads and acting on them, be sure to keep them going. It probably would not cost a lot of money to run ads for the Ink Well on keywords like "writing blog," "publishing blog," "author's blog," and the like. You might even consider purchasing more generic keywords like "writing" and "publishing" if your budget allows and the conversion works.

Writing your blog should be fun. Creating content—text, audio, video, or images—should be fun. Write with your heart on your sleeve, but always remember how powerful the search engines are. Instead of saying, "I'm going to the conference this week," be clearer by saying, "I'm attending the National Writing Association Convention and Trade Show in Austin on September 20–25." This way, anyone looking for information on that specific conference might find your blog and spread the word about it to their friends and associates.

Great content = great word of mouth.

Finally, feel free to spruce up your posts. Keep them tight, short, and lively; use bold in specific areas to draw attention to the words and italics in other places to mix it up and add some visual variety to the text. Link out on the keywords and thoughts; link to other websites, blogs, and online social networks. The power of text online is in the linking. Let people read you and let them have the option to take themselves on a journey through all of the amazing sites and blogs that have inspired you. Adding in a picture is another easy way to get attention (people love looking at pictures), and let your style and flair really shine through.

SIX GENERAL RULES FOR A HEALTHY BLOG (OR ANOTHER FORM OF ONLINE CONTENT)

1. Be a good community citizen.

2. Respond to comments on your space and on others quickly.

3. Define your level of privacy—know what you're willing to put out there and make sure you respect the privacy of your community as well (their level may be different from yours).

4. Some people may be mean and nasty. If you set up a clear blog policy (and post it on your blog) and people don't respect your rules, you can delete, ban, or unpublish them.

5. Embrace the Long Tail of content. Be aware that everything you create will be online forever. I write with two things in my mind: What would my mother think and what would my kids think if they saw this today—or in ten years?

6. Be consistent. Start, continue, and finish what you started.

Always remember that content is not an ad campaign and that all of this requires a serious time commitment beyond your everyday activities. You can't buy community—you have to earn it.

CHAPTER 9

Digital Darwinism

Even with the ups and downs in the economy they're still selling four-dollar cups of coffee, and it's not uncommon to see one person walking down the street with four cups in his hands—someone has to be the one to make the Starbucks run for the office.

But let's face it: splashes happen.

That little sip hole can still do some serious damage to your clothes if you get bumped or if you're walking too fast. Enter the splash stick. Starbucks introduced this little stir stick that actually snaps and covers the sip holes on their cups. It's a simple and brilliant idea. Too bad it wasn't their own idea.

The idea for the splash stick came from their My Starbucks Idea website. The digital channel is a place where Starbucks consumers can sound off and add their own ideas and recommendations. The consumers also vote the ideas up or down, and from there Starbucks can decide which avenues to pursue. Many ideas are filtered through the discussion and user forum site, including free Wi-Fi, a free drink on your birthday, foam with flavor, and the splash stick.

Was Starbucks able to look progressive, smart, and digitally savvy because they created a platform for people to send in their suggestions? The core idea is little more than turning the old office suggestion box into a living and breathing online community that pushes the concept out beyond the office to anybody interested in the company. Or does the idea really work because the community embraced it, added to it, and pushed it forward? Would the site be considered so successful if it attracted no one or if any or all of the suggestions were either goofy or some kind of attack on the company? What makes the splash stick such an obvious success beyond the public acceptance?

WELCOME TO DIGITAL DARWINISM

What will it take for you to be successful in the new media channels?

More often than not, the thought of adding in some of these cooler shiny new objects is seen as the endgame. Companies quickly jump onto YouTube and post videos, they add widgets and downloadable applications to their websites, they start Facebook pages and then sit around the boardroom slapping each other on the back and handing out lollipops for how well they have managed to evolve their digital and online properties from where they were.

Darwin's Theory of Evolution has been morphed and adapted for any and every type of situation (including business). In the pre-social-media Web, where all you could do was read, look at images, and click on links to other pages with similar limitations, websites and companies online "evolved" by adding in functionality. For a time, it was Flash movies that introduced the site (this has become a huge faux pas). Then for a while it was adding video. While all of those tactics worked to keep their visitors' attention for a longer period of time, perhaps even encouraging additional clicks on other pages or gathering user information via registering for a white paper, these types of information-acquisition tactics were how corporate brands evolved online. It was either "Here's a bunch of cool and interactive stuff to check out" or "Give us your information so we can show you some really cool stuff." It was the first phase of digital evolution as we pushed our brands beyond being an online corporate brochure.

As these new channels for communications, connecting, and creating began to take hold, we continued on the same path. The general ideology was that if you added Twitter or a blog into the mix you were able to evolve your digital property by the simple act of having these new channels as a part of your digital ecosystem.

But here's the catch: Digital Darwinism favors the community, not the creator or enabler of the content.

In the past few chapters, we discussed the power of allowing your consumers to connect to one another with your company being the conduit and the enabler to make this connection. There is no doubt that this is still the primary and best course of action for you to take as you build these new marketing channels. The challenge is this: Digital Darwinism will work for you (as evolution, not extinction) based on what your users, community members, and readers do with your content. If you don't have any of those, you won't evolve. If you have readers and users but they're not active (taking part, reading, adding their own comments, passing your information around), again, you will become extinct.

Can you continue to create content in hopes that people will connect with it and help you evolve? Of course, but you have to do the heavy lifting at this point. You have to be the one out there beating the drum and letting people know that it's not a self-promotional environment you have created, but rather one to benefit the community. It's easy to see why this can be challenging. In one breath, we want people to connect to our content so they become loyal customers. In another breath, we have to be sensitive to the fact that the more self-promotional we are with our material, the less likely it will be that a community spawns and extends our evolution.

Here's the other shocker: There is no set formula to follow. There is no set of rules for why a community is created and why others are left to their own devices. There is no industry that is specifically more inclined to be successful by deploying these tactics (it's worked for a guy who sells blenders and has failed miserably for a company trying to promote the latest science fiction blockbuster Hollywood movie) and business to business can be equally successful as business to consumer (and equally sucky). However, there is one common thread that you always find in all successful programs that take on a life of their own: They are awesome. They are smart, engaging, and able to delight. They offer a holistic brand experience.

Everything about it is good, funny, smart, or compelling. I am often asked why an initiative is not working. People will cite how great the design is, the copy, the ease of use, and so on, and I am constantly reminded of the best-selling book by Greg Behrendt and Liz Tuccillo entitled *He's Just Not That Into You*. Much like that guy (or girl) who never calls for a second date or does something even though he said he would not, building community has many more similarities to dating than you might imagine. So if your blog, podcast, or Twitter is getting no traction, more often than not it's simply not what your customers are looking for and, to be blunt, they're just not that into you.

THEY'RE JUST NOT THAT INTO YOU

So how do you reach digital Darwinism panacea? How do you make all of your initiatives evolve, connect, and grow? How do you create and foster an engaged community that is interested in what you're doing and what their peers are doing? How do you enable and empower your community to connect?

What do Facebook and Google know about how to grow and nurture a community? Is it possible to "make" something go viral?

Now that you understand how much business has changed, and what you can do to take part in these conversations and communities, let's look at how to keep pace, grow your community, share it, and help it expand. Let's look at real ways to build your community and ensure that your business evolves (and doesn't become extinct).

TRAFFIC DOES NOT EQUAL COMMUNITY

In preparation for this book, I looked at many "Internet celebrities," people who have built their own personal brands to the point where they have significant amounts of traffic each day and are consistently seen as the go-to people for their perspectives on something new or on some kind of breaking news item. In looking at their traffic, comments, and their visitors who went off on their own to blog about what was being said, it became very apparent that human beings also have a wonderful way of polarizing one another. As much as we want to help, join, and build community, there are many who take great pleasure in leaving negative comments, bashing the blogger, and going off on their own to spout content that is in direct conflict with what's being said.

Everyone loves a villain. Hollywood was built on this foundation of human nature. In order to really push things forward and grow your newfound media properties, it's important to stay focused on why you are doing this. If you're doing it to become Internet famous, or you're doing this strictly as a way to be contrarian, it's going to be very hard to define serious business goals and maintain an ongoing development.

Your site visitors, views, and comments may be increasing, but it could be for the wrong reasons. As part of your ongoing strategy, you will have to define what the difference is between traffic and community.

For example, there are many websites (like Digg and Sphinn) where the community submits links, blog postings, and websites that are interesting, and the community votes these items up or down. The more votes up, the higher the content appears on the page. The more votes up, the more traffic is garnered. Think about it like a newspaper, where the more votes for an article, the higher it appears on the page and the closer to the first section it appears. From a pure numbers game, more traffic is never a bad thing, but that is the mass media complex. You're not looking for sheer mass numbers of people for the sake of traffic. You just want more people who are interested in what you have talked about.

Traffic has levels of quality that only you can measure.

Focus on building community and not traffic. Also, keep in mind that many people who have lots of traffic really don't have much of a community at all. In fact, hunting for the traffic can be a game of diminishing returns. To really evolve and maintain, focus on the five new community members (who will, we hope, become lifetime customers) versus the 55,000 who might float in and right out simply because of an orphan link that someone posted somewhere. Namely, they were interested in your content for about five seconds, but now they are gone.

The long-term game of sustainability in the online channels is one of quality versus quantity. Keep in mind that, with well over 1.5 billion people online, you should be able to find a mass number of high-quality people to connect to, with whom you can forge and develop your programs and initiatives as their needs change and as your industry changes as well. The good news is that by putting the time in now to build your community, you will have equity in your community and the basis for the continuous establishment of value and trust.

ATTENTION DOES NOT EQUAL TRUST

But just as traffic does not necessarily mean you're building any form of community, having attention does not equal trust. Think about how many people you know in the real world who garner a lot of attention but hold little trust. It's easy to point to certain politicians, musicians, and celebrities. There's no doubt we humans have a huge desire to slow down and look at the car accident, but being the target of digital rubbernecking is not sustainable.

Once you've understood these channels and started playing in them, you'll quickly realize that to really push things forward you need to deepen the level of trust you have. This happens through the types of content you create and how you engage in direct contact with your community.

The foundation of having a strong personal brand in these digital channels is in understanding what your reputation is online and how it interacts in the channels. Knee-jerk reactions that lead you to publish a piece of content can be, to a certain degree, very human and engaging, but in the long haul your content will need to stand the test of time.

How do you build trust once you begin receiving attention? By using the Web in a very human way. This falls into two major categories:

1. Be Helpful

Famed motivational speaker Zig Ziglar is known for his quote "You can have everything in life you want, if you will just help other people get what they want," and while it might sound like a modern cliché, being helpful to those in need online is one of the easiest ways for you to turn attention into trust.

Just now, I hopped over to Twitter and noticed this message from Jeff Pulver: "Does anyone have any stats about innovation and discovery in times of recession and/or depression vs. times of economic prosperity?" Jeff is one of the original guys behind the voice over Internet protocol company Vonage and is considered a leading tech business mogul and entrepreneur. He's asking for help. Can you help him out? Do you think if you did he would, at the very least, come over and check out who you are and what you are about? Do you think he might let his whole community know about who you are and how you helped him?

Plugging yourself into others' networks and needs is one of the easiest (and most fun) ways to really start developing trust. Don't do it in the spirit of "I'm going to need something from you, too." Do it in the spirit of sincerity. The Web is built on reciprocity. *If your actions are carried out with sincerity (be they big or small), the community quickly takes notice and repays.* An additional tip: Don't be sincere just to the bigger-named online personas. Help out anyone who makes sense to you.

2. Be Sincere

If your only reason for helping out Jeff Pulver was to get him to notice you so you could pitch him about your telecommunications start-up, he will see right through you, and your efforts will have the opposite effect you intended. Being sincere, being real, and being human (all pretty good ways to act) are the only solution. If you are known in these channels as someone who is helpful and sincere, you become a valuable community member—just like in the real world. Think about your community. Think about your neighbors. Think about who you would trust to watch your kids (and who you wouldn't). Do you trust them because of what they can do for you, or do you trust them because of who they are as human beings? We are all the same. We all have a deep desire to build and expand our community. Most of us are looking for the good in everyone and when that connects, our businesses tend to take flight as well. The general idea is to react and engage in the community the same way you do when someone in your family calls on you for help or information.

Hopping back to Twitter, Beth Kanter says: "Got call from unnamed charity—not asking for donations, but will you write 10 neighbors a letter and ask them to donate?" Beth runs a highly popular blog called "How Nonprofits Can Use Social Media," and is a consultant to the nonprofit sector. All of Beth's content is rife with sincerity and provides countless helpful examples, either through her own anecdotes or examples she blogs about, as to how nonprofits can build their donor bases by leveraging the many interesting and new digital channels. She has become popular (and successful) as an entrepreneur because she spends her time being helpful in a very sincere way. The other side is that her content (like her tweet above) is easy to understand and helpful. You don't have to work in the nonprofit sector to read that content and think about ways that type of strategy could be applied to your business. What if you didn't focus on the next customer call, but instead spoke to ten of your existing and happy customers and asked each of them to refer you two new potential clients?

Beth builds trust by providing real value and information to her community. We all need to be a little bit more like Beth.

THE ETHICS OF LINKBAITING

Part of building your audience will involve ethical linkbaiting. In its simplest form, linkbaiting is the practice of creating content with the intent of generating incoming links from outside sources. Linkbaiting is sometimes perceived as being unethical because inbound links are one of the primary ways a search engine gauges how high they will rank a website. The practice of unethical link-baiting is the creation of content for the sole purpose of gener-ating a bunch of links. Granted, it's not exactly a crime against humanity, but in a world where community and trust are the currency, individuals who linkbait are (to some extent) frowned upon. After all, your content should be of high enough quality that if people see the value in it, they will link to it because it is simply that good.

Some even argue that giving your content a sensational head-line is linkbaiting. Then there are those who say that everything is linkbaiting and that's the whole point of it all—to link to one another. It's the tactic that is often used but rarely talked about. You'll see it primarily in blog posts, but podcasts (both audio and video) have been known to have them, and they're most perva-sive in platforms like Twitter (where you only have 140 characters to speak your mind). Pictures can even be provocative enough to evoke this type of response as well. So, instead of posting a fully thought out idea, you leave the idea hanging, or you leave out some of your thoughts, or you ask a question (even if you think you know the answer). This not only allows your content to breathe, but it usually also sets a word trap for your readers and it incites them to leave a comment and keep your content alive and spreading.

Why are comments so important to the conversation? For one, comments show other readers not only that there's an interesting piece of content to consume, but also that a bunch of additional people have added to the conversation. Second, the people who comment also have the option of leaving a link, so that readers can go and check them out. As described earlier, inbound links still add a tremendous level of credibility to your community. Half-thoughts are good from both an optics and overall operational perspective. They allow your content to be more open and engage the community much more effectively.

Being slightly provocative also helps—not to the point of being seen as a jerk, but being a little edgy does stir and elicit response. Obviously, as a business owner, you have to decide how willing you are to be provocative. The point of these channels is not to polarize your customers. The point is to build a healthy conversation where people feel free to speak their minds and to share opinions. Keep in mind, there is a reason why people stop and look at *People* magazine or *Cosmopolitan* at the checkout counter (think about what makes those tabloids sell). Great headlines do draw attention. As more and more people switch to digital news readers (like Google Reader) and are bookmarking and visiting sites less and less, creating captivating headlines does help illustrate why people need to stop, slow down, and check out whatever you are producing. They're no longer seeing everything if they are finding you in a reader; they're mostly just going to see the text headline. The headline has to catch their attention.

Headlines that will catch people's attention:

- 5 Ways to Recession-Proof Your Business
- The Top 10 Ways to Attract Clients for Life
- Hidden Secrets of Entrepreneurial Success
- How to Change the World Like Bill Gates
- The One Thing Warren Buffett Never Told Anyone about Wealth

Great headlines do bait people in, but you need the content to be meaty to keep your community and get them engaged. *The general rule of thumb is to create a provocative headline only when you have the content to back it up.*

BUILD BY BEING CREDIBLE

There is no doubt that, in a world where anyone and everyone is a publisher of content, the lines are getting a little bit hazy between what is clearly content for the sake of content versus content for the sake of linkbaiting versus content for the sake of advertising. In the print world it is always easy to separate the ads from the content and, even when the publishing industry introduced advertorials in the sixties, the mass public was fairly quick to catch on. That advertising ploy is still used in both magazines and newspapers all over the world. We are even beginning to see advertorials in the online channels.

The assumption here is that whatever it takes to get your message through all of the clutter is fine, as long as you disclose and are transparent about your intent.

But that simply is not the case. All cannot be forgiven just because you wave your hand over a piece of advertising posed as real content and say "Paid," "Sponsored," or "Advertising." It's great to know that what your consumers are seeing is actually a piece of one-sided advertising versus a piece of content, but to really win in the digital channels, something more needs to happen.

You need to be credible.

Clearly, being transparent and disclosing any potential conflicts are still valid (even if they seem like draconian rules from traditional journalism), but the brands that are making the really big advances in the digital channels are the ones that have credibility. It's not only that, but every engagement they create becomes an opportunity for them to continue to build on their credibility, and they do nothing that will affect it or even give the perception that their credibility should be put into question.

Transparency is easy. Credibility is hard.

If your brand is new, building credibility will be one of the most challenging but rewarding activities of your business-building strategy. Embrace the idea that this won't happen overnight. Get comfortable with the notion that you will have several missteps that will feel like you hit the big, bad, long snake in the game Snakes & Ladders that slithers you back to square one. There are a few simple ways you can build your credibility. Be smart, be consistent, and be aware that this is going to take a long time. There is nothing more powerful than being known as a credible source. Your clients feel it and so does your staff. Real credibility moves people to talk, spreads your ideas, and gets people excited to be around your brand.

Here's the opportunity:

Few brands are really embracing the notion of creating a foundation based on credibility in the digital channels. Most of them are looking for quick fixes. They're willing to splatter the Web with banner ads or buy third-party e-mail lists. They're willing to allow their brands to appear in questionable spaces and will randomly add everyone and anyone on Facebook or Twitter. If you can build your brand by starting off with a foundation of transparency and then think about what you can do to create those real interactions between real human beings—understanding that this is a long road—then you are well on your way.

Credibility is everything.

ASK QUESTIONS

One of the easier ways to build your community and keep things moving along is to ask your community direct questions about the content you are producing. Never underestimate the power of what asking a good question can do to create content and to give you ongoing feedback. Many people fear asking questions in their social channels because they are worried they will get no response. They're worried they'll look like a loser if only one person responds. There's no denying that no response is a legitimate concern, but even if no one responds to your question, keep asking and keep trying. Give it some time, but keep asking.

Some of the better pieces of content you will come across will end with a question. Even a simple one like, "What do you think?" or "Do you agree or disagree?" Asking questions encourages participation. Think about conferences when the keynote speaker concludes and the moderator asks if there are any questions. Regardless of whether the room has five or 5,000 people, we tend to get shy. We're worried that others will perceive our own questions as stupid. It's basic human nature, but when the moderator begins with a question himself, it doesn't take long for people to jump in on the conversation. You could also ask one of your readers if he or she would mind taking a stab at answering it. If all else fails and no one does leave a comment, don't be discouraged. Continue developing great content and keep trying. *Only about 2 percent of all people online actually comment.* The question really needs to be provocative enough to spark them to take action.

Asking questions also keeps your content alive for a longer period of time. With well over 130 million blogs floating around, the shelf life of content is quite short. Here's another thought: Create a blog post by posting a question and then answering it yourself:

- Why should you read the latest business books?
- How does reading a business book make you a better entrepreneur?
- If I were going to start a new business tomorrow, what are the five things I would never do again?

Right now, you could easily make up ten questions (ones you have answers for) to use as potential content fodder. Asking questions also allows you to play the role of the contrarian. It's a great platform to bounce around a new idea or a concept you have been thinking about while also empowering your community to take part and be active. You may even be surprised by the amazing and different perspectives your community brings to the fold.

Use your new space for what it really is: one of the biggest focus groups you could ever ask for (and it's free). Use your space to really find out what people love (and hate) about your industry or one of your new business ideas.

Asking questions will also lead you to do a lot more self-analysis of your industry and business. Some of the more provocative questions I've seen (in text, audio, and video) have also led to some amazing pieces of follow-up content. Just last year, I had written a national newspaper business column on my six "must-read" business books. When I cross-posted the column to my blog, it generated about forty additional comments from other entrepreneurs about the books that inspired them. After seeing many similarities in the combined lists, I realized that there were, at least, a dozen more obscure business book titles that also shaped my thinking. The simple act of asking the community which more obscure business books shaped their thinking led to many follow-up blog postings on additional brilliant business books. Some of them were more alternative titles; others were books that had not sold many copies but still offer fascinating insights. These posts generated even more comments, which inspired other forms of content and discussion in both the Twist Image blog and our podcast.

ASKING QUESTIONS IS ALWAYS ONE OF THE BEST WAYS TO START A CONVERSATION

Don't believe it?

What is a better way to get people to comment on your content?

(I bet that question got you thinking—see what I mean?)

EMBRACE THE LONG TAIL OF CONTENT

Most entrepreneurs fail to embrace these digital channels because the channels are very candid and very real; these new channels are as real as it gets. You will see and hear the types of insights and comments you would never normally have access to. Often, people who are asked to speak at an event are given candid feedback provided on the feedback forms by the participants. As you can well imagine, the real purpose is to help the organizers understand what worked (and what didn't), but most conference organizers are happy to share what their audience thought of your presentation. I often get these feedback forms, and I really dig deep into what was said. On one hand, they are an amazing mix of information that helps me tweak and refine my presentation. I take them seriously, and I consider getting access to them a privilege. On the other hand, they provide an amazing glance into the human condition. There is always a person (or two) you cannot impress.

These digital channels can provide the same kind of important feedback, and you need to be prepared for it.

Remember that Brett Hurt from Bazaarvoice said that the average consumer review is a 4.5-plus out of five? This is counterintuitive. You might suspect that only the people who don't like your product or service would review it. Clearly, this is not the case. What we're seeing is that people who love your product are much more inclined to let other people know.

So yes, there's hope for humanity yet.

Digital channels are like that feedback form, only all the reviews are open to the public. Everything is open for everyone to see, comment on, tag, share, and pass along. The kooks and haters have the same volume of voice as the lovers and brand evangelists. Plus, everything that's recorded lies as a permanent record in the Long Tail that is a search result.

Be ready and willing to embrace this type of open forum and conversation (your competitors probably don't have the thick skin or bandwidth to handle and respond to everything that comes in). Ignoring what people are saying about you online is not an option, either, anymore, because the search results that are returned to users who are looking for your goods and services will be tainted with everything but your own perspective.

In the end, you may come to the conclusion that everything we've discussed is, simply, not for you, but then again, you really can't afford to ignore it. It's quite possible that the one person out of 100 with something negative to say will detract from the five-star-plus rating you are getting from the majority, but that, too, is not a reason to dismiss it. We are getting to a point in time where all business owners have to suck it up and set up some Google Alerts and a Technorati Watchlist to hear these voices—whether we like it or not.

Digital Darwinism is very real. Evolution or extinction? It's your call.

CHAPTER 10

From Mass Media to "Me" Media

FINDING YOUR ZEN

Garr Reynolds was simply living his life and doing what he loved. He was born in the United States and, for a time, was working at Apple as the manager of Worldwide User Group Relations in Silicon Valley. Garr's gig with Apple involved working with the brand communities by delivering presentations, software demos, and keynote addresses to the company's most loyal customers all over the world. Through his travels, Garr decided to move to Japan. Currently he lives in Osaka and is an associate professor of management at Kansai Gaidai University, where he teaches marketing, global marketing, and multimedia presentation design. As diverse as his cultural shifts have been, Garr has accidentally also uncovered one of the most powerful realities of the new online channels: *finding and owning your own specific niche.*

Through his teaching and corporate work, Garr realized that most people not only don't know how to present, but they also don't know how to build, design, and deliver a powerful presentation. On January 18, 2005, Garr started a blog called "Presentation Zen" to share his thoughts on the topic with the world.

"Why Presentation Zen?" asks his first blog posting. "Because something has to be done. The current state of business presentations is a disaster of mind-numbing ineffectiveness. I do not have to tell you this. PowerPoint, for example, lends itself to be misused and abused and most presenters fall into its trap. But multimedia or slideware (PowerPoint included) is not the problem. The problem is us. Many experts are trying to do something about this (Tufte at Yale, Cliff Atkinson at Sociablemedia, etc.). Please allow me to be another voice of reason."

With only two comments on that first blog posting (one of which looks like a bunch of spam) and no clear direction, Garr began to dissect what it takes to create compelling presentations. He had a passion for it and because the tools to publish were readily available for him to pursue and share his passion, he went for it.

In the three-plus years since he first started blogging over at "Presentation Zen," Garr has become one of the de facto global authorities on presentation skills. He could have blogged about design. He could have blogged about Asian versus North American culture and trends. But instead Garr became very focused on a small subset of design, *presentation design*, and decided that it would be his niche. He's become the leader of a passionate group of active people involved in the field of presentation skills.

Within a few short years, Garr has already released a bestselling book, *Presentation Zen: Simple Ideas on Presentation Design and Delivery*, and has spoken all over the world on the topic. His blog ranks as one of the most trafficked in the world, and he has built an audience that reaches well beyond the design and communications industry and cuts right into the overall business market with readers from a very vibrant community.

In a world where online content choices are endless, being generic or covering too wide a breadth of content holds no strategic advantage. *The real winners in business are the ones who are building and leading communities from micro-niches that expand and grow as more and more people come online.* Presentation skills are an area of information that, prior to the Web, individuals had to really search out (and whatever they could find was fairly limited in scope). There are just not that many specialized books on the topic, and you don't see many magazine articles or television specials on how to develop a better presentation. Yet it is a skill set that most businesspeople readily admit they need help with. Beyond the basics of good presentation skills, software packages like PowerPoint and Keynote enable anyone to create a presentation, but we all know the reality that "just because you can, does not mean you should." Garr took his passion and insights and created a new cottage industry for himself. He's become known as the "presentation go-to guy." His blog has secured him a book deal and numerous paid speaking engagements and has raised his profile.

Garr delivers consistent and fresh content to your computer on a frequent basis and has managed to create excitement over the art of presenting. One guy. One passion. One question: Why didn't the people running PowerPoint do this?

WHAT IS YOUR NICHE?

We've seen it before (and we'll see it again): A company starts off selling a product they're passionate about, they push things, they become active in their community, but as they grow, in order to sustain the business model, they start to take on additional brands, products, and services. They begin to lose focus. They lose market share. They dilute the power of the niche they had created. "Do one thing great" is, without a doubt, the biggest lesson you should apply to your online endeavors. Even if you're successful at a multitude of products and brands, choose one passion, nurture it, and work it.

DIG DEEP TO DEFINE YOUR NICHE (AND STICK WITH IT)

Finding and defining your niche is not easy. And the truth is, the majority of people who have done it well have probably stumbled upon it rather than strategizing and plotting their success. Most successful entrepreneurs were following a path of passion over a path of professionalism or profit. The endgame is always to create a viable and long-term business, but the road to get there is sometimes muddled with fumbles and foibles.

Being able to define your niche is a powerful step and an essential one. Thinking differently about your business is what inspired you to open shop in the first place. In order to dig back in and uncover your niche, make a list of what got you to this point. What inspired you to start your business—and what did you know about the industry that no one else seemed to see or understand? There must have been a major consumer insight that you uncovered.

More often than not, this list uncovers things that seem, at first, quite odd and unique—and that's the point. That's where the niche is born. How many people were looking at business PowerPoint presentations in boardrooms all over the world and saying, "This is boring"? (The answer is all of us.) But how many people actually had the vision to sit down, think about it, and create a blog about the topic or build a personal mission statement about why this needs to change? Garr found his niche by being a couple of simple action steps ahead of the rest. The lesson is that you don't have to be thinking leaps and bounds into the future.

We're not looking for you to be a wizard with a crystal ball. A few simple steps in another direction (it could be forward, it could be left, and it could be right) are often just enough to uncover your niche.

Don't dismiss how your personal life collides with your business (your personal brand continues to shine). Many people struggle to uncover their niches because what they love to do is not directly linked to what they do professionally. Many times, your unique hobbies or areas of interest *do* intersect with your business and can be adapted to help your business grow. You just may not be able to see it—yet.

ELEMENTARY, MY DEAR WATSON

Scott Monty loves Sherlock Holmes. He hosts an audio podcast called "I Hear of Sherlock Everywhere: The Podcast for Those Interested in the Life and Times of Mr. Sherlock Holmes—Where It Is Always 1895." He also writes a blog entitled "The Baker Street Blog: The Game's Afoot as Scott Monty Writes About the World of Sherlock Holmes"; he even runs an online community in tribute to Holmes called "The Sherlock Holmes Social Network." This is a very small niche. At any given time, Monty's Sherlock Holmes community is directly connecting about 500 people. So with a relatively finite audience, why would Monty keep at it?

For one, he's passionate about Sherlock Holmes, and these free online publishing tools enable him to meet others who feel the same way. Second, and most important, as Scott started using these digital tools, he began to meet others who were using the same tools to talk about what they were passionate about. As he continued he began looking for content on how he could grow his audience. As a marketing professional by day, he saw how both his professional and hobby lives were beginning to collide and come together.

This led him to meet several prominent people in the marketing and communications space (he also has a very highly regarded blog, "The Social Media Marketing Blog"). Eventually Scott was able to make some professional changes in his life to move more toward marketing using these new channels. His latest move brought him to Detroit, where he is the global head of the social media function for the Ford Motor Company. In sticking with his niche for the sole purpose of personal passion, Monty was able to move his professional career forward much more efficiently. It's not just Sherlock Holmes, marketing, and the automotive sector. Scott also runs another blog called "Nothing Could Be Finer than Being in Your Diner," along with another social media marketing luminary and podcaster, C. C. Chapman, where these two self-professed "diner junkies," along with guest commentators, "document their real experiences with real food in diners, roadside restaurants and authentic eateries."

Find your niche and stick to it. After all, if someone can blog about Sherlock Holmes and convert that into a global position at a major corporation, just imagine what you can do.

WHAT IS YOUR "BLUE OCEAN" STRATEGY?

Blue Ocean Strategy is a best-selling book by W. Chan Kim and Renée Mauborgne. This book on strategic planning looked at how some of the most successful businesses ventured off into undefined markets with unknown pricing and market share (a "blue ocean") instead of sticking to the traditional business process of competing with other similar companies for margins (the "bloody red sea"). The basic premise of the book is figuring out a way your business can avoid a competition business model by creating an entirely new market, essentially making competition irrelevant. It's the sort of business development that has made companies like Cirque du Soleil, Southwest Airlines, and Dyson so successful. And, while others have tried to compete with them, these companies continue to have little real competition. These businesses have found new, totally unique ways to serve traditional and significant industries.

Your business is (or must become) driven in a similar fashion. If you can't do it in the real world (figuring out a Blue Ocean Strategy is not something that happens overnight), thinking about how you can add certain "blue ocean" elements to your business using the online channels can change the scope of your business in a short period of time. Imagine being the only plumber blogger. When people are looking online for a solution to a sudden in-home incident, imagine being the go-to person online. Imagine what that would do to grow your business locally. Think about how that kind of positioning might also get a lot of very specific media attention in the markets you serve.

Twist Image is a digital marketing agency. I'd love to say we spend our days developing blogs and social media platforms for companies, but that's not the case. Social media development accounts for about 10 percent of our overall business. Like other interactive agencies, we spend our time developing websites, customer relationship management initiatives, micro-sites, and online promotions for our clients. But because we started our blog back in 2003 and because we have over 200 episodes of our weekly podcast "out there," when media outlets are looking for a quote about how blogging, podcasting, or social media is changing business, they call us. This is part of our Blue Ocean Strategy. This is part of what separates us from other digital marketing shops. None of this was easy to accomplish. It was (and is) hard work and very time consuming, but we have received great results from these efforts, and it has differentiated us and brought us out of the bloody red sea of interactive agencies and into a blue ocean (even though, on some days, it feels more like a pond) of what the agency of the future should look like.

Think about how you can be innovative using these tools and channels to leap ahead of (and away from) the competition. Having a strong Blue Ocean Strategy is about doing more than changing a few things about how you market your business and how it connects to your consumers. By simply thinking about more unique ways to connect, you are, in essence, becoming the leader we spoke about earlier. You are becoming a "category of one" (also the name of a book by Joe Calloway) and you are defining a brand-new niche within your industry.

This is not going to move forward unless you spend a little bit of time up front, building a process for developing your niche and deciding how you are going to grow it over time. Preparation and research are key. You may even find yourself developing a niche only to discover that others have already walked down that path. Do some simple searches online to make sure that your niche is not already owned by someone else, but even then follow your passion—just do it better.

BUILD SOME HOOKS INTO IT

The most common mistake we see in growing a business is adhering to the old "what you see is what you get" idea. The unique businesses, the ones that really push the conversation forward, are those that focus on their specific niches but also build their platforms with enough hooks that they can grow, morph, and change over time or as the community grows.

What are "hooks"?

Hooks are anything you can put into your community that will extend it and take things to another level. Comments on a blog can be hooks. The photo-sharing application part of Facebook is a hook (by the end of last year, over 10 billion photos had been posted to Facebook). In essence, the comments on the blog may spark a whole new kind of conversation. That conversation could lead you to develop newer types of content. For instance, over at the Borders bookstore website you can do almost everything you can do on any other website that sells books. As Borders built out its new online presence (side note: this was a major shift, as for years it decided not to compete with companies like Amazon .com in the online game), Borders began to realize that people go to bookstores for many more reasons than simply to buy books. Historically, bookstores have always held author events—book signings, author readings, musical performances. After watching what people were doing online and getting a sense for the type of content that could add value to the experience (and by snooping to see what their competition was not doing), Borders launched BordersMedia.

With its core site doing what it does best (getting people to buy books) and an audience looking for more and more content, Borders started posting videos of interviews with authors, artists playing in the stores, chefs who have authored cookbooks doing video demos of recipes, and much more. By developing a solid website with good traffic, Borders had the hooks to expand beyond being a simple e-commerce play. And, while all of this content is available only on its website as of this writing, my guess is that the next steps for Borders will be to distribute this content in other online places to drive the traffic back to the Borders website. Imagine seeing some of these videos posted on YouTube and knowing that there would be much more available if you headed over to Borders. Imagine Borders' adding in an RSS component (or even a small e-mail application) where consumers could choose the types of content they wanted and when something was updated, the community would be notified. Imagine what this would do for the brand. Essentially, Borders would be building hooks into its hooks. *The hooks would become a virtual multiplier of the business and extend into other niches and opportunities.*

Look at whatever endeavors you're thinking about taking on and brainstorm about which components need more hooks built into them, and which areas might create their own hooks. The point is, you don't have to worry about hooks right away, but you do need some foresight to make sure that whatever you're doing does have the flexibility and ability to have hooks built into it should you desire to push it further.

USE THE CLOUD

Mark Twain once said, "Find out where the people are going and get there first." Until now, you may be thinking that everything we've talked about is about getting you and your business online. It's not. Getting online is easy. Everybody's doing it. You could take almost every single idea in this book and adapt it to fit your everyday life. That being said, the general population is online and there are plenty of tools readily available at your disposal that can help you identify and nurture your niche.

In engineering and technology schematics there's a graphical image of a cloud at the top of almost all technical designs. This cloud is a representation of the Internet—all roads in all technical designs lead to the Internet. Leverage the Internet. Make it your best friend. Make it your best sales rep. Make it work for you.

Use the cloud.

Seth Godin is not just the author of many amazing marketing books and a famed blogger, he's also the founder of a very interesting company called Squidoo. Squidoo was created with the intent of making things on the Web easier to find through organization. This organization Squidoo calls a "lens." Imagine MySpace, but instead of personal profile pages, your pages are a lens into something you're particularly interested in.

Kate Trgovac (who also runs the excellent multi-authored blog "One Degree") created a lens on Squidoo that is entirely dedicated to cool, funky, and chic laptop bags. That's just one of her many niches of interest. By leveraging the power of the Internet and using the free tools at her disposal, she's not reliant on Web designers and programmers to share the information on laptop bags that she gathers out of passion. Instead, she set up a simple lens page on Squidoo, let some people know about it, and now the word spreads not only organically, but through the search engines as well. People looking for information, reviews, and ratings on which laptop bag to buy find Kate. Kate has had so much success with her lens that she has others, like "Funky, Chic and Cool Laptop Sleeves," "Book List from the *Daily Show with Jon Stewart*," "Book List from the *Colbert Report* with Stephen Colbert," "Funky, Chic and Cool iPod Cases," and "Funky, Chic and Cool Knitting Bags."

Kate found her niche and then found a place and tool (Squidoo) that would let her make some easy pages (for free) and started putting out the content she liked, as others who liked it as well began discovering her. Kate uses the cloud to share and explore her areas of interest and in doing so is also building a name for herself and her business. For Kate, the Internet is all about exposing others to her passionate niches.

THE WISDOM OF CROWDS

Whatever is happening online, you can rest assured that people not only have an opinion about it, but they also think they have a better way of doing it. You might think "there's no rea-son to reinvent the wheel." Online, every day, that's pretty much exactly what individuals are trying to do: not only reinvent the wheel, but figure out a better way to get around.

The Wisdom of Crowds: Why the Many Are Smarter than the Few and How Collective Wisdom Shapes Business, Economies, Societies, and Nations by James Surowiecki was first published in 2004. At the time, word was that Google was encouraging all of its new employees to read it. The top-line thesis is that group-driven instincts are usually better than an individual's. The Web acts as the great amplifier of this concept. Working with the crowd (instead of just pushing things at them) offers a new and dynamic way to uncover your niche.

Example: Twitter became even more mainstream during the tragedy in Mumbai.

Instead of waiting idly by for updates on CNN, many of the people "on the street" in front of the Taj Mahal Palace & Tower hotel began using Twitter to give eyewitness reports about what was going on. Instead of a couple of news sources, Twitter created a virtual network of reporters who were feeding real-time infor-mation, updates, and news to the entire world, in 140 characters or fewer.

The results were fascinating as well as frightening.

This river of news streaming through Twitter added a com-plex layer to our understanding of "news" and "journalism." This unfiltered feed of information demonstrated what happens in a world where the mass media have become completely disin-termediated. *Essentially, Twitter and all of the citizen journalists used free publishing platforms to cut out the media middlemen.* And while the news was unfiltered, unsubstantiated, and, at times, inaccurate, for the most part we have never seen these two very distinct worlds of the big news media collide with the person on the street.

In the good ol' days (two years ago), the mass media would interview people on the street for eyewitness accounts. Now, the mass media rely on Twitter feeds as the de facto source of information for live and "as it happens" moments. In a world where individual publishing platforms are free and big media newsrooms are increasingly expensive to maintain, we're seeing a new era in which everyone (including you) has become a citizen journalist.

More specifically, Twitter continues to demonstrate the amazing power behind the Wisdom of Crowds, not because you can get a quick glance into the psychology of the crowd just by watching what people are tweeting about, but because together, as a group, an interesting functionality came to light that was not part of its original intended use.

The primary function of Twitter was to let everyone know what was happening in your life at that particular moment. But when someone sent a message out to an individual, the content was hard to track (how would that person know that someone, somewhere, had written about him?). Somewhere, someone along the way started adding the @ sign with no space and then the user name of the person they were responding to (it would look something like this: @mitchjoel—I totally agree with everything you say!). From there, everyone was able to do a quick search for the phrase "@mitchjoel" to see if it was mentioned.

As this idea spread, it became a new way of communicating, connecting, and sharing. The Wisdom of Crowds prevailed. Instead of waiting for Twitter to develop a function outside of the original intention of enabling individuals to connect to one another using a 140-character broadcast system, the community developed a primitive workaround. This workaround has now become not only core to the functionality of Twitter, but we're seeing this type of communication pour over into comment sections on blogs, text messages, and more. This type of communication has widened—without Twitter doing much at all.

Your crowd and community will find more new and interesting ways to push your platforms forward than you could have ever imagined. They'll become the digital incarnation of MacGyver, using bits and bytes instead of chicken wire and bubble gum to make your system of communication even more effective for them.

Note: If your new media channels are set up solely as broadcasting systems for yourself and your messages, they will fail. But if you embrace the idea of monitoring, listening, and pushing things forward based on the feedback, insights, and comments from your group—your Wisdom of Crowds—you will become even more effective at not only defining and nurturing your niche, but also creating newer and even more exciting ideas and areas of interest.

EXPAND BEYOND BY ADDING MORE NICHES

David Usher has sold millions of albums worldwide as both a solo artist and the frontman for the rock band Moist. He is a multi-platinum-award-winning musician who has entertained millions. Through his own website, www.DavidUsher.com, David is in constant experimentation mode with online social networks, video-sharing sites, and more. He's not only a passionate artist and musician, but he also understands the power of turning everyday music fans into raving community members. It helped push his last disc, *Wake Up and Say Goodbye*, to number one on iTunes.

If there is one industry in dire need of reinventing itself and getting back to the power of the niche, it is the music industry. David is not just starting out, trying to figure out how to market himself as a musician. He has, literally, been there, done that, and sold the T-shirts. He built his career and rocketed to the top of the charts during the 1990s when the Internet was just taking hold as a commercial channel. As powerful as the Web was back then, it was not yet mature enough to be the powerful community and communications channel it has become. The reality is that Moist, his band at the time, did most of the more traditional marketing to get the word out: postering cities when the band was playing gigs, doing radio promotions, making videos, slugging it out in the clubs. They managed to build up the band, get a huge record deal and big arena tours, and sell millions of records. David has moved on to become a solo artist—also with great success—and has embraced the niche of fans (both old and new) who connect with his modern rock styling.

Over the past several years, Usher has been paying close attention to his fans—specifically, what they're doing online, what they're sharing, and how they are communicating. Along with a very active community forum that is linked off of his website, David quickly realized that his fans were congregating in the usual online social circles as well: MySpace, YouTube, Facebook, Flickr, and so on. For David to connect to his fans more effectively and to find some new ones, he had to take everything he was doing well on his website and add in more opportunities and more niches.

He started by recording some raw ideas for songs off of his MacBook Pro and then immediately uploaded the low-grade videos to Facebook. He used his website as the destination and these other social channels as a way to distribute the content. He began posting more and more pictures to Flickr. He asked that people on Facebook switch from his Fan Page to his personal profile, making the connection that much more personal and real. He's using many niches to get his art out there. He's using more and more niches to find and uncover newer fans. And he's pushed it even further.

In March 2008, David launched another blog called "CloudiD: David Usher's Blog on Art, Technology, and the Communications Revolution." David has a passion for how this space is changing everything we know about connecting and building audience. He's privy to some very interesting stories and brings a unique perspective to the conversation. Along with building his website and serving his niche with great audio, video, text, and information about tour dates, he's expanding into other niches in hopes of showing other musicians (and businesses) how to connect some of these very fragmented pixels. "CloudiD" is not just about his music or those fans; "CloudiD" is about the new business of art in a technology saturated world.

David is not sacrificing his music career to become a new media consultant. He is using and enabling both of his creative passions to connect and build bridges between both spheres of interest. That being said, you can follow David the musician and miss nothing. You can also follow "CloudiD" and not the musician and miss nothing. David built his music community and used all the channels at his disposal to grow it out. When the timing was right, he evolved and added a new niche to his repertoire, and continues to expand his career. It's unique in that if the music thing fizzles he's got something new and exciting on the go. If "CloudiD" takes off, he can maintain both. He's adding niches and building two very distinct and interesting businesses.

The common misunderstanding is that a niche is small and inconsequential. In the online world, this is simply not the case. The challenge will be in not biting off more than you can chew, in not taking on too many channels that require so much time that you wind up not only diluting the online channels, but putting your business at risk because you have shifted so much attention away from it. Discovering your niche is about nurturing it slowly by testing different areas where people congregate online, and by using the many dynamic and free tools that are at your disposal (be it a Squidoo lens or a free Flickr account) to figure out what pace works best for you. This will be the key to finding the right balance.

Focus on building your niche by asking these questions:

- Is your niche a hobby, your profession, or both?
- Do you see any crossover between the two?
- If you could sell only one type of product, what would it be?
- What do you do better than all of your competitors?
- Why do your most loyal customers keep coming back to you?
- What makes you different from others in your industry?
- When was the last time you asked your customers why they keep coming back?
- Is it time to do some quick (and non-annoying) surveys?
- What is your unique selling proposition (USP)?
- How can you communicate your USP more effectively?
- Once you find your niche and build community, what actions do you want your members to take? Read your content? Share it? Give you their personal information? Buy from you?

ALWAYS BE EXPERIMENTING

Experimentation is not a bad thing. It's a common mistake to look at ways to build your new business by doing what someone else has already done but with your own spin on it. It's a common trap, but you should not fall prey to it.

Yes, Technorati tracks over 130 million blogs. Sure, some of them are pure spam, or were set up and never updated, but what you've already learned is that there are tons of gems. Thousands of individuals are building their business by sharing their unique thoughts and perspectives.

The win is not in creating something that appeals to the masses. Your personal win will be in leveraging the power of a very specific and unique niche that you can serve, protect, and call your own. Your personal brand builds your business. You find your own "mass" in your niches.

Remember:

- Take the time to develop your own niche. Be the Cirque du Soleil of your industry.
- Use the cloud. The Internet can and should be one of the most powerful channels to convey your ideas and thoughts.
- Embrace the Wisdom of Crowds. All of us are smarter than any one of us is. Sometimes your community's ideas will be the ones that win.
- Be agnostic (not in the religious way). Don't be the person who gets his Facebook account flagged and then has nothing to show for it. Move from channel to channel without losing momentum. If an avenue doesn't work for you, drop it and move on to one that does.
- Get beyond text. The Internet has evolved. Use everything—images, video, audio, and, yes, text, too.
- Make the search engines love you. Make sure that whatever you create can be found through the search engines. Don't be like the countless individuals (and corporations)

spending millions online only to discover that no one can find them because they are invisible.

- Embrace your community as they become more and more passionate about your niche. Play with the hooks and, overall, have fun.

CHAPTER 11

Burn the Ships

THE LARGEST PUBLISHER OF AUDIO BOOKS IN THE WORLD (IT'S NOT WHO YOU THINK)

One day before a road trip, Hugh McGuire was searching online for free audio books and he could not find any. McGuire, a writer, software developer, and engineer, had always kept a keen eye on the open source movement, and in August 2005, based on some other open source and public domain projects that inspired him, he launched LibriVox.

LibriVox has a simple objective: "To make all books in the public domain available, for free, in audio format on the Internet."

Working off a very simple website and additional free Web-based applications, McGuire started putting the word out about LibriVox and asked for volunteers to come forward and record audio chapters of public domain books that were of personal interest to them. Using a message board to choose the titles and assign the chapters, the community is not driven by a bunch of voice-over professionals with full-on audio recording studios. In fact, it's the exact opposite. Anyone with a computer, a microphone, and some free audio recording software can put the classic words to their own voice. All voices are welcome. No auditions necessary. All audio is accepted, no matter what the voice sounds like. Audio books are created in different languages, as well.

Developed and grown almost exclusively through online communications, the community is the project; there is no hierarchy of management and control. Simply put, if you want to record an audio version of, say, *An Outcast of the Islands* by Joseph Conrad, all you have to do is hop over to the online message boards, leave a message with the chapters you would like to handle, and see how long it takes for others to fill in the rest. Once all of the chapters are completed, the entire audio book is published to the Web and available for free to download.

This fascinating new spin on audio books was recently called "perhaps the most interesting collaborative culture project this side of Wikipedia" by Mike Linksvayer, the vice president of Creative Commons (one of the only organizations that helps assign a certain level of copyright while still enabling certain uses for work—an increasingly important role in the digital world).

Most of the texts used for the audio books are drawn from Project Gutenberg (according to Wikipedia: "a volunteer effort to digitize, archive and distribute cultural works. . . . Founded in 1971 by Michael S. Hart, it is the oldest digital library. Most of the items in its collection are the full texts of public domain books. The project tries to make these as free as possible, in long-lasting, open formats that can be used on almost any computer") and the Internet Archive (again, from Wikipedia: "a nonprofit organization dedicated to building and maintaining a free and openly accessible online digital library, including an archive of the Web. . . . The IA makes its collections available at no cost to researchers, historians, and scholars. It is a member of the American Library Association and is officially recognized by the State of California as a library"). LibriVox's annual budget is $0, "and for the moment we don't need any money," says McGuire.

The principles of LibriVox, as listed on its website, www
.librivox.org, are also as fascinating as the project itself:

- LibriVox is a non-commercial, non-profit and ad-free project
- LibriVox donates its recordings to the public domain
- LibriVox is powered by volunteers
- LibriVox maintains a loose and open structure
- LibriVox welcomes all volunteers from across the globe, in all
  languages

LibriVox has become the largest publisher of audio books in
the world.

Hugh McGuire curates LibriVox along with several other open
source and collaborative projects and start-ups like earideas ("a
collection of the best thought-provoking audio available on the
Web" and edited by human beings), Collectik (a website that helps
you manage, mix, and share audio and video online), datalibre.ca
("Urging Governments to Make Data about Canada and Canadi-
ans Free and Accessible to Citizens"), and a new book-publishing
start-up called the Book Oven.

In order for Hugh to figure out a way to get more books into
audio format, he had to think differently. He could not publish
audio books the way it had always been done before. He had to
get out of his own way and let the community take over, own, and
nurture LibriVox. There was no "thinking outside of the box" because, in truth, there was no box for this strategy. There was no
traditional book publisher who was doing this sort of project. It
became a question of how to change the way people get and listen
to books on audio.

LIBRIVOX BURNED THE SHIPS

In the 1500s, Hernando Cortez was the captain of eleven ships with more than 500 soldiers headed for Mexico to conquer the Aztecs and bring back gold and treasures. As you can well imagine, after his ships arrived in Mexico, the sailors and soldiers were not in the best of shape. Some of them fell ill on the journey, some had lost their motivation, and their quarters were not exactly shipshape. Several of Cortez's crewmates wondered what would happen to them in this strange new land. If they faced challenges or resistance, how would the crew return home? The crew asked Cortez what the plan would be to get back home. The captain had the perfect response: He burned the ships.

There was no going back.

The only direction to go was forward.

The old ways of doing things were about to be rethought.

In fact, there were no more "old ways of doing things"; a new way had to be defined.

The story of Hernando Cortez and the burning of the ships ripples through to the present time. So much has changed in terms of what it means to be a business owner, the global economy, how we connect to our consumers, and the marketing and communications we create to connect more effectively with them. This notion of "being a part of their community" is still new, and, if the truth be told, it is not exactly clear or defined. As we enter this new world of new business, we, as the next breed of entrepreneurs, must do what we can to burn the ships. Every time a new business opportunity arises, be it through blogs, podcasts, or Twitter, we are far too fast to look at ways to monetize and commercialize the channel as though it were print, radio, or TV (the more traditional media).

If print, radio, or TV were a new medium, started today, what do you think they would do? Would they burn the ships?

New channels and new tools, like new lands, call for new strategies. The amazing part of all of the innovations we've discussed in this book is that we can still take the necessary time to understand what they are and how they connect us ever so much closer to our consumers. We can embrace the notion of discovery. As you move forward, take the appropriate amount of time to understand the environment and its elements (but don't sit back and wait forever). Buying Google AdWords may seem like a simple and obvious tactic, but there's still plenty of beauty in some of the more complex concepts that are present as well (or the ones that may at first appear to be complex). Bill Gates once said that he loved to see extremely complex concepts broken down into something simple and easy to understand. There is nothing more beautiful than finding that simplicity in the complexity. Think about the Google home page. Think about how easy it is to upload a video to YouTube.

HOW DO YOU BURN THE SHIPS?

For your business and from a pure marketing perspective, step one is to let go of trying to integrate or adapt your traditional advertising to the Internet. To date, most of the bigger ad agencies are, for the most part, practicing "adaptation." They're looking at the big thirty-second television commercial and are trying to figure out a way to re-create that in the online channels. This might be by producing a similar banner ad, or it might be by adapting the offer for an e-mail marketing campaign. What they're not doing is looking at what the brand truly is, how it connects to their consumers, where those consumers are in the online channels, and how to best reach, communicate, and connect with them.

Now is your chance to look at how your consumers are behaving and creating content for the new channels, and what kind of advertising messages they are looking for during the engagement. Unique content made specifically for them (think about Blendtec's "Will It Blend?") on a click-to-view (and click-to-subscribe) basis is one of the newer lights over the dark horizon as the ships burn. Video, audio, and mobile also start to glow as the blaze from the ships rages on.

You need to lead. You need to be curious. You need to be willing to do whatever it takes to maximize all of these new media channels to best deliver your brand. There are billions of dollars at stake and billions of people connected and watching. Please note: Google, Skype, eBay, Starbucks, and many more of the superbrands we have come to know have all done very little to no traditional advertising to build their empires.

This chapter is all about opportunity for your business. It's all about closing your eyes and taking yourself back to the 1500s. It is truly a New World and you have every single opportunity to make your own choice: You can do things the way you have always done them, or you can burn the ships.

BE VIGILANT AND CONSTANTLY BE MONITORING

Once you have begun to listen to the conversation and have started monitoring what others are saying about you, it's going to open up a whole new dialogue for your business. If you've already begun to respond (maybe you have even started to use Twitter or have set up your own blog), it is going to be increasingly difficult to respond to all of the online and offline chatter—especially if you've done everything effectively.

You must be vigilant. It is both an internal and external action. Early last year, the Pew Internet & American Life Project released a fifty-plus-page report entitled "Digital Footprints: Online Identity Management and Search in the Age of Transparency."

Here is one key finding: "Internet users are becoming more aware of their digital footprint; 47% have searched for information about themselves online, up from just 22% five years ago."

It turns out that Santa isn't the only one finding out who's naughty or nice. It sounds like half of the Internet population is doing their own ego-surf (searching their own name) to see what the score and count is.

The truth is, you should be surprised that it's not more than half of the online population.

And while this may, indeed, be a simple vanity search, managing your personal and company brand in the era of powerful search engines and our desires to connect through online social networks is becoming more of a challenge and a huge necessity. The report also says:

> Unlike footprints left in the sand at the beach, our online data trails often stick around long after the tide has gone out. And as more Internet users have become comfortable with the idea of authoring and posting content online, they have also become more aware of the information that remains connected to their name online.
>
> Nearly half of all Internet users (47%) have searched for information about themselves online, up from just 22%, as reported by the Pew Internet Project in 2002. Younger users (under the age of 50) are more prone to self-searching than those ages 50 and older. Men and women search for information about themselves in equal numbers, but those with higher levels of education and income are considerably more likely to monitor their online identities using a search engine.
>
> Just 3% of self-searchers report that they make a regular habit of it and 22% say they search using their name "every once in a while." Three-quarters of self-searchers (74%) have checked up on their digital footprints only once or twice.

It may be easy to dismiss the statistics and information as applying to a small fragment of the online population. But further consideration reveals that the opposite is true: This is the beginning phase of a trend that is leading toward a shift in business. It will affect what individuals say, do, and publish online. As images, video, and audio become more mainstream online (and more searchable), self-searching will become ever more relevant. Through tagging and the combination of text, the research in this report indicates that managing your brand—as part of an ongoing strategic mandate—will become as important to you as selling and business development are to your company's growth.

Remember, I'm Googling you just like you're Googling me—and it's happening more and more often. As such, you have to keep seeing what the search engines are pushing back. Now that you have the tools, your job is to set a regular schedule to keep on top of this. You must be increasingly vigilant in your effort and know what to look for (and how to respond). Customer service just went beyond the one-to-one interactions we have in our daily business and is now being played out online where the interaction is live, hot, and in the public view—forever.

STAY IN THE LOOP

Earlier on we looked at the many free tools you can use to monitor the conversation and be more effective at understanding what is taking place. As you move past the simple acts of monitoring, your use of these tools should shift and adjust as you transition into ongoing reconnaissance by being present, by staying in the loop.

At first glance, the tools below may seem like the simple monitoring solutions we first discussed in earlier chapters. But they are also powerful ways to be watching for new trends and are some of the best ways to share information with your clients, stakeholders, and other interested parties.

Now we're not just looking at how people feel about your brand, we're moving into a live and organic ongoing conversation, because once consumers realize that you are involved, engaged, and a part of the conversation, the tone of the content will definitely shift. Think about it this way: when someone is talking about another person behind his back, it is usually quite a different conversation than if the speaker knows that individual is listening or will hear what is being said about him.

1. Google Alerts

By this point you're going to notice that some of the links coming back to you will be related to how you reacted in the social channels. Google Alerts becomes a powerful tool to measure whether your input is having a positive effect on your business and the conversation around your brands. One quick trick is to create a spreadsheet and begin to track not only the number of mentions you are getting (which is still a valid indication of how your efforts have evolved), but also whether the conversation is positive, negative, or neutral. There are many paid services you can also use to monitor your social media activity, but Google Alerts will give you a more-than-basic perspective.

Pushing the technology forward, Google Alerts can also be turned into an industry nerve center for you. By simply entering the keyword terms that are relevant to your industry (for example, some of my Google Alerts are for keywords like "blog," "online advertising," and "digital marketing"), you will be able to keep a pulse on what the overall industry is doing. Going even further beyond the trending capabilities that will be delivered to you, you can also take some of the more salient topics and use them in your own content creation.

Personal anecdote: When both Twitter and Second Life started gaining attention in the marketing industry, I was noticing the increase in my alerts on these channels. In turn, I was able to blog about them early on and be seen as an early adopter—even though I was just following what was "hot" in my Google Alerts (there, now you know the real secret).

Beyond helping you stay in the loop, Google Alerts are an effective way not only to track how your brands are doing, but also to see overall trends in your industry that you can then use either to create original content and be seen as a leader or to adapt and adjust your business model.

2. Technorati

While having your Watchlists enabled (much like Google Alerts) to monitor what people are saying on the blogs, Technorati also offers two additional tools that can help you monitor the space and see how valued those individual voices are.

As you know, Technorati ranks blogs. Their rankings are based on an odd concoction of how websites and blogs link to a specific blog—the more links and references, the higher the ranking. If you have a blog of your own, make sure you have "claimed" it in Technorati (it's a simple process that involves a sign-up). If you don't have a blog, the ranks are still important and are relevant advanced information for you to monitor on an ongoing basis. If someone is talking about you, knowing how big his audience is and whom he reaches is an important tool. This doesn't mean you should treat higher-ranked blogs any differently than the lower-ranked ones, but the size of the audience and its overall power to spread a message will play a role in how you respond.

Authority is another important measurement tool. According to the Technorati blog,

Authority is the number of blogs linking to a website in the last six months. The higher the number, the more Technorati Authority the blog has. It is important to note that we measure the number of blogs, rather than the number of links. So, if a blog links to your blog many times, it still only counts as +1 toward your Authority. Of course, new links mean the +1 will last another 180 days. Technorati rank is calculated based on how far you are from the top. The blog with the highest Technorati Authority is the #1 ranked blog. The smaller your Technorati rank, the closer you are to the top.

As you become more engaged in these conversations, you'll notice two things:

1. Technorati often plays with its own algorithm, so blog rankings go out of whack a lot. It's frustrating, but to date, they are still the only real game in town. While some well-known bloggers have abandoned Technorati, it is still the 800-pound gorilla in the room. While the process of ranking blogs may not be perfect, it is still recommended to stay current on what and who is connecting in Technorati.

2. Technorati also uses tag clouds. A tag cloud is a visualization of the words that are used to create a piece of content. The more frequently used words are both bigger and bolder in size. In a quick glance you can get a vibe as to either what's hot or what are the most frequently used phrases in a blog posting. Tag clouds are an extremely useful way to see both what's on people's minds and what gets people talking. You should frequently look at tag clouds to better identify the type of language and words consumers use to talk about you and what they find interesting.

3. Google Blog Search

While Google Blog Search has no ranking or authority systems in place like Technorati, it does have a great RSS subscription service where you can do a quick search and then subscribe to it through your news reader. This way, you will be notified automatically when that set of search results gets updated. Do this for your own key terms, and don't forget about the ones that serve your industry and your competitors.

CENTRALIZE ALL OF YOUR INFORMATION

Most of the tools and programs we have discussed have RSS capabilities. One of the easiest ways to gain ground, stay in the loop, and be able to respond efficiently and effectively will be to manage the mass amount of information that is now available at your fingertips. Google Reader (or iGoogle or My Yahoo! or whatever Web-based news reader you are using) must become your personal NORAD system.

By adding all of this more advanced information (along with the more basic tactics we discussed in the earlier chapters) and organizing it into properly named folders in Google Reader, you will be able to manage your information and news so that you can spend the majority of your time focused on responding and spreading the good gospel, instead of wasting your valuable time going from site to site and searching aimlessly for what's been said about you. Because tools like Google Reader also enable you to mark information as read or to save it, you also will not have to worry about whether or not you responded to something, as you are managing all of this news and information from within one, centralized location. Use these tools to get efficient and organized.

BE WRONG—BECAUSE THERE ARE THREE SIDES (AND MORE) TO EVERY STORY

Is there anything as counterintuitive as telling a business owner to be wrong?

Publishing your thoughts "out there" for the world to see is not only an important part of building your reputation and your business, but it also demonstrates (to yourself and to your clients) what you think and how you think. Blogging and the other more social publishing tools are hugely powerful because they enable you to think about something, write your thoughts down about it, publish it, and then allow the public to comment and add their own perspective. If you embrace the idea that you are going to be wrong (once in a while), you are well on your way to burning the ships.

Being open to the idea that you could be wrong is being open to the idea of risk. Real entrepreneurs risk it all every day. In a world where most people shy away from risk and most people would dread not only the idea of being wrong, but also having it highlighted and out there for the world to see, being wrong suddenly becomes a powerful entrepreneurial force. Putting yourself in a position where you can be wrong and where you not only embrace it but respond to it allows you to be deeply engaged with your community.

CONNECTING IS NOT ENGAGING

Just because you're connected in the digital channels does not mean that anyone really cares. Connecting is not engaging. Do not confuse the two. People think that because they have a presence in an online social network, like Facebook, they are providing something of value to their consumers. Nothing could be further from the truth. Think about the title of this book. Yes, we are all connected now, but that doesn't mean anyone is paying any particular attention to what you are doing or is engaged in whatever you are selling.

You see this time and time again. Think about someone who has requested to be connected to you in an online social network. You may not know him, but after reviewing his profile and some of the people he's connected to, you decide to make him part of your digital social circle. From that moment on, the messages, requests, and sales pitches never end. That individual is abusing your connectedness and is confusing it with engagement.

Engagement online is almost as tough to create and nurture as trust. Being connected is table-stakes, but building engagement is quickly going to evolve into a game of delivering high-value content and becoming widely regarded as someone who continually adds value to others without being perceived as a user and abuser with the end goal of simply getting more sales.

BE RESPONSIVE AND FAST

Your business life just became a high-speed game of virtual paintball. In order not to get hosed with too many paint pellets, there is one very simple tactic you must carry out. It is one that states, without a question, that you, unlike your competitors, have truly decided to make a commitment to respond to your customers.

Never be silent.

If someone e-mails you, blogs, podcasts, or interviews you for an article, do everything in your power at least to leave a comment (or e-mail) letting them know you are reading, paying attention, and, most importantly, appreciative.

Make this the one thing you never fail to do.

Whom do I never forget? I never forget those who respond. Now there are instances when Google Alerts fails or a Technorati-driven ego surf does not pull in every result, so there is a good chance you will miss some of the content being produced about you. If it's an honest miss, there's nothing you can do. If you knew about something and didn't leave a message or follow up, shame on you.

More than anything, digital channels provide a global platform to share. There is the momentum effect that businesses must be paying more attention to, the instances when a consumer mentions your company, brand, product, or service in his or her profile in an online social network and the effect it has in the marketplace. You should find it completely insane that individuals (and companies) who have blogs whose popularity helped them get mass distribution for their products do not take the time to acknowledge when they are mentioned in the exact same types of spaces.

It's a responsibility always to respond to an inquiry. This is why marketing plays such a critical role in customer service and in your business. It's simple: I say "Thank you"; you respond with "You're welcome." But now take some real action here: if someone bought your product and took the time to mention it in his own space, don't you (as the person or company being mentioned) feel obliged at least to drop in a simple "thank you"?

If anything, there's a Raving Fan (as author Kenneth Blanchard calls them) you are all but ignoring. This is further amplified because the feedback is being given in one of the social media channels.

Most companies look at the space and want to dive headfirst into blogging. We've already discussed the importance of monitoring the space, listening to what's being said, and being a part of those conversations prior to trying to start your own. There's a reason: Nothing stinks of insincerity more than a blog or blogger who is not listening to the other conversations.

"People are busy and they can't respond to every comment or posting" is a very common mantra you begin to hear from some of the Internet celebrities who have gained a level of fame in these channels. But in this day and age, can you really still afford to have that kind of attitude, especially when these channels gave you access to business opportunities in the first place?

No chance.

As much as you physically can, respond and be thankful to everyone who takes the time to mention you. If anything, my personal disappointments have only fueled my passionate fire to make sure all of the links in the chain are (and stay) connected.

LET PEOPLE STEAL YOUR IDEAS

Here is a true story about the conception of Six Pixels of Separation:

One of my former employees at Twist Image came up with the line "Six Pixels of Separation." It was a phrase used in developing copy for one of my presentations. While the context of it was totally different from what it is today, I brought my version and what I felt Six Pixels of Separation stands for to one of my business partners. Having a more traditional background and being from an older generation, he suggested we trademark it and not talk about it publicly until this book was ready for publishing. You should have seen his face when I told him I had already blogged about the concept a few months back.

"What if someone steals the idea and writes the book first?" he asked.

"Then they're a thief," I said calmly.

"How would you prove that?" he pushed on.

"Do a search for 'six pixels of separation' in Google and you tell me."

The conversation was over.

I was not afraid to put the idea of Six Pixels of Separation out to the world. I was not afraid to be told that I was an idiot for thinking that individuals would soon have personal brands that would rival even the biggest corporate brands out there, and I wasn't afraid someone could steal the idea, either. The world is no longer about proving in a court of law who was the first to have the idea; a simple search proves everything to everyone.

Let people steal your ideas.

It may sound dramatic, but odds are if your idea is strong and you have shared it in these circles, someone will come along and "adapt" it as his own. Not only will the community know, but beyond that it won't get any further.

Scraping is a part of the digital life cycle. There are many sites and business owners who simply don't have the time to develop their own content, so they troll across the Web and copy and paste whatever content they like and place it on their own web-sites as if it were their own. It's highly illegal but, sadly, never worth the trouble, time, money, and lawyers you need to engage to attempt to get it resolved. Somebody with such low scruples is usually running an operation offshore or in countries with much more lax copyright laws.

It is a dilemma, but it's also a paradox: On one side, everything you have taken the time to create and nurture should be your own and only you should profit from its value. I am a journal-ist, and you can imagine how painful it is to see all of my con-tent floating around on a bunch of websites and blogs without my written consent. On the other hand, with the millions of blog postings and pieces of content being created each and every day, it is very flattering that they choose to steal my content. So, while it's morally impossible to accept this kind of behavior, the reality is that your content will probably get stolen, but the real people, the potential community members or customers you are looking to attract, probably will not be in those other spaces.

GO OUT ON THE FRINGE

Remember: Your primary goal is to be spreading your ideas and thoughts far and wide, knowing full well that the right people will find you and the right people will also know who the real source is for all of the great content they now have in their lives. There are going to be countless times in the online channels where you will not be acknowledged as the source of an idea and someone will not thank you for inspiring an idea that generated business for him or her. With the mass numbers of channels and the amount of content out there, those who really burn the ships are not waiting for credit. They are out there, on the fringe, building, sharing, growing, nurturing, and leading.

CHAPTER 12

Tribal Knowledge

CONTENT IS MEDIA

Arthur Sulzberger is the owner, chairman, and publisher of the *New York Times*. At the World Economic Forum in Davos, Switzerland, in 2007, he said, "I really don't know whether we'll be printing the *Times* in five years, and you know what? I don't care, either."

That statement has become one of the most provocative in the publishing industry's history (some even argue that Sulzberger has since backpedaled). At its core, his reasoning is quite sound. It's not that Sulzberger does not believe in the power or future of the newspaper, he is simply following the money. And whether the money comes from the online channel, the mobile channel, or a collaborative channel is not all that relevant to Sulzberger. The *New York Times* is about delivering great and relevant content to its consumers, and Sulzberger wants to be the intermediary and to ensure his fair share of the advertising cut in the process.

In due order, the *New York Times* also changed their online business model. Originally, you could view certain pieces of their content but had to pay a premium subscription to have access to everything you could read in the printed version. They dismantled this and began offering all of their content for free online.

What had changed?

"With the removal of the pay wall, the audience potential at NYTimes.com, already the No. 1 newspaper website in the United States, is vast," said Denise Warren, senior vice president and chief advertising officer of the *New York Times* Media Group, in a news release. "Advertisers on the site can expect to see an unprecedented number of *Times* readers interacting with their brands."

Sulzberger and his team may not be looking at the next three years to stop the presses, but there is no doubt that they are testing the model of "content as media" in a unique way.

It is the transition to the "content as media" model that is powerful in understanding how your business can use collaborative tools to help build your wealth of content. The three-phase transition works as follows:

1. Content Is Everything

"Content is king." There is still no doubting this. Whoever has and creates the best content wins. This is not just for newspapers, magazines, or any other media outlet, it is true for your business as well. Take a quick glance at the industry leader in your line of work. Odds are they are out there speaking at industry events, contributing articles to the industry trade papers, building white papers, and videotaping testimonials. When a potential customer comes knocking on their door, they are winning the business because of what they do and how much quality content they have put out into the industry. The better the content of a business, the more likely it is to win more business. People want to work with a company that is seen and recognized as the leader in its space.

Creating great content is one of the surefire ways to build that type of reputation.

Great TV shows, smart websites, and brilliant movies win by offering the best content. Your business can, too.

2. Everything Is Content

With the advent of blogging, mobile phones with built-in video cameras, and the many free publishing technologies and channels that are readily available to everyone, suddenly everything has become content. A statement like "Doing the laundry" posted to Twitter is now content. Suddenly, a picture taken at your company BBQ and posted to Facebook is content. If we sat down for a quick phone interview and recorded it, it could then be posted as a podcast. That phone conversation has now become content. Each and every one of us has not only become a content provider, but everything we do, say, and document is content. We are all publishing content . . . always.

There's nothing wrong with that, and some (including me) might argue that it's a good thing to have this legacy of content out there. This is the new reality of our world when it comes to integrating the new media channels into our businesses. Before, the cost of creating and publishing content was out of reach for most of us. In this new world, everything we create can be used as content and as a way to connect us effectively to consumers. It may sound a little like all businesses are doing is creating content clutter, but this is not the case. If no one wants to see and engage in this content, they won't. It is very easy to ignore or avoid. The overarching concept of the shift from "content is everything" to "everything is content" is what you need to consider when you enter this fray.

3. Content Is Media

"Content is media" is more than creating a piece of content and buying advertising space for it (aka an advertorial). If you can engage your consumers by providing them with relevant and valuable content that your brand is powering, you win. If you push it further by building trust and getting your consumers to collaborate on that content with you, just stop and think about the power. What is more valuable: having millions of people see a thirty-second spot on television or getting thousands of really interested people to spend many minutes (maybe even hours) engaged with the content you are either producing or creating in conjunction with them?

Whirlpool has done this with "The American Family Podcast." This weekly audio program provides content about traditional American family values. It may not be specifically relevant to you—and that's the point. Whirlpool creates this twenty-minute audio podcast because their core demographic probably can't get this type of unique content on their local cable TV or radio stations. By creating content, putting it out there, and encouraging their audience to take part, Whirlpool is slowly building out their demographic and is directly engaged with it in ways traditional advertising never could be. Even if you're not a Whirlpool customer but you listen to the podcast and appreciate it, it's not hard to imagine that when the time comes to purchase a new fridge or dishwasher, Whirlpool will be top of mind. "The American Family Podcast" is twenty minutes of great content. That content is their medium.

Your job is to take the many examples of ways companies are embracing their consumers and enabling those consumers to collaborate with them to build loyalty and long-term relationships and chart your own map.

PEOPLE ARE NOT EVIL

There's an evil side to all of this. There's no doubt about it. People do use these social channels to manipulate, steal, hurt, and injure. It has to be said. It has to be understood. Your general assumption should be that 2 percent of the world is inhabited by mean and nasty people. It's probably a little higher in the online channels because individuals have false beliefs that they are, to a certain degree, anonymous. Let's be clear: No one is anonymous online. Without getting too technical, every move you make online is recorded and is accessible by authorities should they decide to take a peek. Yes, there are privacy laws and, yes, there is an elite group of hackers who work around it without being found, but in general, it is not as easy to be invisible online as you might suspect. The old adage that "on the Internet no one knows you're a dog" is very 2002.

Understanding how visible you really are in the online channels is one of the primary things to consider as we begin to look at what is, without question, the most powerful part of the online channels: collaboration. All of the ideas and concepts in this book can be used to do bad things. The tools and channels are neutral.

But, as we know, people are not neutral.

You may be thinking that a bunch of computer servers, power grids, cables, and wireless routers power the Internet. Nothing could be further from the truth. People are what power the Internet. People have taken the very static tools of the first generation of Internet connectivity (clicking, reading, and looking) and have transformed them into a massive collaboration epicenter. Everything from internal business tools to trying to document and share the knowledge of the world is happening online.

If you fear that the Internet is all about individuals preying on our young or dirty old men surfing for girlie stuff, one look at something like Wikipedia should make you feel that there is hope for humanity yet. While Wikipedia is by no means perfect, the editors and people who contribute, correct, and add to Wikipedia are involved in the noble act of preserving human knowledge (as absurd and slanted as it might sometimes seem on their website). And in between those two disparate areas, many entrepreneurs are embracing the world of collaboration to grow not only their communities, but their businesses as well.

The music industry (in terms of selling CDs) is in dire straits. That being said, more and more people are exposed to more and more music than ever before. Part of this has to do with peer-to-peer sharing tools (it all started with Napster, and torrents continue on to this day). Part of it has to do with MP3 players and the iPod generation, and then there is the digital music scene, which encapsulates stores like iTunes and includes the multi-million-dollar ringtone industry. As certain artists complain that people are not buying music anymore, it is hard to dispute that since the advent of the Internet as a commercial engine people are exposed to more music than ever before.

The real question for musicians is not "Why aren't consumers buying CDs?" The real question is "How do we get the general public to notice us with all of this music out there?"

What if you opened up? What if you had a great idea? What if the entire community could help you? What if people worked together to spread the word?

BUM RUSH THE CHARTS

On March 22, 2007, fans of the indie music band Black Lab mobilized online via a blog to attempt to push the band's newest single, "Mine Again," to the number-one position on the iTunes singles chart. Why? As the blog says, it's "a demonstration of our reach to Main Street and our purchasing power to Wall Street. . . . What's more, we're going to take it a step beyond that. We've signed up as an affiliate of the iTunes Music Store, and every commission made on the sale of 'Mine Again' (by Black Lab) will be donated to college scholarships, partly because it's a worthy cause, but also partly because college students are among the most misunderstood and underestimated groups of people by big media. Black Lab has taken it up another notch—50% of their earnings are going to be donated to the scholarship fund as well."

The idea was to turn things around at iTunes. It wasn't about one song or one band; rather, it became a revolution to make iTunes "Mine Again." There was also an underlying subtext to this experiment. People involved in the online channels felt that this might be a chance to prove the power of new media. Nothing would accomplish their goal better than showing corporate media that not only can a group of regular people, who are mass collaborating, exceed beyond their reach and match the purchasing power of the masses, but they can also make a positive difference in the world while doing it.

The project was called Bum Rush the Charts. And that was exactly the intent. Fans of Black Lab (and even those who weren't fans but simply could not resist an interesting opportunity to do something that might change the way an industry works) spread the word—and the word spread well beyond the digital channels into mainstream media as well. Why do people collaborate and do this type of thing? Is there animosity? Were people trying to hurt the music industry? Probably not, but it is becoming increasingly difficult to get behind an industry that never saw Napster coming, then got pillaged again when iTunes took hold, and then really lost it all when online social networking broke and

MySpace turned bands into real-life communities. There's also a small charm in "sticking it to the man."

People collaborated on this project to prove one thing: The everyday person has power.

Some companies believe they have power over the consumers. Some pundits, though, say that the power of brands is shifting to the consumer. Power has, in fact, been balanced because of these digital channels. Companies used to crowd the available media spaces with their messages by spending a lot of money to reach more people than any individual ever could. Now crowds come together and decide how (and what) they want their brands to be.

Say it is because of blogs, podcasts, online social networks, or what have you, but you and your customers have "real power" now—the real ability to effect change, and the very real ability to do magical things through the power of online collaboration. Your customers can spread your message far and wide—whether it's about how a Kryptonite bike lock can be opened with a Bic pen or an idea from a bunch of indie music fans who want to help their band get to number one.

Bum Rush the Charts is a prime example of how new ideologies like the Wisdom of Crowds, connected communities, mass collaboration, and tribes without defined geographies are mashing-up to make a difference in the business world.

How did Bum Rush the Charts do in the end?

According to their blog, the song was sold for $0.99 on iTunes about 6,000 times. It managed to hit number eleven in the U.S., number ten in Canada, number two in the Netherlands, and number twelve in Germany, but failed to make it to number one on any of the charts. That being said, the experiment could never be seen as a failure. Black Lab got a lot of visibility and, without question, gained a few new fans through the sheer volume of chatter online and in the traditional media. The online community validated that it could, in fact, mobilize in a short time frame, connect, and communicate a message to the masses. But, more importantly, this type of exercise has now become commonplace beyond music.

In launching his second book, *Join the Conversation*, new media strategist Joseph Jaffe launched a Bum Rush the Charts–style event that lasted one full day in hopes of pushing his book to the top of the Amazon.com book charts. Along with promoting it through his blog and podcast, "Jaffe Juice," Jaffe also spent the day online using a video conferencing service called ooVoo to connect with fans and get them, in turn, to invite their friends and colleagues to pick up his book and discuss it. Jaffe was able to move the needle by reaching number two in the Business and Investing category on Amazon.com and number twenty-six overall. Prior to "bum rushing the book charts," Jaffe also used something he called UNM2PNM (use new media to prove new media) to launch his debut book, *Life After the 30-Second Spot*. In that initial program, Jaffe engaged his community to review his book in blogs and podcasts by offering a free book to anyone who had an online publishing platform and was willing to create a review.

These types of initiatives were bound to happen. The minute the tools were made available and accessible, we started forming groups and communities and started sharing. The good news is that, like many of the other topics in this book, it is all fairly new and there is plenty of room to experiment, investigate, and take chances.

"The smartest guy in the room is everybody," wrote Steven Levy and Brad Stone in the article "Putting the 'We' in Web: From MySpace to Flickr and YouTube, User-Generated Sites Are Rocking the Internet" in *Newsweek* (April 3, 2006). One of the first people to coin the term "Web 2.0" was Tim O'Reilly of O'Reilly

Publishing. Levy and Stone quote O'Reilly on the power of harnessing all of this collective intelligence:

> This sounds lofty, but [it] is actually happening all the time on the Web. Every time you type in a search query on Google, what's happening under the hood is the equivalent of a massive polling operation to see which other sites people on the Web have deemed most relevant to that term. Magically, it yields a result that no amount of hands-on filtering could have managed.

James Surowiecki, author of the book *The Wisdom of Crowds*, demonstrates throughout his book how this works. Whether it's the story of how a bunch of people were able to predict an Oscar winner better than the so-called experts or how millions of us are able to mass-collaborate and contribute to an online encyclopedia (Wikipedia) and produce results that do, indeed, rival those of *Encyclopædia Britannica*, "we" are better than "you" alone.

There's more from Levy and Stone's article in *Newsweek*:

> Less than a decade ago, when we were first getting used to the idea of an Internet, people described the act of going online as venturing into some foreign realm called cyberspace. But that metaphor no longer applies. MySpace, Flickr and all the other newcomers aren't places to go, but things to do, ways to express yourself, means to connect with others and extend your own horizons. Cyberspace was somewhere else. The Web is where we live.

This is why the companies featured in the *Newsweek* article work. The community guides and collaborates to ensure their success and longevity (like all of your regular customers). Your consumers should be creating and interacting with your business. If you start doing everything right, all you're really doing is just managing the traffic (and making some money along the way). People no longer sit passively and click their way around websites. They do stuff. They blog. They podcast. They collaborate. They share. They comment. They evolve. They tweet.

Web 2.0, social media, and online communities are not just buzzwords. Most business owners are still getting used to banners, search engine marketing, affiliate programs, and e-mail marketing. Now we're all forced to understand better what happens when user-amassed wisdom forms in the shape of communities and meets through the power of technology.

Imagine the new power and knowledge you and your business can now benefit from.

WHAT'S YOUR BIG IDEA?

When businesses exclaim, "Look at me! Look at me!" it comes off as inauthentic. Because this tactic has come to be expected by consumers, when companies do open up and use these channels to connect, there is always a tinge of skepticism—and that's understandable. There are two simple steps any company can do to overcome this:

1. Ask your consumers to share their thoughts, ideas, feelings, and comments.
2. Act on what they are saying.

It may seem simple enough, especially the first part, but it is the second step where most businesses fall down. If you're going to ask that your consumers collaborate with you on ideas or a specific project, you have to be prepared to engage and act on their feedback. Otherwise your efforts will come off as another hollow attempt at marketing to them instead of collaborating with them.

The story of how President Obama used the Internet and online communities to raise money, awareness, and mobilize people to vote is not half as interesting as his first move after he had won the election. Within days, his official website was online and invited everyday citizens to submit their ideas for the future of the United States of America. Under the headline "Open Government" was a section entitled "Share Your Vision." People could simply e-mail in their thoughts or upload a video or create an audio comment. Whether these visions became part of the transition plan or made it to the top of the president's priority list is not nearly as important as the simple act of engaging the community to see what is on their minds and how, together, they could collaborate for a better America. Is there an off chance that a citizen comes up with an extremely clever and strategic solution to the nation's problems? Why not?

These types of collaborative environments are not just for progressive governments. The more progressive businesses that are engaging in these community-driven channels are opening up more and more. Dell has been the gold-standard example of a company that has shifted and now empowers its employees and consumers to be in these channels as a way to communicate and connect more effectively (this has had a direct effect on sales growth and the bottom line). The positive effects of these efforts are well documented. One of the more interesting projects they've created online is called IdeaStorm.

IS IT YOUR BIG IDEA OR OUR BIG IDEA?

The term "crowdsourcing" was coined by Jeff Howe in 2006. He used the term in a *Wired* article to describe a new form of creation that was carried out not by an individual, but by a community of people. While projects in the past have contained crowdsourcing elements, true mass collaboration is really taking off due to the online tools that are now readily available, free, and easy to use.

IdeaStorm is based upon the concept of crowdsourcing, and not only is it a new way for Dell to listen to its customers, it is also a way to leverage the community's knowledge and ideas to help the company innovate and move forward. IdeaStorm is an online community where consumers can post their ideas about what Dell should be doing and, more specifically, should be doing better. The site has a built-in voting mechanism for each idea and an area for discussion. Dell is not only sharing these ideas within the organization, but individuals who submit their ideas are also being judged by their peers. This tends to cancel out the crazier concepts. The project is not unlike what Starbucks is doing with their My Starbucks Idea.

Chairman and CEO Michael Dell explained the reasoning behind IdeaStorm: "We are at our best when we are hearing directly from our customers. We listen, learn and then improve and innovate based on what our customers want. It's one of the real advantages of being a direct company."

You don't need a unique website and complex voting technology for your website to create an IdeaStorm of your own. You can simply ask people to call or e-mail in their information and post their ideas on your website. You can use simple (and free) online survey tools (like Survey Monkey) to ask for people's opinions. You can ask for text, pictures, video, and audio.

The way to really make this work is not just to ask for this content and let it sit there, but to create a space where the information can be posted unfiltered, a place where individuals can comment and connect on one another's thoughts. But remember, you must be committed to making the changes or responding to the feedback that is coming—both the good and the ugly.

THE CHARMS OF WIKIPEDIA

One of the best (and easiest and free) ways to wrap your head around how mass collaboration really lives and breathes online is to spend some time with Wikipedia. Wikipedia has rules. Serious rules. The first one you need to be aware of is that you cannot create your own Wikipedia entry or edit it. The point of all knowledge posted to Wikipedia is that it is written by an impartial third party, someone without any direct vested interest. This causes many issues and complaints from businesses. How knowledgeable about your business can a third party be, and, if there is an error, how can you correct it? While there is process and logic to it all, Wikipedia has been built up over the years and the dynamics and politics of working the Wikipedia system can be both confusing and frustrating. Even the ability to edit Wikipedia has been changing recently.

One of the ways to get listed on Wikipedia is simply to be relevant to enough people that someone, somewhere, takes the initiative to create an entry on your behalf. If there are issues with your entry or you see some errors, there is a "discussion" area where you can post, let people know who you are and what should be updated, removed, or changed. Usually someone within the Wikipedia editing community will see your comment and adjust it. You can also take a chance and make the correction yourself. If you take this path, it might be wise also to leave a note in the discussion section about who you are, why you made the change, and a link (if possible) that substantiates your edits.

There was a terrific article in the *New York Review of Books* (March 20, 2008), "The Charms of Wikipedia," by Nicholson

Baker, that will help you think differently about what mass collaboration is and why it is so important for moving business forward. The article was a commentary and review of the book *Wikipedia: The Missing Manual* by John Broughton. Baker wrote:

> They weren't called "Wikipedia's little helpers," they were called "editors." It was like a giant community leaf-raking project in which everyone was called a groundskeeper. Some brought very fancy professional metal rakes, or even back-mounted leaf-blowing systems, and some were just kids thrashing away with the sides of their feet or stuffing handfuls in the pockets of their sweatshirts, but all the leaves they brought to the pile were appreciated. And the pile grew and everyone jumped up and down in it having a wonderful time. And it grew some more, and it became the biggest leaf pile anyone had ever seen anywhere, a world wonder. And then self-promoted leaf-pile guards appeared, doubters and deprecators who would look askance at your proffered handful and shake their heads, saying that your leaves were too crumpled or too slimy or too common, throwing them to the side. And that too was bad. The people who guarded the leaf pile this way were called "deletionists." . . .
>
> It worked and grew because it tapped into the heretofore unmarshaled energies of the uncredentialed.

Mass collaboration is sometimes more about what it does for the individual than the overall contribution to the greater good of the group. Wikipedia and other mass-collaboration tools enable individuals to accomplish some major personal stuff:

1. Share their knowledge.
2. Contribute to something bigger than all of us.
3. Immediately create a legacy for themselves (and others).
4. Self-actualize and gain status.

And Baker does not shy away from the ugly side of Wikipedia and other mass collaboration tools that have dispersed power as well: "Without the kooks and insulters and the spray-can taggers, Wikipedia would just be the most useful encyclopedia ever made. Instead, it's a fast-paced game of paintball."

Wikipedia is not (and should not be considered) a marketing channel for your business. That being said, your business is validated (to some degree) by the quality of your Wikipedia entry.

TRIBAL KNOWLEDGE

Tribal knowledge is the kind of information that floats around your industry and office but is never documented or discussed. Part of it involves the way things are done and how people in your group operate. When someone new enters the fray, the training (or initiation) begins. It's always a rather long time (usually several months) before someone new understands the jargon, acronyms, and overall mechanics of how your business operates and communicates.

All businesses have tribal knowledge, although, sadly, most of it gets lost in individual e-mails, corporate boardrooms, or on the retail floor. It's the information everyone who works in the organization knows but rarely shares beyond that first phase of new employee training—the unspoken "way things are done." But what happens when someone leaves or someone joins? How is tribal information passed down from one business generation to another? Prior to the advent of these collaborative tools, people passed the stories down. But now you have this amazing technology. Through intranets and wikis, corporate blogs and more, you have all of the tools to share and nurture tribal knowledge within your business.

The first question is, Are you doing this effectively? (Are you doing this at all?)

The second question is this: In this new world, where social media enable us to trust consumers as our co-developers, how can you extend the concept of tribal knowledge to them as well?

Businesses tend to forget that wikis, and the notion of opening up certain Web pages for all to edit, can be one of the most powerful ideas in a marketing world where brands are doing whatever they can to connect to their consumers and are empowering them to connect to one another as well.

SIMPLE IDEAS ARE SOMETIMES THE MOST POWERFUL

Motorola lived the dream of tribal knowledge for the launch of their Moto Q Smartphone. Instead of your everyday, boring instruction manual, Motorola posted the user manual for the Moto Q in a wiki format. This way, their consumers could connect, correct, update, and share quickly and efficiently.

You have the same frustrations everyone else has. Most manuals, especially those for electronic devices, are vague, quickly outdated, and missing all the cool and interesting tricks people who bought the device before you have figured out. All Motorola did was reformat the instruction guide so that their technical writers and users could share their information and findings in an open and collaborative environment.

Tribal knowledge becomes even more engaging when you layer on top of it the many tools and technologies that we all have at our disposal to make our lives easier. It may not have the sex appeal of a fancy ad campaign, but it certainly holds the answer to many of the common questions we all hear about how businesses can—

and should—connect in a world where it seems increasingly difficult to garner anyone's attention.

Two concepts to meditate on:

1. How do you make your business's tribal knowledge accessible to all on your team?
2. How do you extend that shared wisdom to your customers and evangelists?

GIVE IT AWAY

Everything we are talking about could cause some serious business issues in the coming years. Even with the recent economic downturn, people's usage of the Internet continues to rise. That being said, there does have to be some kind of business transaction behind all of this free stuff we're all giving away.

It's nice to know you can download and listen to a podcast for free, but how does that company really win and make money?

Facebook has a big valuation (some say close to $15 billion), and when founder Mark Zuckerberg was interviewed on *60 Minutes*, he said that advertising would be the way Facebook would make its money and be able to continue to provide the services it provides for free. Google makes its money from advertising, so it must be the right way.

Think about that for a moment.

Most people will tell you they hate advertising. And most people will tell you that they also expect all of this online stuff to be free.

If that's the case, advertising eventually will not work.

What does work? Content.

Investing in creating content—text, images, audio, video—not only gives consumers the information that adds value to their lives, it gives them food for thought. It keeps them engaged for much longer than a thirty-second spot, and it's a lot easier to remember than that billboard they whizzed by on the freeway. People also like to talk about stuff they've read, seen, or heard. That's really what we mean when we use the word "conversation." Through these digital tubes, we can reach a lot more people than just the person next door. Through these conversations and collaborative environments, we're seeing the initial formation of real communities in virtual spaces.

The business growth comes because people who are enjoying the valuable content you provide for free are also inclined to follow the theory of reciprocity. It's built into us. For the first few years, e-commerce models were built around providing the lowest prices with no fee for shipping. This is shifting as well. Consumers are always willing to pay a premium online if what they're getting has added value.

You need to see and embrace collaboration as a business opportunity, a business development strategy, and as part of your long-term growth. Don't believe me? Ask your consumers and your existing community.

CHAPTER 13

Digital Nomad

HOW TO MAKE HEADS—OR TAILS—OF MOBILE

Have you ever flipped a coin? Heads or tails? In 2001, the mobile game Flip a Coin was all the rage. There was a small pixelated black-and-white coin icon on your cell phone screen, and when you hit a button on your phone either a "heads" or "tails" would appear. Believe it or not, every time someone flipped that digital coin, the creators of this cell phone game would make money and split it with the wireless carriers. Whether the user knew it or not, by flipping the coin they were calling up more mobile data and were paying (a premium) for every bit and byte.

That was the extent of the technological breakthroughs that were taking place about eight years ago in the mobile marketplace. At the time, I was the director of marketing for Airborne Mobile. Airborne was created by Andy Nulman (the guy responsible for the Just for Laughs Comedy Festival) and Garner Bornstein (the founder of one of the first Internet service providers in Canada). Their first company attempt together was a Web portal called TheFunniest.com, where they were hoping to combine their comedy and Web experience to create the ultimate centralized location for anything funny on the Web. As the dot-com bubble burst, it turned out there was little humor left with investors and the Web, so the guys switched their focus to what they thought would be next: big entertainment on little screens. Nulman used to say that we were "marketing the unmarketable." While we had our mobile content (mostly text jokes or quizzes triggered by SMS, short message service) on all of the decks of the major mobile carriers, it was still a huge uphill battle. As crazy as this sounds, the carriers really didn't care about data back then. To them it was all about voice usage and the churn of consumers to other carriers.

Things have changed dramatically since 2001, and yet, when it comes to looking at what your business should be doing in the mobile channels, little has really changed. When talking about the mobile games and applications Airborne was creating, Nulman used to say that we were trying to suck an elephant through a straw, meaning that there were all these great ideas ("Hey, imagine being able to watch a clip of your favorite TV show on your cell phone!") but the pipe (the tubes, the technology, and the ability to transfer data quickly) just wasn't there yet. Some huge challenges still face the mobile channel—everything from interoperability from the carriers, standards for data, and standards for mobile browsing, to how different handsets have different screens and functionality. As if that were not enough, what can you, as a business owner, actually do in this highly personal and very private channel?

The good news is that the impact of the mobile revolution is happening right now. Cell phones have become the personal remote control for our lives. From personalization to content, this is how more and more people are connecting. There are huge business opportunities to connect, share, and grow with your consumer in the mobile channels. Just look at what Apple is doing with the iPhone and the iPhone App Store. Within its first six months, 500 million applications were downloaded.

WITH TRUE WIRELESS EVERYWHERE, JUST IMAGINE THE POSSIBILITIES

There were some fascinating statistics out of Amherst College in western Massachusetts last year. The following stats were cherry-picked from a bigger list available at the "Academic Commons Blog" on the post entitled "IT Index." The school enrolled 438 first-year students last fall and has a total student population of over 1,600.

- Students in the Amherst Class of 2012 who registered computers, iPhones, game consoles, and other electronic devices on the campus network by the end of the day on August 24th, the day they moved into their dorm rooms: 370 students registered 443 devices.
- Number of students in the class of 2012 who brought desktop computers to campus: 14.
- Number who brought iPhones/iPod Touches: 93.
- Total number of students on campus this year who have landline phone service: 5.

If you don't see the link between your businesses, what you're doing online, and what you're doing in the mobile space, you're going to be in for a huge surprise in the next two to four years. Today's students entering the workforce clearly see having a desktop as being "tethered." From the looks of things, even a laptop seems a little tethered to most of these young people.

We're going mobile, and it's happening fast.

There are more than 250 million mobile phones in the United States and overall usage beyond voice continues to rise. Everything from SMS to mobile browsing is becoming much more commonplace. With this usage quickly comes the marketers' looking at how to send, connect, and advertise in these channels. From a demographic perspective, the most receptive group to mobile marketing is the more tech-savvy seventeen-to-thirty-five-year-olds, both male and female.

CAN YOU HEAR ME NOW?

Being connected is everything. Remember, this is a world of Six Pixels of Separation.

The challenge is that mobile will never really take off until we resolve the issue of overall connectivity. It's not about which company owns which pipes (and which network) or which mobile platforms win the war for the consumer. Instead, for everyone to have a better mobile experience, connectivity needs to become as ubiquitous as the radio. It needs to be everywhere.

It's also not enough for it just to be everywhere. It needs to be everywhere and it needs to be fast.

You're probably seeing that most of the newer mobile devices are Wi-Fi enabled (meaning they can access the Internet through any standard wireless connection). Being able to surf the actual Web on your mobile makes these devices seem pretty sexy, but this is just the beginning. It's great when you are in an area with wireless access. When you're not in a Wi-Fi hotspot, it's a brick, meaning the phone is useless unless you're in some kind of zone.

Mobile is going to be critical to your business, and there's no time like the present to start thinking about what your mobile strategy needs to be. If you think about it logically, the availability of very high speed mobile access everywhere is the last mile. Think about the mobile devices you've seen in the past. The limitations were glaringly obvious. Now think about the newer devices: everything from the iPhone to Netbooks and ultra-portable laptops. The hardware is there; all that's really missing is the access everywhere.

RISE OF THE DIGITAL NOMAD

Because of this mobile usage and the proliferation of connectivity in the standard Internet channels, we're seeing more and more people becoming digital nomads in their professional lives.

Digital nomads don't need an office. They have many offices. In fact, anywhere is an office as long as there is connectivity. They work from Starbucks, the local library, in front of their televisions, in hotel lobbies, in the backseats of cabs, and even in some parks.

We're no longer connected just through the Internet as we have known it to date. Many people are quick to dismiss the power of the mobile device because of its small screen, use of mostly text, and very limited graphics. But from BlackBerry to the iPhone, the next level of engagement and connecting to your customers won't come from a fancy website; it's going to happen in the palms of our hands.

We're not just untethering from workstations; we're untethering from everything. On April 10, 2008, the *Economist* ran an article entitled "The New Oases: Nomadism Changes Buildings, Cities and Traffic." It read, in part:

> The fact that people are no longer tied to specific places for functions such as studying or learning, says Mr Mitchell [William Mitchell is a professor of architecture and computer science at MIT], means that there is "a huge drop in demand for traditional, private, enclosed spaces" such as offices or classrooms, and simultaneously "a huge rise in demand for semi-public spaces that can be informally appropriated to ad-hoc workspaces." This

shift, he thinks, amounts to the biggest change in architecture in this century. In the 20th century architecture was about specialised structures—offices for working, cafeterias for eating, and so forth. This was necessary because workers needed to be near things such as landline phones, fax machines and filing cabinets, and because the economics of building materials favoured repetitive and simple structures, such as grid patterns for cubicles. . . .

. . . Buildings will have much more varied shapes than before. For instance, people working on laptops find it comforting to have their backs to a wall, so hybrid spaces may become curvier, with more nooks, in order to maximise the surface area of their inner walls, rather as intestines do. This is becoming affordable because computer-aided design and new materials make non-repetitive forms cheaper to build.

To further this thought, there are more and more companies that do not have assigned desks and offices for their employees. When the employee shows up in the morning, he or she is simply assigned a workstation. All of the worker's software, documents, and files are digital and secured on the intranet. He simply logs on to his laptop or mobile device and works. These companies are also experimenting with more available areas for open space collaboration and meetings. If that's not a mobile culture, what is?

At the retail level, we're seeing a new line of laptops called Netbooks. These are lightweight, very cheap laptops (anywhere from $200 to $400) with limited computing power but more than enough speed to enable you to work online adequately, be it e-mail, surfing the Internet, or even watching and downloading multimedia files. Netbooks are both wireless and Bluetooth enabled and are meant to do one thing (and one thing only): let you be online everywhere.

MOBILE GOES WHERE OTHER MEDIA CANNOT

People have a very intimate and personal link with their mobile devices. Simplistically, these devices sit on your belt or in your pocket—that's pretty personal. It's the last safe harbor of media that is free from interruption advertising. The price individuals pay for their mobile services also intuitively insinuates that it will be an ad-free experience, so breaking that connection is still considered very taboo unless you have explicit permission. Even when carriers use SMS to warn consumers that their bills have not yet been paid, there is an overriding feeling of being violated and of a lack of trust with unsolicited marketing and communications messages.

KELLY CLARKSON AND PRESIDENT OBAMA

North America really started using mobile devices for something more than phone calls on a mass level around 2002 when *American Idol* first asked audience members to text in their votes. Getting people to actually use a new channel is always the greatest barrier. Think back to when someone first showed you the Internet and how you felt about what it could mean in your life. Getting back to the Airborne Mobile days, the biggest barrier to growing the mobile space was simply getting people to try it. For the most part, people had mobile devices but were simply not able to wrap their heads around anything more than phone calls. The "other stuff" was strange and foreign. Through consistent messaging and demos, *American Idol* was able to get people excited about using their phones for more than phone calls. Millions upon millions of people not only started texting in their votes, but they started texting one another. It was a watershed moment that launched this brand-new style of communication. You can thank *American Idol* (even more so than instant messaging) for changing "be right back" to "brb."

Barack Obama used texting and the mobile channel to announce his vice-presidential candidate in 2008. It marked another moment in time where North Americans opened up their most personal of communication devices beyond their own address books. "Future campaigns will have to integrate text messaging into their strategies in order to be successful," according to Francoise Galleto, senior account manager for grassroots services at Aristotle, which is a political technology firm based in Washington, D.C. (quoted in Amy Syracuse, "Lessons in SMS Marketing from the Obama Campaign," *BtoB* magazine, November 10, 2008).

Mobile is going to be much more disruptive to your business than the Internet. If it was causing you a level of grief that people might go online and read a negative review about you or see a search result that led to your competitor, imagine having consumers stand in your physical space and check online for prices and how close your nearest competitor is at the same time. Check out the SnapTell app for the iPhone. You take a picture of a product and it returns reviews, pricing, and more. Imagine them scanning in the barcode of a product and getting a bird's-eye view into everything about it—including reviews, comparison pricing, and more. Imagine being able to move your online social network to the mobile platform, so your "friends" who are physically close to you at that specific moment in time can help you decide whether or not to make a purchase. Imagine if the platform connected you to anyone in your vicinity who was willing to take part in your purchase decision. None of this is too far-fetched. From a technology perspective, none of this is more than a year away from being an integral part of the mobile channel, and integral to our way of life.

Care for some cowboy boots made out of denim? Nulman

(that Airborne Mobile guy) was away on a business trip when he noticed a really striking pair of cowboy boots. He was not sure if his wife would be into them or not, so he snapped a quick photo of the shoes, MMSed (multimedia messaged— basically, "text" messaging for pictures) it over to his wife, got back her boot size, and picked up the shoes for her in a matter of minutes. It was as if she were standing right there. This changes everything we know and understand about the retail experience.

If you feel like you were not ready for the way the Web has connected us all, mobile is shrinking the pixels ever so much more. Are you ready for Six Sub-Pixels of Separation?

IT'S NOT MOBILE ADVERTISING, IT'S MOBILE MARKETING

It's the lifetime value of the consumer and his or her community versus the immediate sale.

Building a list of customer phone numbers is not about running a traditional advertising campaign, scraping the data, and using it to send consumers messages via their mobile devices. For mobile marketing to truly work, each and every time you run a marketing program it has to be treated like its own little viral marketing campaign (with fingers crossed that it can, indeed, go viral).

To get it right, Andy Nulman created his mobile marketing success program in three simple steps. He calls it his N.O.W. system:

1. Nearby: Customers need to be in your radius, close and local. Thinking hyperlocal means thinking successfully. People using their mobile devices are looking for things in their near vicinity.

2. Only: There has to be a select limit to the offer. It can be in the quantities you are offering (only 29 left) or the time to respond to the offer (valid for only two hours). While scarcity has always been used as a marketing ploy, in the mobile landscape it has to be immediate mostly because that is the nature of how the device is used. Very few people are simply "floating around" their mobile devices.

3. Wow: Make it a surprisingly compelling offer (50% off everything in the store!). It has to be a jaw-dropper. Anything with a scent of regular or "ho-hum" simply won't cut it.

No mobile marketing offer can have anything less than all three steps that are 100 percent complete. Mobile is also about speed. If your offer makes a person stop in his tracks, you have better odds of his acting on it and spreading it. Miss any one of the three steps to N.O.W. and you will either burn that bridge or, worse, consumers will spread the word about how poor your messaging was.

Once you have built your mobile program on the N.O.W. strategy, ask only ten friends (or brand evangelists) if they would be willing to take part. Have those ten friends spread the idea to ten "best friends" (only those people who would really appreciate the offer) via SMS, e-mail, and the like. If you've built it following the rules and received permission from the first ten, it should start to spread on its own.

I know what you're thinking: All of that for only ten people? Is it really worth all the trouble and hard work to build an entire marketing campaign around ten people in hopes that they can spread it?

Yes.

Mobile marketing is still very new, yet there are already way too many brands making big mistakes with this channel. If you thought getting into online social networks or posting your videos to YouTube was new, doing anything in the mobile channel must be treated like you're still in the laboratory. Mobile is small (now we're talking about much more than the screen size), but, if it's done right, respecting the consumer and the relationship he or she has with his or her mobile device, the long-term outcome will be that you've managed to build a new and loyal database with huge growth potential.

In the retail space, getting 100 more people into a store is a big deal. In the mobile marketing space, getting 100 people onto a mobile marketing database is a bigger deal. That being said, if you're just looking to get your message into a bunch of people's faces, you might want to forgo the whole mobile channel, open your office window, and scream your offer out into the street. *The point of mobile is to build relationships with your most loyal consumers and to connect them to your brands ever more effectively.*

I'M LOVING IT

A scavenger hunt, photo gallery, ringtones, wallpaper, and even wireless coupons were all a part of a mobile marketing program by McDonald's called Mobile Whoa.

According to MediaPost's "Out to Launch," by Phyllis Fine, April 19, 2006:

> McDonald's is using cell phone technology to promote its Tulsa, Okla.-area restaurants, whose up-to-the-minute bells and whistles include wireless Internet, cashless technology, and plasma-screen TVs. As part of the "Mobile Whoa" campaign, through the end of April, customers in northeastern Oklahoma can participate in a mobile scavenger hunt, get a mobile coupon

and post photos in a camera phone and Web site picture gallery. The scavenger hunt starts when customers text-message a specific code or register online at a microsite for the promotion. Customers then receive a series of clues via text messages. Besides the coupons for free fries with the purchase of a Big Mac, there's another plus: all customers who submit a photo to the picture gallery will receive a code on their phone to download a free ringtone or wallpaper.

What do you like about this campaign? They're using mobile technology, engaging their customers, and introducing the concept of being marketed to on the mobile device. This speaks volumes for getting marketers closer to the mobile marketing tipping point.

McDonald's walked lightly with this campaign. They were not pushing out that much content (smart) and were much more dependent on the people to really pull the content at their own pace and desire (even smarter).

If you're still shuddering at the thought of being SMS bombarded with coupons offering a free small order of fries when you buy a Big Mac, be prepared. But it's not just about campaigns. Remember, advertising is only a small subset of marketing.

BEFORE YOU MARKET IT, HAVE A SITE FOR IT

How many businesses do you know that do not have a website? Even if it's strictly brochure-ware, even five years out of date, every business worth anything should have some kind of online destination. How many businesses do you know that have a mobile website? One designed specifically for the mobile space? Maybe some of the airlines you frequently fly on? The whole idea may sound a little too premature.

It's not.

More and more people are not at a computer of any kind, but they are doing searches on their mobile devices, and what they're finding is big, bloated websites that are tough to navigate on such a small screen. How hard is it to set up a simple mobile website with your critical information? It's pretty simple and fairly straight-forward. We're not talking about a fully immersive iPhone application (we'll get to that), but we are talking about the basics: how to contact you, directions to get to your location, hours of operation, late-breaking news, and latest specials. Keep it simple. Consider three to five of the most important questions anyone might have of you while he is on the go. How many times have you wondered what time your favorite shop opens up, or if something in particular is on sale? What about trying to find the weather or a show listing? A mobile website is best optimized by being simple with mostly text and limited to no real graphics. Simple, cheap, and to the point. Nobody has time to surf around your mobile site; they just want the most relevant information and they want it now.

Or do they?

D&G (Dolce & Gabbana) is, and has always been, about im-mersing their consumers in the brand. The passion individuals have for the D&G brand can be directly correlated to how effec-tively the brand has moved beyond clothes and into fashion. It's not just accessories like watches and glasses, either. D&G recently launched the D&G Fashion Channel, which is a mobile-only expe-rience that looks at what's fresh in the fashion world. The mobile channel is packed with all kinds of photos, from the runways to product shots. Consumers can spend their spare time on the train checking out the latest fashions from runways all over the world. It's not about text and information; the D&G fashion channel is all about brand immersion. In figuring out who their target consum-ers are, D&G is able to use the new mobile channel to keep them entertained and in the fashion loop. It's also easy to see how this channel will be extended as their consumers start taking mobile pictures and video of their own and will soon be able to share interesting fashion information on the fly with the entire D&G community.

MEDIA, CONTENT, AND MARKETING EVERYWHERE

Some key cultural shifts are driving this mobile revolution, and it starts with people wanting their media (be it content, marketing, and/or communications) on their own time—it's the "where" and "when" part of the marketing puzzle that marketers have been trying to crack for decades. You can call this the TiVo-nation or the on-demand world, but it is becoming an increasingly complex world for you to market your messages in. It's the idea that prime time is anytime. David Neale, senior vice president of Products and Service at TELUS, said it best: "My son still watches prime time TV. But he just doesn't watch it in prime time. And he doesn't watch it on a TV."

Imagine downloading a movie, watching some of it on your laptop, transferring it to your mobile device (wirelessly), and being able to take every kind of medium everywhere. As a content creator for your business, this opens up many doors of opportunity— and many challenges, as well.

The iPhone created a stir in the mobile world that no one has ever seen. At a generic level, think about how much content we all want on these tiny devices (do you remember when people were asking "Why would you need more than five hundred songs on any device?"). Do you think, for one second, that all the rules won't keep changing again as more tools and applications are created and as more and more mobile devices come into the marketplace? The G1 phone available through T-Mobile in the United

States is actually the Google phone. If Google is paying so much attention to the mobile space—and we're not just talking about optimizing search for mobile devices; they are manufacturing and selling handsets—your business definitely needs some immediate strategies to stay ahead of this new and fast-growing channel. People have already moved beyond simple SMS messaging. They are downloading third-party rich-media applications. These include everything from tools and alerts to video games and immersive programs and brand experiences.

Keep in mind that it's no longer a phone or a mobile e-mail device, and it's no longer just an iPod. It's everything. But here's the main reason you as a business owner need to start caring right away: *You have to start thinking about what types of content and media will be best suited for this device in terms of your customers' expectations.* It's not just about creating an SMS mobile marketing campaign (though that could be a part of the puzzle). It also can't be as simple as making a YouTube video accessible by mobile. You have to define how your current content plays out on mobile. What types of text, images, audio, and video work in the mobile platforms for your consumers? What more can you give them in terms of valuable and immediate information and opportunity, and what types of overall brand experience can you extend to the mobile device? As you begin to look at the multimedia nature of the channel and couple that with how much time someone has to use these applications and how easy they are to navigate, imagine how valuable and worthwhile they will be in their lives.

It's not just about asking more questions; it's about understanding the current set of rules that work for those succeeding in the mobile space.

THE NEW RULES OF THE NEW MOBILE MOVEMENT

1. New device = new rules.

2. Think in terms of tribes, not mass. What segment of your customers and community members would use this type of application and how will they spread it?

3. Mobile adds a new dimension to all messages—make it work for the person in control of the device.

4. If you try to port an old way of doing things or content that you're using in another channel to these channels, it will fail. Burn the ships.

5. Think about what we had before podcasts and before PVRs (personal video recorders). Start from there and build with that success in mind.

6. If you can port content from TV to computer to iPhone, think about the level of control the user has. How will you make the time he spends with your brand really count?

7. Start building a permission-based list of people who do want to be contacted via mobile.

8. Think about building a mobile application. Both iPhone and BlackBerry have their own application stores for mobile only.

9. Offer compelling incentives. The list will start off small; if you surprise and delight, you will be able to grow it more efficiently based on the "wow" factor of the offers.

10. Establish conversation. Just look at what people are able to communicate in 140 characters on Twitter. You might just surprise yourself with how much you can share in a short message.

HOW DO YOU USE MOBILE?

The mobile channel is changing and developing day by day. The thoughts in this chapter and the rules should always be seen as a moving target. The highly personal, protected, and private nature of mobile also brings with it changes that are subtle in perception but huge in terms of impact for business owners. Also, bear in mind that real mobile social networking has not yet happened, and creating content on mobile devices is still relatively nascent. The technology and tools do exist to "broadcast" from your phone and have your content distributed in the online channels, but it's not being fully embraced by the masses yet.

Also, platforms will merge more and more. Not that long ago, you could not send an SMS message from one carrier to another. Again, the rules are changing. Some devices and some carriers are still hesitant to allow third-party applications on their devices, but this too is changing at a rapid pace.

WHAT WILL IT TAKE FOR MOBILE TO WORK? TWO COMPONENTS

One component is better usability. The wireless Web is still very nascent (with the exception of how devices like the iPhone allow you to surf the Web). You can't find anything efficiently yet, and most of us are trapped in our carriers' walled gardens with slow connections that usually return interruption errors instead of what we clicked on. Better usability and better-built mobile sites will bring with them a much more accurate and dependable search result with great speed.

The second component is a reason to want ads and to be marketed to on mobile devices. We currently have a strange relationship with our mobile devices. On the one hand, we love being connected; on the other hand, we can't deal with how reachable we always are (go off the grid). This point is more psychological than anything else. Just like Google democratized the Web by making search friendly, easy, and effective, someone will come along and make the mobile device (either through the handset or through the software) so engaging that we'll no longer see it as a shackle around our collective necks, but rather the hammer and nail that will free us all from cubicle, desk, or home office slavery.

Microsoft with Windows did it for the personal computer. Someone will do it for mobile.

Last, for mobile to really connect with your consumers, it needs to move from a content play into context. If you can best learn the context that your consumer is looking for, marketing your brands, products, and services by delivering the right messages and the right types of content at the right time will be significantly easier.

If content is king then context is queen.

CHAPTER 14

Participation 2.0

I AM TECHNOLOGY

There was an unsubstantiated urban myth that said that 40 percent of people watching television admitted that they were sleeping at the same time. There's also a very famous line that says, "Half of my advertising works, I just don't know which half." If you put those two pieces of information together, the shift away from mass media becomes ever more compelling. Why are we sleeping while the television is on? It's not because we're bored, and it's not because there's not that much interesting television to watch. With more and more specialty channels and movie networks, we could argue that the content has never been better and more relevant (thank you, Long Tail). Because of the Internet and how we engage with this medium—really manipulating it, changing it, creating for it—when something comes on and we become passive users, our brains are starting to shut off. Our brains are falling asleep and our bodies are following.

Do you remember the old, first-generation television remote controls, the ones that were beige or brown boxes with big, clicking buttons and dials that were connected to the television via a long wire? Now they seem almost laughable. Technology shifts and changes at such a rapid pace that we hardly even notice anymore the subtleties of how things evolve. Before those remote controls existed, my father used to ask me to get up and change the channel. In effect, I was the remote control. It was not too long ago that I was technology. Looking forward, it's important to remember where we've been.

LIVE FROM HUNTER VALLEY

One of the most powerful things about any podcast is the audio comment line. This turns the podcast from a one-way monologue into an audio community. Because podcasting is not live but pre-recorded and then published, one of the few ways you can have community and conversation is to allow and embrace audio comments. There are only two ways to accept audio comments:

1. Someone records the audio comment on their own computer and e-mails or FTPs it over as an MP3 or WAV file.

2. You set up an audio comment line—much like setting up a voice-mail line. There are many services (like K7.net—it's free and they assign you a number, which is not toll-free). This way when someone calls in and leaves a message (as you would on any standard call answer system), you will receive the comment as a WAV file in your e-mail.

If you would like to try it out, feel free to call in a comment or question on my podcast right now: +1 (206) 666-6056. No, I'm not pushing for more audio comments on my podcast. I am merely going to provoke you to keep your eyes forward on the future by becoming an active participant in the existing online communities. One of the ways you will best be able to see what is coming next is by getting involved. By sharing your thoughts and asking a question, you immediately become a part of a very vibrant and vocal global community. On any given episode of the "Six Pixels of Separation" podcast you will hear from people in places like Ireland, Singapore, Russia, South America, Germany, and beyond. This is not your local talk radio on the AM dial; this is a hungry-for-information audio community from very diverse backgrounds. Instead of simply saying "Hey, e-mail me and we can connect," why not share what information or questions you have with the world? That's exactly what Jared Madden did.

All the way from the Hunter Valley in Australia, he talked about where the marketing industry is in Australia and how hard it is to find people to connect with. Jared was especially interested in the unconference movement and the use of blogs and podcasts. Beyond the cachet of having someone from Down Under on the podcast, his thoughts were passionately presented and what happened next was even more interesting.

The day after the new episode of the podcast was published with his audio comment, an e-mail from Adam Purcell arrived. Adam also lives in Hunter Valley and had been looking desperately for someone near where he lives to connect to. He asked if I would mind making an e-introduction.

Over the course of the months that followed, the two not only connected but agreed to organize the first Podcamp Australia, which took place in Perth on November 3, 2007, and hosted nearly 150 people from all over Australia who were interested in new media and communications. It hasn't ended there. The two have been referring each other business and most recently have become very active in digital media literacy within their home-towns.

It took a small podcast from a small city in North America to connect two guys who live in Hunter Valley on the other side of the world.

That is the spirit of Six Pixels of Separation and our interconnectedness. Stories like that help illustrate how powerful a tool this is for you to connect, to contribute, and to establish yourself and build your business.

DIGITAL IS THE GREAT DISRUPTER

If you look at some of the industries that are facing the biggest challenges and financial strains because of these changes, you will be able to pull some key indicators that can help you refocus by focusing on what's next. The music industry continues to think people will somehow wake up one day and want to buy full-length CDs. Their industry is seeing, firsthand, what happens when technology disrupts so much that it shifts the final products from something physical into something digital. The same is currently happening in the film industry, in the publishing industry, and the list goes on. *Whenever the final product shifts from its physical form to a digital one, all hell breaks loose.*

The first lesson in understanding "What's next?" is in embracing the very real possibility that your final products might go digital too, and if it's not your final products it may just be the way they are purchased, produced, and managed from a business perspective. Learn from others. Here's what we do know: The industries that have faced this dramatic shift have all responded in the worst way possible. At first they continued like it was "business as usual" and when the overall consumer adoption hit the tipping point and they were forced to change, their gut instinct was to charge the same price for the new digital products that they charged for their physical products (sometimes they even try to charge more). No more packaging, packaging design, logistics, transportation, retail fees, or internal sales rep salaries, and they wanted everybody to pay a premium because of how easy it was to receive it. Yes, there are other enormous costs associated with digital business: technology infrastructure, distribution rights, connectivity, fulfillment, and customer service, to name a few, but (and here's the bigger question) what choice do you have?

Do you think the music industry made the right choices? It is the consumers' final choice if they want a physical CD or twelve MP3 tracks they can download, but the product (the music) is all worth the same amount, right?

Wrong.

And the problem with it being wrong is that no one really knows what the right answer is. That being said, we do know, with 100 percent certainty, that the answer is definitely not "Charge them the same amount."

IN LOOKING TO THE FUTURE, THE ONLY CONSTANT IS CHANGE

We all love quotes about how change is good, it's the only thing that is inevitable (along with death and taxes), and "If you don't like change, you're going to like irrelevance even less" (General Eric Shinseki, secretary of Veterans Affairs), but no industry can handle or deal with dramatic change—like when a product goes from physical to digital.

On a recent trip to a speaking event, the driver was pointing out to me how the local area had once been a great industrial port where ships came to load and unload their stock and filled the whole northeastern part of North America with goods. The city was bustling, the local economy was swelling, and families were moving into the neighborhoods. He went on to say, however, that the shipping had slowed down in recent years to the point where that port was now empty because the demand was not there anymore. He felt it was a shame and a sad state of affairs for the world at large. I had one simple and lucid thought as I stared at the rusted cranes and dilapidated harbor area: We're still shipping tons of stuff, but we've shifted from crates and barrels into bits and bytes now. Yes, this creates change and, in this town's economy, real human distress. It's sad, very sad. But the pace of change continues to increase and all of us have to get much better at spotting these trends or, at the very least, doing our best to stay informed and connected.

We also have to accept another very real concept: *It's going to shift from bits and bytes into something else as well and we are not (and cannot be) prepared for that, either.*

Here's the future business challenge: This is all so new that most companies would rather hold on to what they know with everything they have than dip some toes into the brave unknown that is partly the present, but mostly the future. Getting better and more refined with your business can shape that future. You need to focus, accept this new reality, and get much more efficient with your analytics and industry trends. If you do this, surely you will be able to help shape not just your own company, but the industry you serve as well.

In looking at where this is all going, you will need to strategize and optimize everything. The best way to do this is to take a few minutes to think about your company and the industry you're in. How well would you be able to cope, change, and evolve if the very product you sold changed entirely overnight? What are tools like your Web analytics and Web research packages telling you? How quickly are you able to turn that data into an action item and then make it happen? How able are you to bend and flow with these changes on an organic and concurrent level?

NEW BUSINESS MODELS

There are lots of little ways to tweak your business using the many online channels. The problem gets increasingly complex when the channel changes the way your business operates. Many traditional businesses think it's about how they market online through this change or disruption and not about how their business model works in this new channel. That's when the tragedy usually strikes.

We keep seeing big companies make the same big mistakes over and over again in a whole bunch of different industries. Think back to what we discussed in chapter 13, "Digital Nomad." The big mobile carriers were worried about voice and churning consumers to other carriers; they were not even thinking about what data might do to change and add value to their business. When other companies came in and focused on data (like RIM with the BlackBerry and Apple with the iPhone), the carriers started fighting for what they felt they were entitled to. This always makes a company look sad, desperate, or greedy (or all of the above). The music industry did not want to stop selling plastic CDs and they really didn't want to go back to the single-song format. Then iTunes came out with songs for $0.99 by download and changed everything. Taking that a step further, some people didn't even want to download the song at all, but simply wanted to use it as a ringtone.

These are all examples of companies holding on to the past, not embracing the idea of experimenting with new business models, and focusing on the "way things used to be."

Don Tapscott (author of *Wikinomics* and *Grown Up Digital*) says this about the music industry: "How sad that the same industry that gave us The Beatles is now suing their consumers because they can't figure out a new business model." More recently, Seth

Godin was interviewed for a blog about the book publishing industry entitled "The 26th Story," in a post ("Tribes Author Seth Godin Discusses Free Content and the Publishing Industry"). He said:

> First, the market and the internet don't care if you make money. That's important to say. You have no right to make money from every development in media, and the humility that comes from approaching the market that way matters. It's not "how can the market make me money" it's "how can I do things for this market." Because generally, when you do something for an audience, they repay you. The Grateful Dead made plenty of money. Tom Peters makes many millions of dollars a year giving speeches, while books are a tiny fraction of that. Barack Obama used ideas to get elected, book royalties are just a nice side effect. There are doctors and consultants who profit from spreading ideas. Novelists and musicians can make money with bespoke work and appearances and interactions. And you know what? It's entirely likely that many people in the chain WON'T make any money. That's okay. That's the way change works.

WHAT A NEW BUSINESS MODEL LOOKS LIKE

Threadless is a website where the community is asked to design T-shirts. All entries are posted and the ones that receive the most votes after being posted on the website are turned into T-shirts for everybody to buy. The company has become a runaway success.

Does Threadless sell T-shirts—or do they sell design and the celebration of the creative spirit of the individual (with a passionate community)?

Lulu does not see themselves as book publishers. In fact, their corporate profile states, "It's a digital marketplace guided by a vision of empowerment and accessibility, and built on a business model that has proven wildly successful. . . . Lulu eliminates traditional entry barriers to publishing, and enables content creators and owners—authors and educators, videographers and musicians, businesses and nonprofits, professionals and amateurs—to bring their work directly to their audience." Through Lulu anyone can have his work published into a legitimate book. In fact, they have over 15,000 new registrations a week and more than 100,000 unique visitors every day. They have published thousands of books. Lulu does not publish one book for 10 million people; Lulu sells 10 million books to 10 million people.

Both of these companies have one thing in common: They looked at the shifts in the markets and how consumers were behaving, and they then laid that against how most businesses were fielding the needs and decided on some form of new business model that would be more in line with how consumers were acting.

The problem is that all new business models look weird and act weird because they are weird. Odds are that a new business model will look nothing like the ones you have used to make your money to date. The reason most companies are stuck is because they keep thinking: "That's the way it has always been." What would happen if you sat down with your business colleagues and thought back to how it all got started? What made your business what it is today? What shifts were happening at that time that set the stage for your business to open and mix things up? Who else has come along and been successful? What did they do? Before your business was around, who was the industry leader? What got them that title? You'll quickly realize that the reason you are in your present business is because, at some level, you saw a new way of doing things. It could have been better, cheaper, more efficient, cooler, whatever—your new way of doing things had a place in the economy and it was a new business model.

We live in interesting times. We're seeing some unique and new business models. It's hard to believe that people made millions selling ringtones for mobile devices and it's equally hard to look at something like Wikipedia, which is not a commercial entity, and wonder why it isn't. It should be fascinating to you that there are individuals who were consultants who left the area of "being paid to write their thoughts" for blogging and in doing so have become the de facto recognized authorities in their industries. These people now command huge consulting fees and have extended their businesses into speaking appearances, book writing, and even selling premium content through the Internet.

What if all classified ads were free (except for the ones related to employment and real estate)? This is exactly what Craigslist (the free online classified marketplace) has done. Take a look at what the value of Craigslist is (*Silicon Alley Insider* said in April 2008 that Craigslist brought in $80 million in 2008 revenue and has an estimated worth of $5 billion) and compare that to any major newspaper's classified business over the past five years. Maybe newspaper publishers should have looked at what Craigslist was doing to grow and expand instead of sticking to their traditional models. Craig Newmark, founder of Craigslist, is probably very happy they didn't.

IT'S ABOUT SIMPLICITY, NOT COMPLEXITY

Here's the really scary part: A new business model does not have to be complex. Google changed the entire advertising world without bringing out advertising models for rich media, audio, images, and videos (which they could have done). Google AdWords has nothing to do with high-end directors, special effects, celebrity endorsements, and Super Bowls. It has to do with a fistful of text-based words that are targeted based on the searches that someone is doing and then presenting that relevant, small text-ad at the right time and in an unobtrusive fashion. Google even pushed advertising a step further by charging their advertisers only when someone clicks on one of their ads instead of charging them based on how many impressions are served, perceived value, or estimated audience size.

New business models will look insane to you at first. Here's the good news: Failure is relatively cheap in this day and age (just ask Google).

BUSINESS OF ACTION—START YOUR OWN

Before looking at some of the emerging trends for your business to watch, please reflect the mirror back on yourself. Let's make a future trend something that only you can control. You may think that some of the channels discussed have seen their last day, but that is simply not the case. There has never been a better time to start your own path than right now.

Start your own blog—now.

Every day someone calls and asks for more information about your company and how you can help them. Every day you contemplate going to a trade show but then get stuck by trying to figure out how your business can rise above all of the other similar businesses at the event. At multiple points over multiple years someone (either in your marketing department or your next-door neighbor) has told you it's time to update your marketing materials and to create a new brochure. In the past, while trying to secure a big sale, your potential client has asked for either references or a white paper to help him validate his choice of working with you. To quote Hugh McGuire from LibriVox and the Book Oven, "Don't blog to get known; blog to be knowable."

There are enough people out there with the "look at me" syndrome. They are using these free publishing channels to push more sales and not build loyalty, community, and conversation. The real future of these online channels is that each and every individual will be the gatekeeper of his or her own elite social network. We would all agree that the best and more authentic conversations happen in small groups. Those small groups transcend and help spread messages they know will interest their individual peer groups.

The ultimate beauty of these social channels is that the cost of entry is next to nil, and beyond the personal commitment you have to make to keep it fresh, vital, and personal, blogging is still a critical channel to look at. It enables you to find a voice of distinction. Blogging gets that voice "out there" and starts the foundation for a solid digital footprint that will immediately demonstrate to potential clients how you think and why you think this way, and, in return, it will demonstrate your thought process and your true humanity, if you are being sincere and transparent.

In a chapter dedicated to what's next, you might be questioning why blogging should be considered a future trend. Don't be fooled by the few who are looking at the next shiny objects. Blogs still matter, because regardless of what you call it (and, indeed, the term "blog" might be passé by the time you read this), a blog is a tool to publish fast, efficiently, and to the world. People still read. People are still looking for relevant content, and even with the 130 million blogs in circulation, there is only a handful that each individual can wrap their head (and heart) around. New ones come out every day and rise to the top. Why? Because they're good. Make yours a good one. It's not too late.

If it's not a blog, fine. Start your own "anything": a podcast, a Twitter account . . . something. It is one of the smartest moves you, as a business owner, can make, and business owners' becoming media channels and publishers is a growing and important trend.

PUSHING OUT ONTO THE HORIZONS

The following are ten emerging trends in a Six Pixels of Separation world. Some will affect you personally, some will affect you because of changes in technology and media, and some others will be driven by your customers. All of them will have a direct impact on your business as we move forward.

1. Personal Brands Rise

There are many people talking about personal branding and there are many people talking about how the new digital channels are changing everything we know about growing a business. This is not going to stop. In fact, quite the opposite. It is going to intensify in the coming months and years. Instead of individuals' being concerned about how they act within an organization, we're going to see individuals use these many channels to self-publish, develop a platform, audience, and community, and when all of it is combined, this is going to provide a tremendous value to either their own business or the companies they work for.

The result of this is going to be staggering. All indicators are pointing to a day where anybody and everybody will be broadcasting their messages to the world. Brands will soon become subservient to their consumers and employees, instead of the other way around. We are currently cultivating a culture where any individual (including you) could be the next superstar of whatever it is you work at.

2. Attention Crash

Way too much of everything is everywhere. Text, audio, video, and images—some are professionally produced and others are full-on amateur. If you lived the rest of your life online, you could never see, hear, and read all of the content out there. One of the few ways to manage the sheer volume of this content is through a news reader. Most who deep-dive into their readers find it challenging not only to manage them, but also to really take the time to digest and think about a lot of the content. Most are simply skimming through it at best. There is going to be an attention crash, and that is not a bad thing.

Once we get beyond the mass volume of everything being produced, there will be a slight dip as the world adjusts itself and begins to focus not on the amount of content but on the quality of it. Aggregation will be everything. The difference will be that the quality will not reside in the hands of the few, but it will be about many people connected to unique content being created by many people. The adjustment from the attention crash will be a shift toward less content created by individual sources that are trusted by individuals. It's also going to force the more traditional mass media channels to shift and morph regarding how they report and produce content. Context will be everything.

3. Micro Social Networks

Instead of massive and all-encompassing online social networks like MySpace and Facebook, there will be fatigue within these channels, and individuals are going to start looking for more specific and focused online social networks that satisfy their needs. People will begin to seek out and create their own micro online social networks that focus on the quality of the connections and the conversation and less on the quantity.

This is also going to have physical geographical implications. Because we're already seeing individuals wanting to connect in the real world and not just online (think PodCamp or BarCamp), these micro social networks are also going to have some hyper-local flair and focus. People in Idaho interested in new business models for the automotive industry are going to have their own space to connect, share, and grow. In turn, people from other parts of the world who are traveling will also be able to connect with those who have similar interests through a simple online search. Ning, a place where anyone can set up his or her own social network, provides a glimpse into how this will work. That platform will expand once the audience and the community managers shift their focus from quantity over to quality. Many of the social networks within Ning are doing just that, and the results speak for themselves.

4. Levels of Connections

Not all "friends" are created equal. Somewhere, someone (hopefully skilled in both the art of computer programming and in how networks are formed) is beginning to unravel what would be considered strong links that individuals have versus very weak ones.

Because many people are focused on "how many" friends they have instead of the quality of the links, understanding whom to trust (and who trusts them) is very complicated.

The best connections are the real and authentic ones. For your business to grow by using online social networking and the other digital channels, you are going to need a way to understand more about the individuals you are connecting to than how many connections they have. The key to success is in understanding the quality and different levels of trust the individuals have within their own social graphs. Just like search engine results have some kind of algorithm behind them that quantifies why some things rank higher than others, soon the same type of indexing will be done on individuals and the company they keep. How highly would you and your network rank in this type of environment?

5. Analytics and Research

Analytics can be sexy. Understanding what people are doing on your space and changing and adapting it to suit their goals better has been the promise of the online channel since its inception. The real analytics and research packages going forward will also look at the semantic (or natural language) content to help you better understand the more human side of why things are happening in the online channel. On top of that, the tools will get much better at indicating how you can change and adapt your course for better conversion and optimization. Most people see this side of the business as boring, and that is going to change as well. Through better visuals and more immediate information, analytics and research are going to push the smart businesses to get much better at targeting their consumers and engaging them.

6. Content as Media

We're beginning to see the scales of advertising slide in this direction, but it is still very nascent. The future is going to be about not focusing on banner ads as the primary online advertising model. Even when the first banner appeared on HotWired in 1994 (thank you, AT&T), people's first reaction was not to click, but to ignore. Up until that point, it looked like the Internet was going to be a different type of medium and, potentially, even one that would be free of interruption-based advertising. So much for that idea. Instead, media companies saw this channel as another place to plaster their messages.

But in the midst of that, several other interesting and powerful digital marketing channels arose—like the ability to create very powerful content as media. All of those channels are multi-million-dollar opportunities to grow a business and to become much more effective at marketing, yet when we hear about digital marketing, the default is to think about banner ads. Going forward, content will be the new media. When we shift that first impression, we change the landscape.

The reason we're not there just yet is because the online media are controlled by publishers and agencies that own and operate mass media companies. This is what makes up the online marketing channel: people with big properties along with the audience and inventory to help an advertiser reach a bigger target market. The trick is that publishers need to convince advertisers to buy space based on how many "eyeballs" they can deliver and how that stacks up against their traditional media buy. The discussion goes something like "You're going to get X number of people with your TV buy, and I can deliver X number of people in the online channel as well."

Future trending looks like we will move away from this and aim toward a place where publishers are helping businesses to promote their unique content to a broader but more targeted audience. Think of how a newspaper's online edition can create a holiday gift-giving guide for your retail operation instead of just selling you a banner ad in their lifestyle section.

On top of this, all content will become more and more portable. As easily as you can cut and paste text today, all kinds of content online will be portable to mix, match, and publish at will. This is going to make issues like copyright even more important and complex, but it's going to create a world where your content can be anywhere someone wants it to be.

7. Consumer-Generated Brands

Consumer-generated content is very real and very powerful. Whether it is the ability for an individual to share his creativity or to use his creativity to sell something, more and more people will be generating brand- and marketing-related content, and this content will continue to play a vital role in the consumer's final purchasing decision.

We are going to see companies start producing, marketing, and selling more and more consumer-generated brands. Be it by design or via crowdsourcing, a shift toward more generic "non-branded" items is coming as well. Consider this: Why would anyone want to wear your brand and be like others when she can have you produce for her her own branded items that illustrate, highlight, and display her uniqueness (and from that, perhaps, others will also want to be a part of these new micro-brands). Consumer-generated brands are going to shake the very foundations of even the newer channels we have been discussing. With design technologies making it easier for someone to mock up a quick design and have it produced in a short period of time for a fairly cheap price, we're going to see more consumers take branding into their own hands not just by talking about it or creating digital-only products, but also by shifting it toward real-world goods and services.

If the idea that consumers were taking your brand and creating videos or reviewing it and sharing it with the world was a little unnerving, how is your day going to look when those consumers start creating their own brands and are marketing them and selling them to the world much more efficiently than your business ever could?

8. Virtual Worlds

In 2006, many people (including me) got very excited about an online virtual world called Second Life. While it initially grew in popularity, the complexity of the usage and the technological challenges that the owners faced to scale the environment caused it to shrink back into a small niche of interested people. But don't count out the power of what an online environment can be versus the very static nature of the Internet as we know it today.

Once we resolve the ease of use and the technology issues, the idea of virtual worlds is going to make a huge comeback and see mass acceptance. Just look at the growth of online social networks. It took many iterations from Friendster to MySpace to Facebook to create a compelling, fun, and, most importantly, easy-to-use environment (and there are still plenty of complaints floating around). Virtual worlds will go through a similar transition.

After having spent some significant time in Second Life, I do believe it to be one of the main ways we will "surf" the Web in the coming years, but we're just not there yet. And, like all great things, it will just take some more time. The first telephone, phonograph player, radio, TV, personal computer, and mobile phone were not perfect.

The key indicator of this is looking at the younger generation and seeing how their Web experiences (areas like Webkinz, Club Penguin, and World of Warcraft) are, for the most part, all about virtual experiences. Young people today see no difference between spending time in Habbo Hotel or checking out the Black Eyed Peas' website.

9. Web and Mobile Connect

"Convergence" was a very naughty word after the dot-com implosion. The idea that we would watch TV on the Internet or download full-length movies created great disruption and confusion in the media. In recent years, we're seeing more and more unique content for each different kind of channel rather than one piece of content that migrates across multiple platforms. One area that must begin to embrace some form of convergence is the Internet and mobile space. For everything to move toward the idea of cloud computing and to really help your consumers to buy from you, we are going to need a further level of untethering, and it's going to have to come from the creation of one platform for mobile and Internet as those two individual channels today become one channel tomorrow.

As more and more people become digital nomads, we are going to see that mobile will lead the connectivity (as it does in certain parts of the world, like Korea) with an Internet backbone. For this to happen we're going to need better interoperability among the telecommunications carriers, who will then need to sit down with people at companies like Google, Cisco, and Microsoft to make it become a reality.

An additional prediction for this merger is that it will be led by the sheer demand of the consumer and not because technology people like to introduce newer tools and applications and disrupt the general masses with them.

10. Openness . . . Will Make Us Very Private

When you Google yourself, what do you see? Before any modern form of technology, people lived in villages and, with the exception of drawing the blinds in your home, everyone in the community knew about what everyone else in the community was up to. It wasn't just the basics, but the really deep stuff. There was nowhere to hide, nowhere to run, and so your life was an open book to the people who surrounded you. Over the decades, this changed. But, due to technology and these first-generation online social networks, we are going back to that day and age where everybody can (and does) know a lot more about one another than we ever did before. Isn't it amazing what you can learn by checking out the newsfeed in your Facebook profile?

This shift is going to do two things. One: It is going to force businesses and government to open up even more. It's going to force them to be more naked and transparent than we ever thought possible. We're going to demand accountability and even more openness in regard to what they are doing with our money. Two: Many individuals are going to recoil in an effort to protect their privacy more and more. Individuals are so open online with everything from where they live to their relationship status that marketers are going to pounce and inundate them with messaging. This bombardment and use of personal data for targeting will be one of the key factors in why people are going to "wake up" en masse and be much more careful about what they put online and where. There is no doubt that people are willing to give a tremendous amount of personal information in exchange for products and services that add value to their lives, but going forward that will shift slightly as they become more aware of just how "naked" they are in the online channels. Businesses will need to build trust through permission and be increasingly diligent about their consumers and the sensitivity of their personal information.

WELCOME TO PARTICIPATION 2.0

The shifts we have discussed in *Six Pixels of Separation* are very real. The fact that mass media have spent the past eighty years convincing large groups of people to think and buy the same things will mean very little in the grand scheme as we move forward into these new and exciting channels. Prior to mass media, how did messages spread? People shared stories, they got together, they connected, and they participated in one another's actual lives. Welcome to Participation 2.0. Welcome to this very unique moment in time—it's just a pixel past mass media—and now the technology exists to express ourselves freely and to connect not just within our geographical social circles, but with anyone, anywhere in the world, who shares in our values and thoughts.

Six Pixels of Separation is not about how you can connect your business more efficiently in these online channels to be successful. It's too late for that. We are all intrinsically connected. *In this world of interconnectedness, the bigger question is, How are you going to spread your story, connect, and add value to your life and the people whose lives you touch?* How are you going to explore your network to grow your net worth? How are you going to add tremendous value to a brand, product, or service that can always be made cheaper and faster by someone else? How are you going to connect and stay connected?

Everyone is connected. Connect your business to everyone.

Acknowledgments

Mom and Dad—For your love, support, and belief . . . and for buying that first Atari 800.

Bubby and Zaida—This would have really blown them away.

Arn, Winn, Jerry, Marnie, Reesa, Jessie, Lianna, Noah, Rachel, Jake, Rebecca, Beverley, André, Martine, Annabelle, Yahav, Jacques, Natalie, Ella, Maya, Ethan, Tristan, Olivia, Marcia (and the whole Shuster clan), and Sam—Online social networks are great, but nothing trumps the interconnectedness of our family.

Mark Goodman, Mick Kanfi, Aubrey Rosenhek, every team member at Twist Image, and all of our amazing clients—Thanks for letting me do what I do and be who I am. Some say that "it's nothing personal . . . it's just business." I disagree; we spend most of our days together and strive for what we all, collectively, want to accomplish at Twist Image . . . It's not just business, it's personal. Thanks for taking it personally.

This book would have never happened if Dan Ariely (the amazing author of *Predictably Irrational*) had not introduced me to James Levine, my literary agent. Jim, thanks for being my partner on this venture. I could not have done it without your help, support, and guidance. The entire team at Levine Greenberg Literary Agency rocks—thank you. I look forward to a long and healthy partnership on this and every other literary adventure you're willing to go on with me.

It's great to have an agent, but ultimately nothing gets into print without an interested publisher. I am forever thankful that Jim introduced me to Rick Wolff and the amazing team at Business Plus. The adventure is just getting started!

After spending almost fifteen years in the music industry watching bands release albums with huge "thank you" and "dedication" lists, I've seen that it's inevitable that someone gets left off, feels insulted, or is simply forgotten. That won't happen here. So, thank you to all of my family, friends, business associates, industry association and community group professionals, and laypeople. I loved writing this book, but the words would have failed me had you not been a part of my life.

A special mention does go out to all readers, listeners, and community members of the blog and podcast, "Six Pixels of Separation." Thanks for the sharing, the community spirit, and even for challenging me on some of the more half-baked postings. Everyone (yes, including you) is free to read, listen, share, and join here: www.twistimage.com/blog.

Index

"Academic Commons Blog," 236
achievement, and self-worth, 19
adaptation, by ad agencies, 201
advertising
    adapting to online world, 28–29
    banner, 28, 267–68
    blogs and, 159–60
    building credibility and, 172–73
    interruption-based, 240, 267
    paid media vs. earned media,
        156–60
    pay-per-click, 12–14, 28–29, 46, 159
    ripples vs. splashes, 76–77
    simplicity vs. complexity, 261–62
    "vicious cycle" effect of, 32
Advertising Age, 92
advertorials, 172, 218
affiliate marketing, 29
affiliation, and sense of community, 20
agnosticism, 195
Airborne Mobile, 234–35
Alba, Jason, 134
alerts, 60–61, 115, 205–6
Allstar, 65–66
Amazon, 23, 29
American Idol (TV show), 240–41
Amherst College, 236
analytics, 69, 267
Anderson, Chris, 6–7, 33, 78–79

Andreessen, Marc, 72–73
anonymous user names, 36–37
Ariely, Dan, 9–10
Asacker, Tom, 157
ASPCA Online Community, 73
attention crash, 265
audience. *See* community
audio, in blogs, 145
audio books, 197–99
audits, personal brand, 139–42
authenticity, 15–16, 79, 168–69
autonomy, and self-worth, 19

Baker, Nicholson, 228–30
"Baker Street Blog," 182–83
bandwidth speeds, 65–66
banner advertising, 28, 267–68
BarCamps, 110
Bazaarvoice, 81–83, 176–77
Behrendt, Greg, 164–65
Bianchini, Gina, 72–73
big idea, and collaboration, 225–28
Bing, 12–14, 62
BlackBerry, 249
Black Lab, 220–23
Blanchard, Kenneth, 41
Blendtec, 145–46
Blogger, xii, 150
blogs, 29, 143–60

blogs (*cont.*)
  adding value to conversation, 39–40
  authority and know control, 87–91
  building overarching strategy,
    147–49
  comments, 84, 139, 160, 170–71,
    185–86
  designing, 51–53, 150, 179–80
  equality of content on, 105–6
  finding right name and people,
    150–52
  finding your voice, 152–53
  focusing on your passion, 146–47
  four types of content, 143–46
  future trends, 262–64
  general rules for, 160
  marketing, 155–60
  setting up, 148–50
  staying in the loop, 204–8
  updating, 153–55
  vigilance and constant monitoring,
    202–4
Blue Ocean strategy, 183–85
Blue Ocean Strategy (Kim and
    Mauborgne), 183
Book Oven, 199
Borders Books, 186–87
Bornstein, Garner, 234–35
"branding," use of term, 128
brands
  consumers playing with, 100–102
  core values of, 128
  equal treatment by search engines,
    6–7
  See also personal brands
Brennan, Chris, 87–88
Brogan, Chris, 124–26
Broughton, John, 229
buff, being, 100
building community, 68–86
  asking questions, 174–76
  consumer to consumer, 80–84
  credibility and, 172–73

building community (*cont.*)
  faith-based initiatives, 68–71
  Long Tail of content, 78–79
  participation and leadership, 84–86
  ripples vs. splashes, 76–78
  traffic levels vs., 165–67
  viral expansion loops, 71–76
building trust, 34–43, 266–67
  adding value to conversation,
    39–40
  choosing global user name, 36–37
  choosing one good picture of
    yourself, 38–39
  consistency and, 35–36
  credibility and, 172–73
  responding quickly and honestly,
    40–42, 210–12
  sincerity and, 130–31, 168–69
  speaking like a human being vs.
    press release, 42–43
  vigilance and constant monitoring,
    202–4
Bum Rush the Charts, 220–23
Bunker Hill Community College, 108–9,
    112
burning the ships, 197–214
  centralizing of information, 208
  connecting vs. engaging, 209–10
  embracing idea you could be wrong,
    209
  going out on the fringe, 214
  responsiveness and speed, 210–12
  staying in the loop, 204–8
  stealing your ideas, 212–14
  vigilance and constant monitoring,
    202–4
Bush, George W., 91
business models, new, 258–62
business speak, 42–43
business-to-business marketing (B2B),
    80–81
business-to-consumer marketing (B2C),
    80–81

Canadian Marketing Association (CMA), 148–50

candor, in communication, 15–16

Carnegie, Dale, 130

cell phones. See mobile

Center for Media Research, 19

Center for the Digital Future, 15

change, and digital future, 256–57

Chapman, C. C., 183

Cirque du Soleil, 184

citizenship, 123, 160

city hosts, for unconferences, 119–20

Clarkson, Kelly, 240–41

classified ads, 261

cloud, using the, 187–88, 195

"CloudiD," 193–94

Club Penguin, 270

CNN, 91

collaboration, 219–33
    Bum Rush the Charts, 220–23
    giving content away, 232–33
    IdeaStorm, 226–28
    tribal knowledge, 230–32
    wikis, 31, 228–31

Collectik, 199

comments
    audio, on podcasts, 253–55
    on blogs, 84, 139, 160, 170–71, 185–86

commerce, 57–58

community, 14–15, 56–57
    building. See building community
    favoring of the, 162–64
    traffic levels vs., 165–67

complexity vs. simplicity of advertising, 261–62

conferences. See unconferences

connecting (connections), 19–21, 53–54
    engaging vs., 209–10
    levels of, 266–67

consistency, and building trust, 35–39

consumer-generated content, 30–31, 95, 97, 100–102, 269. See also collaboration

consumer reviews, 22–23, 81–83, 176–77

consumer-to-consumer marketing (C2C), 80–84

content as media, 137, 215–18, 267–68

content creation, 54–55, 143–60
    building overarching strategy, 147–49
    building trust, 167–69
    finding right name, design, and people, 150–52
    finding your voice, 152–53
    focusing on your passion, 146–47
    four types of content, 143–46
    giving it away, 232–33
    setting it up, 148–50
    updating content, 153–55

contextual advertising. See pay-per-click (PPC) advertising

control
    of message, 93–94, 95, 97, 100
    See also know control

convergence, 270–71

conversations, 55–56, 79, 97, 135
    adding value and building trust, 39–40

"Copy Blogger," 155

Coremetrics, 69, 82

core values, of brands, 128

Cortez, Hernando, 200–201

CPC (cost per click), 28–29

Craigslist, 261

creating content. See content creation

Creative Commons, 198

credibility, and building community, 172–73

cross-channel promotion, 28

crowds, wisdom of, 23, 188–91, 195, 224

"crowdsourcing," 226–28

D&G (Dolce & Gabbana), 246–47

Darling Buds, 80

Darwin, Charles, 162–63

datalibre.ca, 199
degrees to pixels, xiv, 4–5
Dell, 226–27
Dell, Michael, 227
democratization of media, 95–96
design of blog, 51–53, 150, 179–80
Dickson, Tom, 145–46
Digg, 77, 166
digital Darwinism, 161–77
    asking questions, 174–76
    building community vs. traffic,
        165–67
    building credibility, 172–73
    building trust, 167–69
    embracing Long Tail of content,
        176–77
    ethics of linkbaiting, 170–72
    favoring of the community, 162–64
digital footprint, 131–32, 202–4
digital marketing. See marketing
digital nomads. See mobile
direct marketing, 28
direct questions, 174–76
display advertising, 28, 267–68
disrupter, digital as great, 255–56
Dopplr, 76
downloading
    mobile content, 247–48
    music, 24–25, 145, 258
Due Maternity, 70
Dyson, 184

earideas, 199
earned media vs. paid media, 156–60
eBay, 22–23, 72
Eckstut, Arielle, 10–11
Economist, 238–39
editing your blog, 153
editorial calendars (ed cals), 154
e-mail marketing, 28, 81
emerging trends, 264–72
    analytics and research, 267
    attention crash, 265

emerging trends (cont.)
    consumer-generated brands, 269
    content as media, 267–68
    levels of connection, 266–67
    micro social networks, 265–66
    new business models, 258–62
    openness and privacy, 271–72
    personal brands rise, 264
    virtual worlds, 270
    Web and mobile connect, 270–71
"Engadget," 88–89
engaging vs. connecting, 209–10
Entrepreneurship 2.0, 45–63
    building a website, 51–53
    five C's of, 53–58
    global scale, 46–47
    Google as model, 48–49
    six free online tools, 58–63
    strategic plan, 45–46, 49–51
    technology and tools, 47–48
etiquette online, 40–42
everything is content, 216–17
experimentation, 194–96

Facebook, 30, 55, 72, 85, 136–37, 140,
        232, 265
Facebook Lexicon, 62–63
faith-based initiatives, 68–71
faith in trust economy, 43–44
Fallis, Terry, 121
Farmery, Anna, 134
Fast Company, 126
fear of technology, 16, 219–20
"Financial Aid Podcast," 112–14
Fine, Phyllis, 244–45
five C's of Entrepreneurship 2.0, 53–58
    commerce, 57–58
    community, 56–57
    connecting, 53–54
    conversations, 55–56
    creating, 54–55
flexibility, 49, 187
Flickr, 30

Flip a Coin (game), 234
focus group, online world as, 100–101
focusing on your passion, 146–47
Ford, Henry, 12
"Foreword Thinking" (podcast), 9
"For Immediate Release" (podcast), 122
free hugs online video, 1–4
free online tools, 58–63, 204–8
free publishing, 7–8
Friedman, Thomas, 67
"friends," levels of connections,
    266–67
future trends, 264–72
    analytics and research, 267
    attention crash, 265
    consumer-generated brands, 269
    content as media, 267–68
    levels of connection, 266–67
    micro social networks, 265–66
    new business models, 258–62
    openness and privacy, 271–72
    personal brands rise, 264
    virtual worlds, 270
    Web and mobile connect, 270–71

gadgets (widgets), 31, 70
Galleto, Francoise, 241
Gates, Bill, 64–65, 201
Geek Dinners, 120–23
giving content away, 232–33
Gladwell, Malcolm, 104
global user names, 36–37
Godin, Seth, 10–11, 187–88, 258–59
Google, 6–7, 48–49, 62, 141
Google AdWords, 201, 261–62
Google Alerts, 60–61, 141, 205–6
Google Analytics, 69
Google Blog Search, 61, 208
Google Reader, 59–60, 208
Google Trends, 62–63
grammar, on blogs, 153
Grateful Dead, 259
great disrupter, digital as, 255–56

Halvorson, Christine, 77
Hamlin, Kaliya, 120
Hart, Michael S., 198
headlines, 171–72
helpfulness, and building trust,
    135, 168
He's Just Not That Into You (Behrendt
    and Tuccillo), 164–65
hiring for blogs, 151–52
Hirshberg, Gary, 77–78
Hobson, Neville, 122
Hollywood, 165–66
Holtz, Shel, 122
honest feedback, 40–42, 87–90
hooks, 185–87
Hotmail, 71
HotWired, 267
Howe, Jeff, 226–27
Huffington, Arianna, 91–93
"Huffington Post," 91–93
Hurt, Brett, 81–82, 176–77

IdeaStorm, 226–28
Identi.ca, 29–30
iGoogle, 59–60
illegal downloading, of music, 24–25,
    145
images. See photos (images)
individualism, 12, 137
Ink Well, 147–48, 155, 157
In Rainbows (Radiohead), 24–27
Internet Archive, 198
interruption-based advertising, 240, 267
iPhone, 89, 235, 247
iPhone App Store, 235, 241, 249
iPod, 80, 95, 145
Israel, Shel, 136
"IT Index," 236
iTunes, 26, 85, 145, 220–21

Jaffe, Joseph, 223
"Jaffe Juice" (podcast), 223
Jaiku, 29–30

Jobs, Steve, 95
Join the Conversation (Jaffe), 223

Kanter, Beth, 169
Kaushik, Avinash, 68–69
Kerry, John, 91
Kim, W. Chan, 183–85
know control, 87–107
    "Huffington Post," 91–93
    levity and humility, 104–5
    Long Tail of content and, 104
    mass media vs. mass content, 105–7
    mobile devices and, 103
    online world as focus group,
        100–101
    passionate people doing passionate
        things, 95
    resigning your privacy, 98–100
    responding to online channels,
        87–90
    speed challenge and, 93–94
    user-generated content, 95, 97,
        100–102
    volume of voices, 95–96
Kryptonite bike lock, 87–88, 90

"Law of Two Feet," 110–11
leaders (leadership)
    participation and, 84–86
    of unconferences, 116–17
Learmonth, Michael, 92
Lee, Tommy, 65
Leopard, 89
Lerer, Kenneth, 91
Levine, James, 10–11
Levy, Steven, 223–25
LibriVox, 197–99
Life After the 30-Second Spot (Jaffe), 223
linkbaiting, 39–40, 170–72
LinkedIn, 30, 85, 140
Linksvayer, Mike, 198
Little MissMatched socks, 10–11
Long Tail, The (Anderson), 78–79

Long Tail of content, 78–79, 83, 104,
    105, 160, 176–77
"look at me" syndrome, 262–63
Lucas, George, 100–101
Lulu, 259–60
lurking, 40, 102

MacDonald, Kyle, 133–34
McDonald's Mobile Whoa, 244–45
McGuire, Hugh, 197–99, 262
Madden, Jared, 254–55
Malone, Michael S., 138–39
Mann, Juan, 1–4
marketing, 155–60
    adapting to online world, 28–29
    business-to-business (B2B), 80–81
    business-to-consumer (B2C), 80–81
    consumer-to-consumer (C2C),
        80–84
    mobile, 242–45, 247–48
    paid media vs. earned media, 156–
        60
    Radiohead initiative, 24–27
    ripples vs. splashes, 76–77
    search engine, 12–14, 28–29, 46, 159
    slowness and speed, 31–34, 93–94
    viral, 71, 73–74
Marketing, 93–94
Maslow, Abraham, 19
mass collaboration. *See* collaboration
mass content, 143–60
    building overarching strategy,
        147–49
    finding right name, design, and
        people, 150–52
    finding your voice, 152–53
    focusing on your passion, 146–47
    four types of content, 143–46
    marketing, 155–60
    mass media vs., 105–7
    setting it up, 148–50
    updating, 153–55
Masters, George, 80, 95

Mauborgne, Renée, 183–85
meet-ups, 108–23
    Geek Dinners, 120–23
    good citizenship and, 123
    turning online relationships into,
        108–9
    Tweet-ups, 121
    See also unconferences
Megadeth, 65
"me" media, 178–96
    adding more niches, 191–94
    Blue Ocean strategy, 183–85
    building hooks, 185–87
    experimentation, 194–96
    finding your niche, 180–83
    presentation skills, 178–80
    using the cloud, 187–88
    wisdom of crowds, 188–91
micro-blogs, 29–30, 157–58
micro social networks, 265–66
Microsoft, 12–13, 62
"Mine Again" (Black Lab), 220–23
Mitchell, William, 238–39
mobile, 103, 234–51
    connectivity, 237–38, 270–71
    media, content, and marketing,
        247–48
    new rules of, 249
    rise of, 238–39
    unsolicited marketing, 240
    usability, 250
mobile marketing, 242–45, 247–48
Momentum Effect, 41
monitoring blog, 202–4
Monty, Scott, 182–83
Moore, Shimon, 2–4
Mötley Crüe, 65
Motorola, 231–32
music industry, 24–27, 220–23, 255–56,
    258
MySpace, 30, 72, 265
My Starbucks Idea, 227
My Yahoo! 59–60

Naked Conversations (Scoble), 136
name
    of blog, 150
    global user names, 36–37
    nicknames, 37
Napster, 220
Neale, David, 247
needs, hierarchy of, 19–20
netbooks, 239
Netvibes, 59–60
networking, 17–18. See also building
    community
new business models, 258–62
Newmark, Craig, 261
news alerts, 60–61, 115, 205–6
newspapers, 138–39, 215–16
news readers, 59–60, 79, 208, 265
Newsweek, 223–25
New York Review of Books, 228–29
New York Times, 88, 93, 215–16
niches, 180–83, 191–94
nicknames, 37
Ning, 72–73, 266
nomadism, 238–39. See also mobile
notebook, for recording ideas, 154–55
N.O.W. (Nearby, Only, Wow) system,
    242–43
Nulman, Andy, 234–35, 241–43
Nussbaum, Emily, 99

Obama, Barack, 226, 240–41, 259
Omniture, 69
OneRedPaperClip.com, 133–34
One to One Future, The (Peppers and
    Rogers), 81
online advertising. See advertising
online etiquette, 40–42
online marketing. See marketing
online relationships, into real-world
    meet-ups, 108–9
online social networks, 19–20, 30,
    265–66, 270
    micro social networks, 265–66

online social neworks (*cont.*)
    viral expansion loops, 72–73, 75
ooVoo, 223
openness and privacy, 271–72
O'Reilly, Tim, 223–24

paid media vs. earned media, 156–60
Participation 2.0, 272–73
participatory culture, 23
partnership with consumers. *See*
    collaboration
passion, focusing on your, 146–47
pay-per-click (PPC) advertising, 12–14,
    28–29, 46, 159
peer reviews, 22–23, 81–83, 176–77
Penn, Christopher S., 112–14, 117
Peppers, Don, 81
permission, on digital channels, 27–28
personal brands, 124–42
    audits, 139–42
    for building a business, 132–33
    building trust, 167–69
    embracing digital footprint, 131–32
    networking and, 17–18
    questionnaire, 129–30
    rise of, 126–28, 264
    sincerity and, 130–31
    strategy vs. tactics, 135–36
    three-dimensional, 134–36
personal profile pictures, 38–39
Peters, Tom, 104, 126–27, 259
Pew Internet & American Life Project,
    202–4
photos (images)
    in blogs, 144
    personal profile, 38–39
Pink, Dan, 130
Planet Earth (Prince), 26
PodCamp Boston, 108–9, 112
PodCamp Montreal, 116–17, 118–19
PodCamp Ottawa, 116
podcasts, 9, 30, 85, 145
    audio comments, 253–55

podfading, 153–54
PowerPoint, 179, 180
Predictably Irrational (Ariely), 9–10
presentation design, 179–80
Presentation Zen, 179–80
Presentation Zen (Garr), 179
presenters at unconferences, 111,
    115–16
Prince, 26
privacy, 98–100, 160, 271–72
"ProBlogger," 155
profile pictures, 38–39
programming schedule, 132
Project Gutenberg, 198
"prosumers," 55. *See also* consumer-
    generated content
Provencher, Sebastien, 136
publishing industry, 7–8, 258–60
Pulver, Jeff, 168
Purcell, Adam, 254–55
Purple Cow (Godin), 10–11

quality vs. quantity, in online channels,
    166–67
questions, asking, 50–51, 174–76
quick feedback, 40–42, 87–90

Radiohead, 24–27
Raving Fan, 41–42, 211
readers, 59–60, 79, 208, 265
reciprocity, 168, 233
recognition, and self-worth, 19
recording ideas, 154–55
relationships, building. *See* building
    community
reputation, 20, 22–23. *See also* building
    trust
research packages, 267
responding (responsiveness), 40–42,
    87–90, 210–12. *See also*
    comments
Reynolds, Garr, 178–80, 181–82
ripples vs. splashes, 76–78

Rogers, Martha, 81
Roosevelt, Franklin D., 16
RSS (Really Simple Syndication), 40,
    59–60, 208
Rubel, Steve, 137
Rubicon Consulting, 81

Scientific American Mind, 22
Scoble, Robert, 136–37
scraping, 213
search engine marketing, 12–14, 28–29,
    46, 159
search engines, 62, 195–96
    defining your brand, 6–7
    personal brand and, 16–17
Seaton, Michael, 120–21
Second Life, 206, 270
Seinfeld, Jerry, 115–16
sharing sites, 30, 145–46
"Sherlock Holmes Social Network,"
    182–83
simplicity vs. complexity of advertising,
    261–62
sincerity, and building trust, 130–31,
    168–69
Six Pixels of Separation, origins of idea,
    212–13
six social needs, 19–20
Skype, 72
SlideShare, 30
slowness, of digital marketing, 31–34
"snackable" content, 107
SnapTell, 241
social networks. See online social
    networks
Southwest Airlines, 184
speed to publish information, 33–34,
    93–94
spell-checkers, 153
spelling, on blogs, 153
Sphinn, 166
splashes (splashy advertising
    campaigns), 76–77

sponsored links, 12–13
sponsoring unconferences, 111, 119–20
Squidoo, 187–88
staffing blogs, 151–52
Starbucks, 96, 161–62, 227
Star Wars (movies), 100–101
stealing your ideas, 212–14
Stone, Brad, 223–25
Stonyfield Farm, 77–78
strategic plan, 45–46, 49–51,
    147–48
Student Loan Network, 112–14
Sulzberger, Arthur, 215–16
Surowiecki, James, 23, 189–91, 224
Syracuse, Amy, 241

tag clouds, and Technorati, 207
tags, and unconferences, 118
Tapscott, Don, 99–100, 258–59
Technorati, 84–85, 140, 195, 206–7
Technorati Authority, 61, 206–7
Technorati Watchlist, 61, 140, 206
television remote controls, 252–53
text, in blogs, 143–44, 195
text messaging, 240–41
Threadless, 259
three-dimensional (3D) personal brands,
    134–36
"time-shifting," 132
T-Mobile, 247–48
tortoise and the hare, 36
traffic levels, 165–67
Trgovac, Kate, 188
tribal knowledge, 230–32
TripIt, 75–76
trust economy, 22–44
    faith in, 43–44
    overall tool kit, 27–31
    in praise of slowness, 31–34
    Radiohead's pay-what-you-want
        experiment, 24–27
    See also building trust
Tuccillo, Liz, 164–65

Twain, Mark, 187
Tweet-ups, 121
Twist Image, xi–xii, 9–10, 120, 127–28, 151, 158, 184–85
Twitter, 29–30, 72, 106, 157–58, 189–91, 206
Tyrangiel, Josh, 25–26

Uhlhaas, Christoph, 22
unconferences, 108–20
    creating local, 110–11
    finding out about, 114–15
    leadership of, 116–17
    presenters at, 111, 115–16
    sponsoring, 111, 119–20
    using every channel possible to connect, 118–19
unique selling proposition (USP), 194
UNM2PNM (use new media to prove new media), 223
Upcoming.org, 115
updates (updating), 153–57, 159–60. See also comments
user-generated content, 30–31, 95, 97, 100–102, 269. See also collaboration
user names, 36–37
user reviews, 22–23, 81–83, 176–77
Usher, David, 191–94
using the cloud, 187–88, 195

value, adding to conversation, 39–40
vanity, 17, 141
Vaynerchuk, Gary, 58
"vicious cycle" effect, 32
videos, in blogs, 145–46
video-sharing sites, 30, 145–46
vigilance and constant monitoring of blog, 202–4
viral expansion loops, 71–76
viral marketing, 71, 73–74

virtual worlds, 270
voice, for blog, 152–53
Vonage, 168

Wall, John, 113
Wall Street Journal, 138
Warren, Denise, 216
Washington Post, 93
watchlists, 61, 140, 206
Web Analytics (Kaushik), 69
web-design shops, 52
Webkinz, 270
websites, 245–47
    building your own, 51–53
website stats, 140
WebTrends, 69
Weinberger, David, 105–6
Whirlpool, 218
Whole New Mind, A (Pink), 130
"Why" questions to ask, 50–51
widgets, 31, 70
Wi-Fi, 237
Wikipedia, 31, 220, 228–30
Wikipedia: The Missing Manual (Broughton), 229
wikis, 31, 230–31
WineCamps, 110
Wine Library, 58
Wired, 32–33, 226–27
Wired.com, 32–33
Wisdom of Crowds, The (Surowiecki), 23, 189–91, 224
word of mouth, 71, 159–60
World of Warcraft, 270

Yahoo! 12–13, 59–60, 62
YouTube, 30, 97, 101, 145–46

Ziglar, Zig, 168
Zuckerberg, Mark, 232

About the Author

When Google wanted to explain digital marketing to the top brands in the world, they brought Mitch Joel to the Googleplex in Mountain View, California. *Marketing* magazine dubbed him the "Rock Star of Digital Marketing," and in 2006 he was named one of the most influential authorities on blog marketing in the world. Mitch Joel is president of Twist Image—an award-winning digital marketing and communications agency. He has been called a marketing and communications visionary, interactive expert, community leader, blogger, and podcaster. He is also a passionate entrepreneur and speaker who connects with people worldwide by sharing his insights on digital marketing and personal branding. In 2008, Mitch was named Canada's Most Influential Male in Social Media and one of the top 100 online marketers in the world. He was also awarded Canada's prestigious Top 40 Under 40 Award.

Mitch is a board member for the Canadian Marketing Association, an executive for the National Advertising Benevolent Society of Quebec, and an instructor of the CMA e-marketing professional certificate course. He is also a former board member of the Interactive Advertising Bureau of Canada. He sits on the content committee for both Shop.org and the Web Analytics Association.

Mitch speaks frequently to diverse groups like Starbucks,

Microsoft, Unilever, Procter and Gamble, and The Power Within, and has shared the stage with former president of the United States Bill Clinton, Anthony Robbins, and Dr. Phil.

He co-launched Distort Entertainment, the only hard music label in Canada to have major label distribution (Universal Music) and whose roster features the platinum-plus-, Juno Award–, and MuchMusic Video Award–winning acts Alexisonfire and City And Colour.

Mitch is frequently called upon to be a subject-matter expert for CTV National News, Canada AM, CBC Newsworld, *Marketing* magazine, *Strategy* magazine, the *Globe and Mail*, the *National Post*, and many other media outlets. His newspaper business column, New Business—Six Pixels of Separation, runs bi-monthly in both the *Montreal Gazette* and the *Vancouver Sun* and his monthly column, Ultra Portable, is featured in *enRoute* magazine.

You can find Mitch at www.twistimage.com/blog.

BUSINESS PLUS

Recognized as one of the world's most prestigious business imprints, Business Plus specializes in publishing books that are on the cutting edge. Like you, to be successful we always strive to be ahead of the curve.

Business Plus titles encompass a wide range of books and interests—including important business management works, state-of-the-art personal financial advice, noteworthy narrative accounts, the latest in sales and marketing advice, individualized career guidance, and autobiographies of the key business leaders of our time.

Our philosophy is that business is truly global in every way, and that today's business reader is looking for books that are both entertaining and educational. To find out more about what we're publishing, please check out the Business Plus blog at:

www.businessplusblog.com